Developing Psychotherapeutic Innovation and Imagination through Phenomenology and Qualitative Research

This book presents contemporary studies in qualitative psychotherapeutic research, examining their effectiveness in developing psychotherapeutic innovation and imagination. There is a focus on phenomenology, particularly given the growing prominence of interpretative phenomenological analysis (IPA). The book explores the tension between different forms of therapeutic knowledge—theoretical explicit knowledge, practice-derived explicit knowledge, and the crucial yet elusive tacit knowledge that emerges through clinical experience.

While qualitative research methods attempt to transcend the limitations of quantitative approaches and access the communities of practice where tacit knowledge resides, the book questions their effectiveness in this pursuit. It argues that although phenomenological approaches offer valuable insights into both explicit and tacit dimensions of therapeutic practice, their increasing psychological orientation—rather than adherence to philosophical foundations—may ultimately constrain psychotherapeutic innovation and imagination.

This volume will appeal to psychotherapists, clinical psychologists, qualitative researchers in mental health, and graduate students in psychology and counselling. It addresses key subject areas, including psychotherapy research methodology, qualitative approaches in mental health, IPA applications, philosophical underpinnings of therapeutic knowledge, and the ongoing debate around evidence-based practice in psychology. Academics researching psychotherapy and practitioners seeking to understand knowledge development and innovation in therapy will find this work particularly valuable.

The chapters in this book were originally published as a special issue of *European Journal of Psychotherapy and Counselling* and are accompanied by an updated Introduction and a new Endnote.

Del Loewenthal is Emeritus Professor of Psychotherapy and Counselling at the University of Roehampton, London, UK. He is an existential-analytic psychotherapist, photographer, and chartered psychologist, with a particular interest in phenomenology.

Angela Abela is Professor and founding Head of the Department of Child and Family Studies, University of Malta, a clinical psychologist, a UKCP registered family therapist, and a supervisor.

Developing Psychotherapeutic Innovation and Imagination through Phenomenology and Qualitative Research

Edited by
Del Loewenthal and Angela Abela

Routledge
Taylor & Francis Group
LONDON AND NEW YORK

First published 2026
by Routledge
4 Park Square, Milton Park, Abingdon, Oxon OX14 4RN

and by Routledge
605 Third Avenue, New York, NY 10158

Routledge is an imprint of the Taylor & Francis Group, an informa business

British Library Cataloguing in Publication Data
A catalogue record for this book is available from the British Library

ISBN13: 978-1-041-08068-8 (hbk)
ISBN13: 978-1-041-08069-5 (pbk)
ISBN13: 978-1-003-64359-3 (ebk)

DOI: 10.4324/ 9781003643593

Typeset in Minion Pro
by Newgen Publishing UK

Publisher's Note
The publisher accepts responsibility for any inconsistencies that may have arisen during the conversion of this book from journal articles to book chapters, namely the inclusion of journal terminology.

Contents

Citation Information

The chapters in this book were originally published in the *European Journal of Psychotherapy and Counselling*, volume 26, issues 3–4 (2024). When citing this material, please use the original page numbering for each article, as follows:

Chapter 1

Psychotherapeutic research and practice: Do we need to talk about 'efficacy'?
Patricia Talens, Del Loewenthal and Onel Brooks
European Journal of Psychotherapy and Counselling, volume 26, ssues 3–4 (2024), pp. 220–234

Chapter 2

Travelling in time: Using interpretative phenomenological analysis (IPA) to examine temporal aspects of the personal experience of issues in health and well-being
Jonathan A. Smith
European Journal of Psychotherapy and Counselling, volume 26, issues 3–4 (2024), pp. 235–252

Chapter 3

Uncertainty and existential thinking
Tamás Ullmann
European Journal of Psychotherapy and Counselling, volume 26, issues 3–4 (2024), pp. 253–266

Chapter 4

Using medical records in qualitative research. Advantages and limitations
Antonina Bryniarska
European Journal of Psychotherapy and Counselling, volume 26, issues 3–4 (2024), pp. 267–288

Chapter 5

Developing reflexivity and self-compassion in group psychotherapy: A dialogical and narrative approach
Maria Viou and Eugenie Georgaca
European Journal of Psychotherapy and Counselling, volume 26, issues 3–4 (2024), pp. 289–312

Chapter 6

Exploring the grief journey of bereaved spouses: Insights into the impact of sedation within palliative care
Livia Sani, Yasmine Chemrouk, Rozenn Le Berre, Marthe Ducos, Delphine Peyrat-Apicella and Marie-Frédérique Bacqué
European Journal of Psychotherapy and Counselling, volume 26, issues 3–4 (2024), pp. 313–332

Chapter 7

"Lost in space and time": Fathers' experiences of preterm birth
Dóra Monostori, Kinga Lampek and Marta B. Erdos
European Journal of Psychotherapy and Counselling, volume 26, issues 3–4 (2024), pp. 333–351

Chapter 8

Body as mediator: Case understanding in salutogenic-oriented general practitioner consultation
Ottomar Bahrs
European Journal of Psychotherapy and Counselling, volume 26, issues 3–4 (2024), pp. 352–369

Chapter 9

School organisational trauma during student suicide crisis
Clare Finegan
European Journal of Psychotherapy and Counselling, volume 26, issues 3–4 (2024), pp. 370–390

Chapter 10

Living with and living by tattoos – discursive analysis of a bodily practice
Csilla Csekő, Anna Csekő Szél and Péter Bodor
European Journal of Psychotherapy and Counselling, volume 26, issues 3–4 (2024), pp. 391–410

Chapter 11

Towards a psychotherapy publishing ethics concordat
Gary Winship, Ann Scott and James Edgar
European Journal of Psychotherapy and Counselling, volume 26, issues 3–4 (2024), pp. 411–427

Chapter 12

Wished I'd been there: Reflections on the special issue's articles as refracted through my appreciations for qualitative researchers' innovativeness
Tom Strong
European Journal of Psychotherapy and Counselling, volume 26, issues 3–4 (2024), pp. 428–443

Chapter 13

Reading with love: Developing therapeutic imagination through purposeful engagement with qualitative research
John McLeod
European Journal of Psychotherapy and Counselling, volume 26, issues 3–4 (2024), pp. 444–458

Notes on Contributors

Angela Abela is Professor and founding Head of the Department of Child and Family Studies, University of Malta, a clinical psychologist, a UKCP registered family therapist, and a supervisor.

Marie-Frédérique Bacqué is a French psychologist, a professor of psychopathology at the University of Strasbourg, France, and psychoanalyst. She is interested in the psychopathology of grief, the psychopathology of somatic patients (especially in psycho-oncology), the assessment of psychoanalytic psychotherapies, and mentalization and projective methods. She is the author of numerous national and international articles and volumes, editor-in-chief of the *Études Sur La Mort* journal, and member of the Parental Bereavement Research in European Framework, International Psycho- Oncology Society, International Center for Death Studies, and French Balint Medical Society.

Ottomar Bahrs is affiliated with the University of Düsseldorf, Germany, as well as the Department of Health Sciences, University of Applied Sciences Fulda, Germany, and the Umbrella Organisation Salutogenesis.

Rozenn Le Berre is a doctor of philosophy at the Center for Medical Ethics (EA 7446 ETHICS) at the Catholic University of Lille, France. Her interests include the experience of bereavement from a philosophical and ethical perspective, narratives of serious illness, clinical ethics interventions with health care professionals, and palliative care training.

Péter Bodor is a full professor at the Department of Sociology, Eötvös Loránd University, Budapest, Hungary. His research interest is directed on various topics located at the intersection of a social constructivist psychological framework and micro-sociology. Currently, he is working on the discursive construction of identity, memory, and emotions. In these works, he aims to reconstruct the conversationalists' various identities, remembering and emotional claims as they evolve within the interaction order and their relationship to institutional arrangements.

Onel Brooks is particularly interested in philosophy and psychoanalysis. He is a core member of the SAFPAC (www.safpac.co.uk) teaching team and was a senior lecturer in psychotherapy, counselling and counselling psychology, Psychology Department, Roehampton University, London, UK. He is BACP-accredited and UKCP registered as a psychoanalytic psychotherapist and as an existential analytic psychotherapist. As well as working in universities, he has worked for many years with adolescents and adults, in therapeutic communities, the NHS and in voluntary organisations. He also contributes to the teaching at The Philadelphia Association, London.

Antonina Bryniarska is a psychologist, clinician, systemic therapist, and assistant in the Chair of Psychiatry at the Jagiellonian University's Faculty of Medicine, Kraków, Poland. As a researcher, she is interested in eating disorders, therapy processes, and cultural studies. She is currently pursuing her PhD regarding the cooperation between professionals and parents of young adolescents with anorexia nervosa. She works at the University Hospital in Krakow providing mostly family therapy and also in the private sector as a couple and family therapist. She conducts research with both quantitative and qualitative methods.

Julia Cayne is Chair of Training with the Southern Association for Psychotherapy and Counselling and practices as a psychotherapist in the South West. She is particularly interested in phenomenology and post-phenomenology and its implications for practice and research and in particular how it can contribute to our consideration of learning and the kinds of knowledge that emerge through experience.

Yasmine Chemrouk is a clinical psychologist. Since 2015, she has been working in the field of psycho-oncology. Her main areas of interest concern serious illnesses, accompaniment and support for patients and caregivers, work with healthcare teams, and ethical issues, including the end of life.

Csilla Csekő is a doctoral student at the Doctoral School of Psychology, Faculty of Humanities and Social Sciences, University of Pécs, Hungary. She graduated in ethnography, language, and literature. In her doctoral research, she explores the physical, pictorial, and linguistic possibilities of processing crises and significant life events in a discursive psychological approach through tattoos and tattooing. She has experience in family therapy and literature therapy methods in praxis.

Marthe Ducos is a clinical psychologist and works in Mobile Palliative Care Team in a Cancer Center. Her topics of interest and research involve the family when a member is seriously ill and family reorganisation. She is also interested in the grieving process within the family, again with the issue of family reorganisation.

James Edgar is Assistant Research Integrity Auditor, Wiley. James Edgar has ten years' experience at Wiley, beginning in journals' editorial supporting psychology titles. He was Publishing Manager for *British Journal of Psychotherapy*, *International Journal of Applied Psychoanalytic Studies*, and *Journal of Analytical Psychology*. He now works full-time in publishing ethics and research integrity at Wiley.

Marta B. Erdos, PhD, is Associate Professor in Mental Health and Clinical Social Work at the Department of Social and Community Studies, Faculty of Humanities and Social Sciences, University of Pécs, Hungary. She obtained her MA in mental health and earned her PhD in social communication. Her main areas of research interest are life transitions, crisis states, and recovery. She is leader and founder of Social Innovation Evaluation Research Centre at the University of Pécs, Hungary, affiliated with Social and Health Evaluation International.

Clare Finegan's academic journey started with the study of French, German, and Irish at NUI Maynooth, Ireland, followed by The Ludwig Maximilian University of Munich, Germany, and Université Toulon, France. She worked as a language teacher where she developed a strong interest in counselling and psychotherapy. Further studies in psychotherapy and clinical supervision at master and doctoral levels in Iona, New York, and DCU, Ireland, led to clinical work in two medical practices, guidance counselling in several schools, and clinical supervision for the Department of Education. She uses an eclectic blend of therapeutic techniques from multiple therapy models, including Family Systemic, CBT, Gestalt, and EFT, and integrate new creative techniques.

Eugenie Georgaca is Associate Professor of Clinical Psychology at the School of Psychology of the Aristotle University of Thessaloniki, Greece. She teaches and researches in the fields of clinical psychology, psychotherapy, and mental health. Specifically, she is interested in utilising constructionist, dialogical, and biographical narrative approaches for the study of the construction, negotiation and management of mental distress, as well as of psychotherapy process. She has published in international journals, including *Journal of Constructivist Psychology*, *Feminism & Psychology*, *Journal of Mental Health*, *Mental Health & Prevention*, *Psychosis*, and *Qualitative Research in Psychology*. She co-organised conferences on qualitative psychology research (EQuiP & QRMH).

Kinga Lampek, PhD, is a college professor in public health at the Faculty of Health Sciences, University of Pécs, Hungary. She is Head of Department of Health Promotion and Public Health and Associate Dean for General and Strategic Affairs at the Faculty. Her main area of research interest is the sociology of health with special regard to vulnerable groups and equality of opportunities. She is a member or advisor in several doctoral schools at the University of Pécs (Doctoral School of Demography and Sociology, Doctoral School of Health Sciences, and Doctoral School of Educational Sciences), Hungary.

Del Loewenthal is Emeritus Professor of Psychotherapy and Counselling at the University of Roehampton, London, UK, and is Chair of the Southern Association for Psychotherapy and Counselling (SAFPAC), London, UK. He is an existential-analytic psychotherapist and chartered psychologist, with a particular interest in phenomenology. His books include *Existential Psychotherapy and Counselling after Postmodernism* (Routledge, 2017). www.delloewenthal.com; www.safpac.co.uk

John McLeod is a counselling educator, researcher, and author who is committed to the development of flexible, co-created ways of working together in therapy, that build on client strengths and resources. He has published widely on a range of topics associated with research and practice in counselling and psychotherapy.

Dóra Monostori is a PhD student at the Faculty of Health Sciences, University of Pécs, Hungary. She is an instructor at the Preventive Health Care Department at the Faculty of Health Studies and Social Studies, University of Szeged, Hungary. She obtained her first degree as a health visitor and then as a health social worker. She earned further qualifications as Mental Health Expert and a Bereavement Counsellor. As an expert and practitioner, she also works for the Premature Arrival Southern Great Plane Regional for Perinatal Intensive Care Unit (PICU) Foundation. Her main area of research interest is the life-transforming experience of preterm birth.

Delphine Peyrat-Apicella is a clinical psychologist and doctor of psychology at the University Sorbonne Paris Nord (UTRPP – UR 4403), France. Her interests range from narratives of serious illness to psychological issues of the care relationship at the end of life and palliative care issues for health care professionals and psychologists in France.

Livia Sani is a clinical psychologist and researcher at the Department of Clinical Psychology, University of Strasbourg, France. In clinical practice and research, her main areas of work concern loss, death, and severe illness.

Ann Scott is Senior Member of the British Psychotherapy Foundation (Psychoanalytic Psychotherapy Association) in private practice, a training therapist for the Independent Psychoanalytic Child and Psychotherapy Association (ICAPA – BPF), and a part-time doctoral researcher, University of Nottingham, UK. She was Editor-in-Chief of the *British Journal of Psychotherapy*, 2009–2022. She is co-author, with the late Mary Barnes, of

Something Sacred: Conversations, Writings, Paintings, and author of *Real Events Revisited: Fantasy, Memory, Psychoanalysis*. She has a longstanding interest in the dynamics of the acute in-patient setting, having worked on the PICU in a state mental hospital in the USA before training clinically in London. She is the literary executor of Isabel Menzies Lyth.

Jonathan A. Smith is Professor of Psychology at Birkbeck University of London, UK, where he leads the interpretative phenomenological analysis research group (IPARG) and teaches qualitative methods. He developed IPA as a distinctive experiential qualitative methodology and has employed it to examine many topics primarily in health and well-being. He is lead author of *Interpretative Phenomenological Analysis: Theory, Method, Research* (2nd ed., 2022; co-authored with Flowers and Larkin) – the primary text on IPA.

Tom Strong is a professor and counsellor-educator who recently retired from the University of Calgary, Canada. He writes on the collaborative, critical, and practical potentials of discursive approaches to psychotherapy – most recently on concept critique and development (particularly with respect to therapy and research), and critical mental health. Among Tom's books are *Medicalizing Counselling: Issues and Tensions*, *Patterns in Interpersonal interactions* (co-edited with Karl Tomm, Sally St. George, and Dan Wulff), and *Social Constructionism: Sources and Stirrings in Theory and Practice* (co-authored with Andy Lock). Currently, he is coediting the *Routledge International Handbook of Postmodern Therapies*. https://wpsites.ucalgary.ca/tom-strong/.

Anna Csekő Szél, MD, PhD, is a full-time psychiatric resident in Central Jutland. She defended her PhD thesis in 2023 at Semmelweis University in Budapest, Hungary. Her research interest are health inequities and mental health. She conducts research in the fields of psychology and psychiatry.

Patricia Talens is a therapeutic practitioner working both privately and within the charity sector in London. She graduated with a BA (Hons) in criminology and applied psychology before spending six years working in forensic mental health. She completed her MSc in counselling and psychotherapy with a special interest in the role of therapeutic research and practice. This research has continued as she is currently working towards her PhD with a focus on technique and method in psychotherapy.

Tamás Ullmann is Professor of Philosophy at the Eötvös Lóránd University, Budapest, Hungary. His publications include a book on Husserl's genetic phenomenology (*La genèse du sens*, Paris, 2002) and several books in Hungarian on the problems of contemporary phenomenology.

Maria Viou is a PhD student at the School of Psychology of the Aristotle University of Thessaloniki, Greece. She is a systemic and family therapist. Her research interests include qualitative research and the process of psychotherapy. Specifically, she is interested in using narrative and dialogical concepts to understand the mechanisms of change that take place in group psychotherapy. She is also a researcher at the Training and Research Institute for Systemic Psychotherapy (logopsychis.gr). She has published in international journals, including *Theory and Psychology*, *Journal of Constructivist Psychology*, *Journal of Creativity in Mental Health*, and *European Journal of Psychotherapy and Counselling*.

Gary Winship is Professor of Trauma, Education and Mental Health University of Nottingham, UK; Course Leader of MA in Trauma Informed Practice; Chair of Ethics and Integrity, School of Education, University of Nottingham; Senior Fellow, Institute of Mental Health; Editor-in-Chief, *British Journal of Psychotherapy*; and UKCP Psychoanalytic Psychotherapist.

Introduction: Developing psychotherapeutic innovation and imagination through phenomenology and qualitative research with particular reference to the nature of therapeutic knowledge

Del Loewenthal and Angela Abela

"What psychotherapeutic research has been of benefit to your practice?"

I (Loewenthal) was asked the above question on completing many years as the Founding Research Chair of a national psychotherapy organisation. Partly to my amazement, and partly with a dawning realisation that this was something I had always known, I realised my answer was (and is) 'not much'!

However, this answer is dependent on what is regarded as 'research'. At the time then, and even more so now, research, at the very least in the case of psychotherapy, was becoming and has become synonymous with 'empirical' research. Yet there is also research that is 'theoretical' and research that is based in 'practice'. In both of these latter cases, I can give far more examples where I think such research has benefitted my work innovatively and imaginatively with clients/patients. These three distinctions of 'practice', 'theoretical', and 'empirical' research might sometimes be seen as having some loose similarity to the 'exploratory', 'descriptive', and 'causal' research types denoted in the classic text by Selltiz et al. (1959).

Evidence-based practice (EBP; Masfield et al., 2001) can be seen as within the 'causal'/'empirical' category. Whereas the 'descriptive' type can be seen more to do with phenomenology (Brentano and such philosophers as Husserl, Heidegger, Levinas, Merleau-Ponty, Sartre, and Derrida) and the 'exploratory' can be seen more to do with case studies that can also be phenomenological. Indeed, with psychotherapy, there is an argument that case study is our prime research method (see Winship et al., Chapter 11 of this book, and Loewenthal, 2022) it is the phusis/physis, the natural, what comes out of itself. This is as in Husserl's (2001) 'to the things themselves' and does not have to aim to become a general theory and can be helpful to those practitioners who seek to invent psychotherapy each time with every client/patient.

Yet, the empirical basis of EBP can be seen as an essential if we want to know *What Works for Whom* (Roth & Fonagy, 2006). Otherwise, there is the argument that we have various cultural practices at best backed up by the theories of our modality gurus.

But what is the nature of the psychotherapeutic knowledge being researched? Psychotherapy can be seen to draw on theoretical knowledge as a type of explicit knowledge and the knowledge that emerges from experience in practice both explicit and tacit (Polanyi, 1967). Whereas EBP can be seen as primarily drawing on explicit psychotherapeutic knowledge derived from empirical research.

Surely, in order to be psychological therapists, we need the time and space to consider not so much explicit knowledge, but what Polanyi (1967) terms 'tacit knowledge'. Tacit knowledge cannot be taught and learnt but can be imparted and acquired. In some ways similarly, Oakeshott (1962) distinguishes 'practical' from 'technical' knowledge. Such practical knowledge cannot really be learnt just through a manual, but emerges through relationships.

More recently, Lave and Wenger (1991) spoke of such 'tacit', 'practical' knowledge in 'a community of practice' that focuses on social participation. Here, learning occurs when the trainee/student acquires knowledge, not only from the master but also from 'advanced apprentices' and 'fellow novices'.

Qualitative research may help us get closer to tacit, practical knowledge, including 'communities of practice'. Phenomenology lends itself very well to this form of knowledge and links with the aforementioned descriptive research. The potential importance of phenomenology in psychotherapy training has been considered in a previous editorial (Loewenthal, 2019), some of which will be repeated and built on here.

In psychotherapeutic theories, phenomenology can be seen to have influenced the founders of most modalities: existentialism (Binswanger, Boss, etc.) and psychoanalysis (Laing, Freud, Lacan, etc.). Yet, perhaps the Humanism of Carl Rogers person-centred therapy (which can be also seen to be influenced by Kierkegaard) is at least the poor person's introduction to phenomenology and may have had the greatest phenomenological influence on the psychological therapies (and education).

But what is phenomenology? There are numerous answers (see Moran, 1999). For my own part what is important in phenomenology is what emerges in the between by starting with practice and theories may come to mind as implications rather than applications (Loewenthal, 2011). Many have also found Spinelli's (1989) exploration of phenomenology helpful with his use of 'describe don't explain', bracketing/epoche, and 'rule of horizontalisation'.

So can phenomenology with its greater ability to allow in tacit knowledge enable greater possibilities for developing innovation and imagination in psychotherapy; and if so what sort of phenomenology? The chapters presented in this Special Issue are considered to also be an indication of the current use of qualitative psychotherapeutic research methods; and phenomenology is the research method that predominates. They are from the International Research Conference *Qualitative Research in Mental Health 2023* held in Budapest [https://qrmh9.com]. All those presenting at this International Conference were able to submit their papers to the *European Journal of Psychotherapy and Counselling*. The book editors (Loewenthal and Abela, together with grateful thanks to Zsuzsa Kalo) then chose those papers considered most relevant to psychotherapy to go through our journal's review process. (The chapters presented here are for the most part those that successfully completed the review process by the time of publication.)

It will be seen that the main research method was indeed phenomenological. Furthermore, of the various phenomenological research methods that have been developed (by for example, Colaizzi, Giorgi, Moustakas, Smith), it was the interpretative phenomenological analysis (IPA) by Smith (2003) that now predominates, and this reflects our experience with overall submissions to our journal. We assume that one reason for IPA's popularity is that it also provides a semi-structured way of attempting to explore psychotherapy's tacit dimension.

Yet, is not there something of a misnomer in adding the word 'research' to the concept of phenomenology? In philosophy, 'phenomenology' includes the notion of research. Thus, the likes of Heidegger, Merleau-Ponty et al. are actually carrying out phenomenological research in their philosophical writings. So does adding 'research' to 'phenomenology', and in so doing, transforming phenomenology to more psychological research, not only usefully add and come alongside our ever-changing and current notions of how we legitimise knowledge; but, might it also take away from some fundamental notions of philosophical phenomenology? Could a compromise that might still appeal to some current research sensibilities, at least in descriptive research, be inspired by the phenomenological work of Montaigne (1800) through his essays? Though would this require an even more different mindset regarding what it might mean to work psychotherapeutically, whereby we do not attempt to generalise but more attempt, as mentioned, to reinvent psychotherapy each time for each client/patient? This way, findings from psychotherapeutic research would not be regarded as providing a framework from which to practice but rather ideas that might thoughtfully come to the psychotherapist when working with what emerges in the therapeutic hour?

As a European journal we have a particular interest in European ideas and with Husserl, Heidegger et al. continental philosophy; but, here is the rub! Anglo Saxon psychology, in particular, has moved away from its philosophical base and is moving psychotherapy similarly. This would appear to be in line with the cultural move of psychotherapy from their more phenomenological, often Rogerian, base in university education departments to primarily psychology departments.

So what is gained and lost by phenomenology being considered through an increasingly psychological rather than philosophical lens? In order to provide a further exploration of the crucially tacit nature of psychotherapeutic knowledge and attempting to do this in a way that is more consistent with this idea itself, we have included for this book the 'Endnote' by Julia Cayne.

What is regarded as essential in this Endnote 'The possibility of phenomenology and psychotherapeutic knowledge?' is what might emerge for the reader from not only what Julia is writing but how she is writing it, for without tacit psychotherapeutic knowledge, which phenomenology can potentially open up, there is the concern that what too often is considered as psychotherapeutic research can fundamentally get us in the wrong place.

Before introducing all the chapters plus those from our distinguished respondents, we very much want to thank the following for their invaluable assistance in developing this book:

Athena Androutsopoulou, Eszter Beran, Betty Bertrand, Peter Bodor, Marie-Cecile Bertau, Gauri Chauhan, Marilyn Clark, Ellen Dunn, Anastasios Gaitanidis, Desley Hennessy, William Horsnell, Zsuzsa Kalo, Ramar Kapur, Anthony McSherry, Danny McCarty, Bren Neale, Elizabeth Nicholl, Ioannis Papadopoulos, Sally Parsloe, Judit Nóra Pintér, József Rácz, Francesca Robinson, Emma Salter, Carla Penna, Erin Wehrman, Jean Wells, and John Wilson.

Our first Chapter is 'Psychotherapeutic research and practice: Do we need to talk about 'efficacy'?' This book continues to develop this other, more philosophical notion of phenomenology by exploring the question of efficacy in psychotherapeutic research. Here, the authors, Patricia Talens, Del Loewenthal, and Onel Brooks, argue how standardisation in psychotherapeutic research and practice can create a 'procrustean bed' which leads to conformity rather than an ethical response to what emerges in the moment. They consider how the therapist may be rendered 'ineffective' in the name of 'efficacy'; and explore how the industry of funded therapies places measurement at the very foundation of research in 'EBP'. In doing so, they draw out some implications for idiosyncratic practices and research which are rooted in philosophies such as phenomenology.

> Reviewers' comments include: This is an interesting article with some very valid points, refreshing to hear the energy with which you organise the challenges to the narrow dominant paradigm of funded therapies.

We consider ourselves very fortunate to be able to include Chapter 2: 'Travelling in time: Using interpretative phenomenological analysis (IPA) to examine temporal aspects of the personal experience of issues in health and well-being'. Here, the author, Jonathan A. Smith, describes a model for thinking of how participants make sense of temporal aspects of their lived experience and argues for the input that IPA can make to exploring this experiential timeline.

Descriptions are provided of both IPA as an experiential research methodology and what is considered its growing use for longitudinal research among qualitative researchers.

Reviewers' comments include: The article provides a very novel perspective on the IPA research design and, in general, on the longitudinal use of the method. The presentation of the topic and the research is very thorough and precise, and provides very important insights.

Chapter 3 is 'Uncertainty and existential thinking'. The author, Tamás Ullmann, innovatively argues that a clearly articulated set of concepts of existential thinking can be useful for qualitative psychological research. In this context, the main question considered is whether our existential problems are changing historically and, if so, what is specific to our era. This article provides a meta-perspective on the context in which research is taking place which can be very useful for qualitative researchers.

Reviewers' comments include: Excellent text, well elaborated. It is clear that the author has a deep philosophical understanding. The clarity of the statements and explanation is exemplary. We need more articles of this kind, giving a meta-perspective, in the science of psychology. This critical psychological approach can also be very useful for qualitative researchers to not take psychological constructs for granted.

Chapter 4 is 'Using medical records in qualitative research. Advantages and limitations' by Antonina Bryniarska. In this chapter, the author argues that cooperation between professionals, adolescent patients on a psychiatric ward with anorexia nervosa, and their parents is essential for the treatment outcome, and this is why it has been studied using qualitative research. Such research has previously mainly concentrated on self-report methods. Instead, the author describes and evaluates, using both combined Consensual Qualitative Research (CQR) and Comparative Case Study (CCS) methodologies to obtain important clinical implications, a multidimensional and in-depth picture of cooperation in such difficult circumstances.

Reviewers' comments include: The paper is an interesting attempt to utilise medical record via qualitative analysis.

In Chapter 5, Developing reflexivity and self-compassion in group psychotherapy: A dialogical and narrative approach, the authors Maria Viou and Georgaca Eugenie apply dialogical concepts to understand the development of self-reflexivity and self-compassion during psychotherapy. In presenting a study that mapped clients' voices and explored their changes in group psychotherapy, Thematic Narrative Analysis was used to study 20 two-hour group therapy sessions of a systemic informed approach. After presenting their important analysis, they suggest that, in parallel with focusing on the presence and amount of the reflexive processes that occur in psychotherapy, psychotherapy research should also focus on the changes in the quality of these processes, and particularly the development of self-compassion in psychotherapy. The research has intriguing clinical implications and the topic of self-compassion is highly relevant to contemporary clinical work on trauma irrespective of approach.

Reviewers' comments include: This is an interesting and well-written paper with an elaborate qualitative methodology to track changes in group psychotherapy based on the notion of reflexivity and polyphony. The research has intriguing clinical implications and the topic of self-compassion is highly relevant to contemporary clinical work on trauma irrespective of approach.

Chapter 6 is 'Exploring the grief journey of bereaved spouses: Insights into the impact of sedation within palliative care' by Livia Sani, Yasmine Chemrouk, Rozenn Le Berre, Marthe Ducos, Delphine Peyrat-Apicella, and Marie-Frédérique Bacqué. Here, this French research team comprising clinical psychologists, philosophers, and physicians describe an ongoing study focused on the emotional and affective complexities experienced by bereaved spouses after the loss of a loved one due to oncological diseases within the realm of palliative care and Continuous Deep Sedation until Death (CDSD). The preliminary data concerns nine semi-structured interviews analysed using ALCESTE software, a tool for statistical analysis of textual data based on word co-occurrences. Analysis and comparison of the thematic categories that emerged showed that social support, deep loneliness, and the preservation of memories emerged as central elements of the marital bereavement experience. In addition, the study highlights vital information for clinical practice, the critical role of comprehensive palliative care in France, and the delicate nature of sedation experiences, revealing intense emotions such as helplessness and anger. This paper had some significant strengths in its unique approach to data analysis and its attention to a significant and understudied research topic.

Reviewers' comments include: This paper had some significant strengths in its unique approach to data analysis and its attention to a significant and understudied research topic. I applaud the authors for using data within a timely relationship to the loss of the spouse, as this is a significantly understudied period.

Chapter 7, Lost in space and time": Fathers' experiences of preterm birth, is by Dóra Monostori, Kinga Lampek, and Marta B. Erdos. They found, through using IPA, that these fathers live their lives in extended liminality, characterised by chaos and unpredictability, and are struggling with new, often unusual roles and responsibilities that may completely upset their private life–work balance. The authors conclude that targeted intervention by trained counsellors could help the fathers overcome these traumatising experiences. Here, the use of IPA to analyse an understudied topic was an appropriate methodological choice.

Reviewers' comments include:

> This is an interesting qualitative study that provides valuable insights into the experiences of fathers whose infants were born prematurely. The use of IPA to analyse the interview data was an appropriate methodological choice given the goal of understanding the lived experiences and meaning-making of the fathers.

Chapter 8 is 'Body as mediator: Case understanding in salutogenic-oriented general practitioner consultation' by Ottomar Bahrs.

This chapter uses sequence analysis (according to structural hermeneutics) to explore a video-documented conversation between a general practitioner and his patient, in which the overall shape of professional interactional patterns resulting from the rating procedure for solution-oriented interventions is evaluated. It is concluded that shared decision-making must be preceded by mutual understanding and that the health-promoting potential for a sense of coherence can be strengthened by interpreting symptom formation as a possible voice of the body if this expression is taken seriously. Through a sophisticated and detailed methodology, the article highlights the fundamental importance of a good doctor–patient relationship and contributes to the area by also helping us to reflect on access to treatment for difficult patients.

Reviewers' comments include: Through a sophisticated and detailed methodology, your article highlighted the fundamental importance of a good doctor–patient relationship, as Balint taught us. Today, the number of difficult patients and iatrogenic treatments abound. Your article contributes to and improves the quality of GP approaches for this clientele ameliorating the access to treatment for difficult patients.

Chapter 9 is entitled 'School organisational trauma during student suicide crisis'. Here, the author, Clare Finegan, carried out a qualitative IPA study, which privileged the voices of Irish school guidance counsellors regarding student suicide. Semi-structured interviews generated descriptions of what was indicative of vicarious and secondary trauma, moral injury, organisational trauma and lack of containment, systemic disconnect, ambiguity and organisational double-bind used as a defence strategy, which appears to have comprised crisis recovery for the entire system. The paper takes into account the impact of emotional trauma in schools.

Reviewers' comments include: By integrating the existing organisational literature into the paper you have produced a strong publication and case to take seriously the impact of emotional trauma in schools.

Next, Chapter 10 is 'Living with and living by tattoos – discursive analysis of a bodily practice'. In this case study, Csilla Csekő, Anna Szél Csekő, and Péter Bodor present a discursive analysis of tattoos related to significant autobiographical events, examining their pictorial, interpretative, embodied, and discursive characteristics in a remembering process. This study presents the connection between motif choosing and individual motives, as well as the embodied positions of tattoos with their discursive consequences. Through these discursive identity positions, that are assigned both in everyday conversations and in wider social-cultural discourses, persons construct more positive self-images, thus creating a device for coping with crisis situations. This is an interesting paper on a cultural practice gaining increased attention in the academic community.

Reviewers' comments include: This is an interesting paper on a cultural practice gaining increased attention in the academic community. The paper effectively examines tattoos linked to noteworthy autobiographical experiences, delving into their visual, interpretative, physical, and communicative aspects.

Chapter 11, our final chapter, is the potentially ground changing: Towards a psychotherapy publishing ethics concordat by Gary Winship, Ann Scott, and James Edgar. Following the changing landscape of data management and privacy, the authors report discussions among international psychotherapy journal editors regarding ethical guidelines governing publishing qualitative case study research. Here areas for debate are set out as a base for further discussion towards the development of what they term a 'Psychotherapy Publishing Ethics Concordat'. Hence, more recent notions of confidentiality are preventing psychotherapy's main research method of case study (which can be seen as fundamental for us in terms of both the aforementioned exploratory and descriptive research categories). This has already led to psychotherapy's diminution though stalling the development of appropriate psychotherapeutic knowledge.

The argument here on how current notions of confidentiality are preventing psychotherapy's main research method of the case study can be seen as fundamental for us in terms of both the aforementioned exploratory and descriptive research categories. Here is a very grave warning of the increasing risk of psychotherapy's diminution through stalling the development of appropriate psychotherapeutic knowledge.

Reviewers' comments include: This is a very timely piece, so thank you for putting it together. The issue is important and hopefully this article will stimulate further discussion.

Next, our two eminent published respondents. The first, Chapter 12, is Tom Strong in 'Wished I'd been there: Reflections on the special issue's articles as refracted through my appreciations for qualitative researchers' innovativeness'. Here, the author brings an appreciative view of the recent history, regarding what he considers the innovativeness and critical responsiveness of qualitative researchers in studying psychotherapy and mental health, to comment on the above chapters. He considers this history shows qualitative researchers developing and refining their methods to pose new questions and ways of answering them in line with therapist curiosities about meaning making; as well as becoming a tool for surfacing social justice concerns, or for answering or addressing questions in novel contexts.

Reviewers' comments include: This well-written paper provides an illuminating account of the history of, and trends and issues in, qualitative research, highlighting its innovativeness, before going on to comment on each of the papers in the special issue.

In Chapter 13, 'Reading with love: Developing therapeutic imagination through purposeful engagement with qualitative research', the author John McLeod, our final published respondent, discusses the above chapters in relation to the question of how counsellors and psychotherapists can make use of routinely reading published research reports to support and enhance their work with clients. In particular, reading strategies are described that promote the development of therapeutic imagination.

Reviewers' comments include: This response to the papers in the special issue is well written and raises interesting points.

Finally we have, as previously mentioned, our Endnote. Here, the author Julia Cayne is concerned with drawing attention to the importance of the kind of knowing that emerges through the tacit, contextual, contemporaneousness of human experience seen as of particular relevance to psychotherapeutic practice and research. Without disregarding theory, the author argues that it is important to question the nature of theory in that it has been abstracted from human experience meaning there are limitations when it is applied without understanding the uniqueness of every situation, whether practice or research. The aim is to attempt to show, with the help from Kierkegaard, Derrida, and psychoanalysis, how seemingly coincidental experiences can lead to a creative process of thought, seen here as a phenomenological approach to inquiry about human being.

We hope you will enjoy reading the research presented here. Qualitative research in the area of psychotherapy is crucially important and the use of increasingly innovative methodological approaches sheds an important light not only on the psychotherapeutic journeys that are depicted in this volume but also the meaning making of our clients and how this can be captured in all its complexity.

John McCleod's above Chapter 13 has 'love' in its title and as Tina Turner has sung 'What's love got to do with it'. Even if we do not know what love is can we research it, let alone measure it! Yet there appears a growing movement to only teach trainees psychotherapy that is evidence based. Does that mean such trainings are without love? So if quantitative research is loveless can qualitative research as in the chapters of this book, and particularly phenomenology, help us be open to such dimensions as tacit, practical knowledge that does not exclude 'love' but rather adds to 'evidence based practice' though enabling innovation and imagination in psychotherapy? Furthermore, are those phenomenologies based on psychology or philosophy more appropriate or do some, at the very best, get us closest to only a 'second-hand emotion'?

References

Husserl, E. (2001). *Logical investigations* (D. Moran, Ed., 2nd ed., Vol. 1). Routledge.

Lave, J., & Wenger, E. (1991). *Situated learning: Legitimate peripheral participation*. University of Cambridge Press.

Loewenthal, D. (2011). *Post-existentialism and the psychological therapies. Towards a therapy without foundations*. Routledge.

Loewenthal, D. (2019). Phenomenology, personal therapy and the training of psychological therapists. *European Journal of Psychotherapy & Counselling, 21*(1), 1–4. https://doi.org/10.1080/13642537.2019.1565667

Loewenthal, D. (2022). Is psychotherapy fundamentally threatened, with the demise of published case studies, to become neither an art and/nor a science? *European Journal of Psychotherapy & Counselling, 24*(3), 263–268. https://doi.org/10.1080/13642537.2022.2115646

Masfield, A., Addis, K., & M, E. (2001). Manual-based treatment part 2: The advantages of manual-based practice in psychotherapy. *Evidence-Based Mental Health, 4*(4), 100–101. https://doi.org/10.1136/ebmh.4.4.100

Montaigne. (1800). *Essays*. Luke Hanford.

Moran, D. (1999). *Introduction to phenomenology*. Routledge.

Oakeshott, M. (1962). *Rationalism in politics*. Methuen.

Polanyi, M. (1967). *The tacit dimension*. Anchor Books, Double Day and Company. Qualitative Research in Mental Health Conference, 31 August to 2 September 2023, Hungary. https://qrmh9.com

Roth, A., & Fonagy, P. (2006). *What works for whom: A critical review of psychotherapy research*. Guildford Press.

Selltiz, C., Jahoda, M., Deutsch, M., & Cook, S. W. (1959). *Research methods in social relations* (Revised One-Volume Edition). Henry Holt and Company.

Smith, J. A. (2003). Interpretative phenomenological analysis. In J. A. Smith & M. Osborn (Eds.), *Qualitative psychology: A practical guide to research methods* (pp. 51–80). Sage.

Spinelli, E. (1989). *The interpreted world: An introduction to phenomenological psychology*. Sage.

OPEN ACCESS

Psychotherapeutic research and practice: Do we need to talk about 'efficacy'?

Patricia Talens, Del Loewenthal and Onel Brooks

ABSTRACT

In this article, we address how standardisation in psychotherapeutic research and practice can create a 'procrustean bed' which leads to conformity rather than an ethical response to what emerges in the moment. Articulated, three points of conflict in which we discuss how the therapist or researcher may be rendered 'ineffective' in the name of 'efficacy'. We explore some of the implications for idiosyncratic practices in psychotherapy, which are rooted in a foundation of ethics and philosophy, when the paradigm of empirically 'evidence-based practices' (EBP), which are rooted in measurement, takes centre stage and are overwhelmingly favoured in the industry of funded therapies. The first point of conflict is in relation to conversation itself; exploring the place of hermeneutics and interpretation within therapeutic dialogue and research. The second point explores what it means to take up a discovery-oriented stance and the implications this has for 'evidence'; further delving into the way our demand for 'evidence' may be impacting how psychotherapeutic research and practice is carried out. The final point aims to explore the infrastructure and work environment of funded therapies in the United Kingdom.

Introduction

> I see you and you see me. I experience you and you experience me. I see your behaviour. You see my behaviour. But I do not and never will see your experience of me. Just as you cannot 'see' my experience of you.
>
> (Laing, 1967, p. 15)

In psychotherapy, one might say the therapist is concerned with emerging experience. And yet, increasingly, there is a great deal of research within psychotherapy which is geared towards a scientifically proven formula that stipulates and demonstrates 'efficacy'. This cultural shift towards a calculative and measurable sense of people's experience draws a concern in relation to its systematising application of psychotherapy. In particular, there is concern towards psychotherapeutic research and practices, which offer 'evidence' towards an outcome measure but which fail to articulate the complex, multi-layered, unmapped and unmeasurable aspects of psychotherapy. Nevertheless, contemporary psychotherapy appears to be marked by a restrictive idea that there is an inherent goal of 'symptom' reduction whilst the ways to attain such a goal have exponentially grown and diversified. For decades, there has been a gradual reorientation toward finding the most 'efficient' ways to achieve this reduction in 'symptoms' which has in turn become its own goal (Dunne, 1993).

Within this article, the word 'psychotherapy' is purposely used as a flexible umbrella term which encompasses all psychotherapeutic paradigms and practices rather than one definitive definition. Therefore, we are able to lend ourselves to a wider understanding which encompasses countless frameworks, individual viewpoints, and disciplines such as philosophy, art, literature and science to name a few. It starts us from the position that what psychotherapy is and what it does is a complex task which can vary depending on time, place, paradigm and situation.

Within this broad spectrum of psychotherapy sits a paradigm of approaches which are increasingly concerned with ideas of 'efficacy' through repeatable 'manualised methods'. As such, using 'randomised controlled trials' (RCTs) as the preferred methodology is often considered the 'gold standard' and is increasingly becoming the go-to for researchers and practitioners (Dalal, 2018; Dobson, 2010). This has led to growing uncertainty regarding the nature of evidence-based practice (EBP) and the effect this has on practitioners, clients, the therapeutic space and research itself (Masfield & Addis, 2001).

It seems that despite the divergence in thought and theory regarding the purpose and ways in which psychotherapy is carried out, it continues to undergo a systematising process which answers to the demands of quantitative 'evidence' (Waller et al., 2012; Wampold et al., 2017). The outcome of which is an '. . . increasingly sophisticated calculus of efficiency and economy in assembling means towards ends' (Dunne, 1993, p. 177). Simultaneously, there is a growing body of work which stipulates how variation in treatment models has little impact or effect on improving outcomes in psychotherapy (Brown et al., 1999). Instead, disadvantages are encountered due to the inadequate mapping of psychotherapy on a more complex and hermeneutic level, because ' . . . manualizing psychological interventions as if they were independent of those administering and receiving them, does not reflect what is known about psychotherapy outcome' (Duncan & Miller, 2006, p. 4).

Through this, we consider the implications for psychotherapeutic practice and research, when it is forced into paradigms which define and reduce complexity. We ask if a crisis point has been reached in psychotherapy; when training, standardisation and professionalisation monopolise the psychotherapeutic space which at its core holds the therapeutic relationship as its most valued asset and often as a prerequisite for therapy?

Hermeneutics as 'openness' in conversation

To define and instruct what a therapist does and the ways in which one goes about therapy is a tension point which has existed since Sigmund Freud but which is potentially reaching a critical point in psychotherapy today; too far towards the needs and wants of an industry which holds its own agenda risks personal disengagement. Simultaneously, showing up and taking one's own unique action without any sense of responsibility, reflection or accountability is equally problematic. It is the tension between these places that this article considers to be the 'ethical'. We engage with the ethical when we can respond to the environment whilst sustaining the unique and innate capacity of other possibilities available (Orange, 2014). With this in mind, we ask how, if at all, we can consider meaningful traditions and rituals in psychotherapy whilst still allowing each therapeutic encounter to change and influence our way of being? Here, a phenomenological understanding of language and dialogue might be seen as a potential avenue.

Within phenomenology, conversation and understanding can be seen as an adventure through its uncertainty which offers a multiplicity of meaning. Through lending ourselves to a fluid and unrestrictive hermeneutical encounter, we can broaden the horizon of self-knowledge and human experience (Gadamer, 1989). Central to the idea of expanding horizons is the notion that conversation requires a form of 'openness' within language and positions itself as an unfinished event. Showing how the ongoing nature of discourse offers a foundation of potentiality when dialogue is not restricted or pre-established.

Through conversation, we find a source of growth and self-discovery when space is given to explore one's own language and possible meaning. This recognises that '... meaning is not simply something "expressed" or "reflected" in language: it is actually *produced* by it' (Eagleton, 1990, p. 60). From this perspective, language and the world are entwined and bound to each other in a cyclical ongoing process making being-in-the-world essentially linguistic (Gadamer, 1983). Here the argument is that we are in essence brought into existence through language or even a lack of language and as such, it holds a creative power as well as a revelatory nature (Gadamer, 1983). In this sense, language is linked to a 'happening' or emerging event which is positioned as a form of 'becoming' (Vandevelde, 2014). In this, language creates the potential to hold pre-established meaning whilst simultaneously allowing a different understanding to emerge in the moment.

Consequently, whilst language and meaning are to some degree inherited, we are always in some way part of the language from which we speak as it speaks us into 'being'. This identifies the need for psychotherapy to hold space for a renewed sense of self through speech, articulating how '. . .the role of the therapist is that of a conversational artist – an architect of the dialogical process – whose expertise is in the arena of creating space for and facilitating a dialogical conversation' (Anderson et al., 1992, p. 27).

This emphasises the importance of facilitating a space of 'not-knowing' in practice and research, as new meaning and understanding can emerge through re-evaluation. This is not to say that we standardise this particular practice as a rule, as this in itself would become a fixed interpretation (Anderson et al., 1992). Instead, in the case of research, it is to recognise the rich and diverse ecosystem of theory which exists, not as a single way of practice but as a potentiality. Equally, in the case of psychotherapeutic practice, to recognise how allowing fluidity in language with no fixed interpretation can be of benefit. This, however, can create a conflict with paradigms that are based on measurement and require a fixed understanding of terms and conditions. Consequently, could the demand for ostensible reliable 'scientific' outcome measures in funded organisations be causing a form of ecocide? Tilting the balance towards evermore defined and calculative ways of being.

The scope of this article cannot fully articulate the breadth and significance of ethics and philosophy within psychotherapy. What can be articulated, is the importance of therapeutic paradigms which explore the capacity to 'be with' rather than 'doing to' as a source of ethics, learning and development in psychotherapy. For example, theory which speaks to the ungraspable nature of the 'Other' and the ethics of our response (Lévinas, 1967). Or the connective and creative power of play in psychotherapy as being unique and spontaneous (Winnicott, 2005). The philosophy of embracing engagement with otherness in such a way that we meet the other in all its uniqueness, not the perceived or known, but in what emerges in the moment (Buber & Smith, 2013). Or ideas of how the body is seen as the primary sight of knowing (Merleau-Ponty & Landes, 1945/2014)

These references are just a glimpse toward paradigms which see the researcher and practitioner not simply as an object in the world but instead as a source of possibilities for action within different environments. Embodying qualities through practice and therapeutic encounters can offer skills and knowledge in a way that cognitive models cannot: 'Acquiring a habit (is) the reworking and renewal of the body schema' (Merleau-Ponty & Landes, 1945/2014, p. 143). It emphasises the call to step into and allow unknown and unpredictable aspects of ourselves to be discovered through a leap into that which cannot be mapped. A call which can be considered an ethical demand; 'Abstract thought requires him to become disinterested in order to acquire knowledge; the ethical demand is that he become infinitely interested in existing' (Kierkegaard, 1941, p. 117).

Therefore, if we become habitual in the way we carry out tasks and practices, do we risk developing a predisposition to acting in particular repeatable ways despite being presented with various situations? In essence, praxis shows that our skills, thinking, and perceptions are embodied activities which can shape the ways in which we feel and act in the world (Merleau-Ponty & Landes, 1945/2014). Hence, whilst research which is based on 'efficacy' outcome offers one form of knowledge to the therapist, could they also be hindering praxis in the therapeutic encounter? This is especially poignant when considering that we cannot know every situation which will emerge in the therapy room. Thinking we can prepare with techniques will never offer the sufficient, ethical judgements needed to be responsive to the context of the situation (Finlay, 2013).

Practice and research as formula over discovery

Psychotherapeutic research and practice increasingly have a propensity towards EBP due to their calculable outcomes. Meaning the current situation faced in psychotherapy is one of being engulfed in an evidence-based race (Guilfoyle, 2008) leaving us to ask where is the finish line? EBT, in the form of manualised practices, fails to account for the nuance and tailored understanding which emerges in the therapy room as this is essentially always unique within the context of the individual. Criticism has been levelled up at manualised approaches for their restrictive nature which can impact the responsiveness of the therapist in real time and situation (Marshall, 2009). As such, we risk negating a wealth of information and understanding in relation to practice and what is considered 'effective' psychotherapy. By 'effectiveness' we are speaking about the therapist's capacity to carry out a practice in a way which is informed and yet responsive to the context and situation directly in front of them, not solely knowing through metric outcome. Highlighting the difference between what it means to inquire and what it means to seek: '…for in inquiry there is no end to be gained and held. Inquiry does not seek answers' (Heaton, 1997, p. 95).

This raises the question of how we use methods to order the world around us and how this might result in our obtaining knowledge that simply fits the paradigm within which it sits, rather than lending itself to something else. For Thomas Kuhn (1970) this meant 'normal science' stating how it ' … is a solver of puzzles, not a tester of paradigms' (p. 144). A community is established within a paradigm which conducts its practice without pushing the boundaries and creates adaptions for any anomalies. Within this 'Normal science does not aim at novelty but at clearing up the status quo. It tends to discover what it expects to discover' (Hacking, 2012, p. xxvi). This is different to revolutionary science which essentially causes a paradigm shift when anomalies build up and interrupt 'normal science' with unavoidable crisis and turmoil.

The issue sits in our use of methods to gain a measure of 'truth' or 'evidence' rather than testing out the paradigm. The implication is that the method itself is applied from a foundation which is essentially built by the community attempting to ascertain knowledge, as such, it is always starting from a pre-established position (Kuhn, 2012). Significantly, it is the claim of 'truth' which is brought into question because 'normal science' does not progress in the way we think it does. It is not slowly making its way to the ideas of 'truth' but instead reinforcing what it already knows. With this in mind, could manualised practice in some way be seen as problem solving rather than shifting and testing the paradigms in which they are situated? It is here that phenomenological perspectives may be helpful in challenging paradigms. Phenomenology does not disentangle and as such, offers a move from efficient and parameter setting methodologies. Instead, it embraces the uncanny, the unexplainable and allows for an embodied sensibility to emerge (Finlay, 2015).

It is the formulating in to concrete and repeatable practice which becomes problematic rather than allowing elasticity through discovery and a reshaping of understanding. One can even become critical of attempts to utilise hermeneutics as a tool or an ancillary method within the human sciences when this too becomes prescriptive (Applebaum, 2012). This is because things begin to show up as orderable and placed into an inventory or reservoir of options rather than the 'embodied sensibility' of a situation (Wrathall, 2019). This lends itself to the idea that science can be an alienating practice when dogma and traditional methods are neither challenged nor considered as a paradigm. In essence, the production of rules and processes which give no opportunity for challenge can become a hindrance to the openness of inquiry both in research and practice.

What is posited here are the ways in which a challenge to methodological rules and boundaries can elicit core discoveries. Paul Feyerabend (2010) challenges the traditional view of science and its standardised methodological approach as providing reliable and objective frameworks, in favour of a pluralistic approach for inquiring. Increasingly, there is a call for diversity and difference with a particular focus on a dialog across difference (Maxwell, 2004). This in essence means that we must be able to dialog with that which is other to us. Concluding that a particular meaning in dialogue cannot be objective or universally valid but instead is situated in a 'fusion of horizons'. This leads to the nature of understanding as an infinite process without a final goal or result, in essence, it is this fusion of possible meaning which allows growth as different interpretations are brought together (Gadamer, 1989).

One's ability to come off course and take up a different experience or interpretation is of importance for the ways we are shaped in practice and for the ways in which research is conducted. Through the idea of 'calculative' and 'meditative' thinking (Heidegger, 1959) we are introduced to the ways we encounter and think about our environment. Through 'calculative' thinking the world takes on a mechanistic view, but over time, this can create a hindrance and dull our meditative capacities as it forces our actions.

Holding space for 'meditative' thinking, which can move through tensions, complexities and paradoxes, is paramount to psychotherapy. This is not in the name of obscurantism but rather a giving room for what might emerge as opposed to seeking 'evidence' to reaffirm the status quo. Allowing ourselves as practitioners and researchers to tolerate 'being adrift' (Ogden, 1997) could be helpful in connecting to situations with a deeper level of complexity and creativity. Through this, we can reconstitute, reconsider, revaluate and essentially keep open the possibility for new understanding to emerge. However, what happens when our environment erodes the space for any thought which is not calculative?

Making it fit at any cost

With little to no empirical support for the idea that manualised interventions are more effective than interventions which are non-manualised, a case is put forward that they should not be promoted as advanced or clinically superior (King & Moutsou, 2010; Truijens et al., 2019). And so, if the science isn't there as some would suggest (Shedler, 2018) we are left to wonder why there has been such a shift towards calculative and manualised practices?

One explanation for the evolution of manualised practices in psychotherapy concludes that efforts are being made to reduce complexity by recommending it to practitioners on the basis of efficacy (Wampold et al., 2017). With the professionalisation of psychotherapy as a discipline, a greater demand has been placed on the institution to establish a more authoritative answer toward what psychotherapy is and what it is for (Mahrer, 2009). Drawing a division between exploring the implications of theory as possibilities and the application of theory for 'evidence' (Loewenthal & Snell, 2003). In turn, we see psychotherapy moving towards monitoring and instructing practices that fit rather than promoting critical engagement with the philosophical and ethical underpinnings of psychotherapy.

This cultural shift towards a calculative and measurable understanding of people's experiences raises a question regarding the nature of knowledge and ethical stance in psychotherapy (R. Miller, 2004), prompting the argument that manualised practices and research are increasingly aligned with a calculative industry which is potentially motivated by good numbers rather than good science. This has the potential to create a form of scientism when metrics devoid of context are utilised as 'evidence' to paint a picture of reality. It: '. . .misunderstands science. Good scientists are well aware that there are many ways of understanding reality' (Heaton, 2014, p. 34).

Of particular interest is the notion that manualised approaches receive widespread recognition not because of their effectiveness in psychotherapy but because they comfortably integrate with social networks of power (Guilfoyle, 2008). The repeatability of manualised practice lends itself to already existing infrastructures built for the medical model and as such can be distributed under cost-effective and time-efficient policies, becoming a politically convenient form of technology (Guilfoyle, 2008). In essence, psychotherapy is being caught up in a metric game for which the production of outcome is politically and economically motivated (Jackson & Rizq, 2019).

This is perhaps most visible through the development of governmental schemes such as 'Improving Access to Psychological Therapies' (IAPT), which was seen as a way to address the economic, social and individual cost of mental health in the United Kingdom (Layard & Clarke, 2014). The question of how to apply mental health support on such a scale was answered by utilising a blueprint of the medical model which seeks to deliver treatment with rigour and efficiency. The critique, however, is that this reliance on a medical model, which dominates in the paradigm of RCTs, is not a satisfactory model of psychotherapy. Instead, utilising practices and methodologies from a model which seeks conformity and regulation might obstruct or hinder the development of psychotherapeutic research and practice (King & Moutsou, 2010).

With monitoring systems and the collection of minimum data sets (MDS) built into the very fabric of IAPT, we see a wide spread system of frequent screening and monitoring become second nature for the people who use the service (Bendall & McGrath, 2020). Numerous screening tools provide a constant stream of evaluation and the ordering of provision in relation to outcomes. These highly bureaucratic stages of development belong to the third wave of professionalisation which threatens creativity and risks a self-promoting industry (Davies, 2009). For therapists in highly monitored institutions such as IAPT: '. . .extensive monitoring and practices or accountability have come to undermine psychotherapeutic efforts to care for patients as "people"' (Bruun, 2023, p. 313). As such, we have established and standardised an audit culture and a managerialism of care. From this, meeting institutional targets has increasingly become the goal, which in turn has created a tension for practitioners and impacted practice, showing '. . .the implementation of strategies that defeat the purpose of delivering effective treatment' (Marshall, 2009, p. 117). This is because the paradigm of evidence-based manuals and research depends on an empirically reduced conceptualisation of psychotherapy (Berg and Slaattelid, 2017) and so: '... manuals focus attention toward a wasteland and away from fertile ground' (Wampold, 2001, p. 212).

Conclusion

What we have explored here, is a need to recognise that therapy is a source of potentiality in which to create and encounter through articulating one's own language. That the therapist learns through a combination of processes which are not simply cognitive but also embodied through practice. Within all these domains, there needs to be a level of engagement and openness for a 'fusion of horizons' both in practice and research paradigms. There are, of course, mandates and expectations which organisations both public and private are ascribed to fulfil; this, however, does not mean that a negotiation of space and openness cannot be met.

What is advocated for is a practice of critical engagement with our relationship to methods and techniques in research and practice. It is an encouragement that we continue running the borders of theory and practice in the hope that we can attempt to have some awareness of our 'embeddedness' to the situation which presents. This requires that we acknowledge how we are in some ways always entangled in method, theory and practice rather than separate from it (Willig, 2008). In this sense, 'efficacy' is not an arbitrary tool that simply provides a clinician with the best available data. It is also a shaping force that is shifting to the very culture of psychotherapy when we allow 'efficacy' to favour the system over the people within it.

Disclosure statement

No potential conflict of interest was reported by the author(s).

References

Anderson, H., & Goolishian, H. (1992). The client is the expert: A not-knowing approach to therapy. In S. McNamee & K.J. Gergen (Eds.), *Therapy as social construction* (pp. 25–39). Sage Publications, Inc.

Applebaum, M. (2012). Phenomenological psychological research and science. *Journal of Phenomenology Psychology*, *43*(1), 36–72. https://doi.org/10.1163/156916212X632952

Bendall, C., & McGrath, L. (2020). Contending with minimum data set: Subjectivity, linearity and dividualising experience in improving access to psychological therapies. *Health*, *24*(1), 94–109. https://doi.org/10.1177/1363459318785718

Berg, H., & Slaattelid, R. (2017). Facts and values in psychotherapy: A critique of the empirical reduction of psychotherapy within evidence-based practice. *Journal of Evaluation in Clinical Practice, 23*, 1075–1080.

Brown, J., Dreis, S., & Nace, D. K. (1999). What really makes a difference in psychotherapy outcome? Why does managed care want to know? In M. A. Hubble, B. L. Duncan, & S. D. Miller (Eds.), *The heart and soul of change. What works in therapy* (pp. 389–406). American Psychological Association.

Bruun, K. M. (2023). A factory of therapy: Accountability and the monitoring of psychological therapy in IAPT. *Anthropology & Medicine, 30*(4), 313–329. https://doi.org/10.1080/13648470.2023.2217773

Buber, M. & Smith, R. G. (Trans.). (2013). *I and Thou*. Bloomsbury Academic.

Dalal, F. (2018). *CBT: The cognitive behavioural tsunami. Managerialism, politics and the corruptions of science*. Routledge.

Davies, J. (2009). Psychotherapy and the third wave of professionalisation. *European Journal of Psychotherapy & Counselling, 11*(2), 191–202. https://doi.org/10.1080/13642530902978652

Dobson, K. S. (2010). *Handbook of cognitive behavioural therapies* (3rd ed.). The Guildford Press.

Duncan, B. L., & Miller, S. D. (2006). Treatment manuals do not improve outcomes. In J. Norcross, R. Levant, & L. Beutler Eds.(2005). *Evidence-based practices in mental health: Debate and dialogue on the fundamental questions* (pp. 1–21). American Psychological Association Press.

Dunne, J. (1993). *Back to the rough ground: Practical judgment and the lure of technique*. University of Notre Dame.

Eagleton, T. (1990). *The ideology of the aesthetic*. Oxford.

Feyerabend, P. (2010). *Against method*. New Left Books.

Finlay, L. (2013). Unfolding the phenomenological research process: Iterative stages of "seeing afresh". *Journal of Humanistic Psychology, 53*(2), 172–201. https://doi.org/10.1177/0022167812453877

Finlay, L. (2015). Sensing and making sense: Embodying metaphor in relational-centered psychotherapy. *The Humanistic Psychologist, 43*(4), 338–353. https://doi.org/10.1080/08873267.2014.993070

Gadamer, H. G. (1983). Hermeneutics as practical philosophy. In F. G. Lawrence Trans. *Reason in the age of science* (pp. 88–113). The MIT Press.

Gadamer, H. G. (1989). *Truth and method* (2nd ed.). J. Weinsheimer and D. G. Marshall Trans. Stagbooks.

Guilfoyle, M. (2008). CBT'S integration into societal networks of power. *European Journal of Psychotherapy & Counselling, 10*(3), 197–206. https://doi.org/10.1080/13642530802337884

Hacking, I. (2012). *Introduction: A role for history the structure of scientific revolutions, 50th anniversary edition*. In T. S. Kuhn (Eds.), University of Chicago Press.

Heaton, J. M. (1997). Pyrrhonian scepticism: A therapeutic phenomenology. *Journal of the British Society for Phenomenology, 28*(1), 80–96. https://doi.org/10.1080/00071773.1997.11007185

Heaton, J. M. (2014). *Wittgenstein and psychotherapy. From paradox to wonder*. Palgrave Macmillan.

Heidegger, M. (1959). *Discourse on thinking* (J.M. Anderson & H. E. Freund, Trans.). Harper. Row.

Jackson, C., & Rizq, R. (2019). *The industrialisation of care: Counselling, psychotherapy and the Impact of IAPT*. PCCS Books.

Kierkegaard, S. (1941). Concluding unscientific postscript. In M. S. Friedman Eds. (1991). (Ed.), *The worlds of existentialism: Critical reader with new preface* (2nd ed., pp. 114–117). Humanities Press International.

King, L., & Moutsou, C. (2010). *Rethinking audit culture. A critical look at evidence-based practice in psychotherapy and beyond.* PCCS Books.

Kuhn, T. S. (2012). *The structure of scientific revolutions* (50th ed.). University of Chicago Press.

Laing, R. D. (1967). *The politics of experience and the bird of paradise.* Penguin.

Layard, R., & Clarke, D. M. (2014). *Thrive: The power of evidence-based psychological therapies.* Penguin Books.

Lévinas, E. (1967). *Totality and infinity: An essay on exteriority* (A. Lingis & Pittsburgh, Trans.). Duquesne University Press.

Loewenthal, D., & Snell, R. (2003). *Post-modernism for psychotherapists a critical reader.* Routledge.

Mahrer, A. R. (2009). What is psychotherapy for? An almost official answer. *The Humanistic Psychologist, 37*(3), 223–234. https://doi.org/10.1080/08873260903206347

Marshall, W. L. (2009). Manualization: A blessing or a curse? *Journal of Sexual Aggression, 15*(2), 109–120. https://doi.org/10.1080/13552600902907320

Masfield, A. K., & Addis, M. E. (2001). Manual-based treatment part 2: The advantages of manual-based practice in psychotherapy. *Evidence-Based Mental Health, 4* (4), 100–101. https://doi.org/10.1136/ebmh.4.4.100

Maxwell, J. A. (2004). Reemergent scientism, postmodernism, and dialogue across differences. *Qualitative Inquiry, 10*(1), 35–41. https://doi.org/10.1177/1077800403259492

Merleau-Ponty, M. & Landes D. A. (Trans.). (1945/2014). *Phenomenology of perception.* Routledge.

Miller, R. (2004). *Facing human suffering: Psychology and psychotherapy as moral engagement.* American Psychological Association.

Ogden, T. (1997). Reverie and interpretation. *The Psychoanalytic Quarterly, 66*(4), 567–595. https://doi.org/10.1080/21674086.1997.11927546

Orange, D. M. (2014). What kind of ethics? Loewald on responsibility and atonement. *Psychoanalytic Psychology, 31*(4), 560–569. https://doi.org/10.1037/a0038062

Shedler, J. (2018). Where is the evidence for "evidence-based" therapy? *The Psychiatric Clinics of North America, 41*(2), 319–329. https://doi.org/10.1016/j.psc.2018.02.001

Truijens, F., Zühlke van Hulzen, L., & Vanheule, S. (2019). To manualize, or not to manualize: Is that still the question? A systematic review of empirical evidence for manual superiority in psychological treatment. *Journal of Clinical Psychology, 75* (3), 329–343. https://doi.org/10.1002/jclp.22712

Vandevelde, P. (2014). Language as the house of being? How to bring intelligibility to Heidegger while keeping the excitement. *Philosophy Compass, 9*(4), 253–262. https://doi.org/10.1111/phc3.12117

Waller, G., Stringer, H., & Mayer, C. (2012). What cognitive behavioural techniques do therapists report using when delivering cognitive behaviour therapy for the eating disorder? *Journal of Consulting & Clinical Psychology, 80*(1), 171–175. https://doi.org/10.1037/a0026559

Wampold, B. E. (2001). *The great psychotherapy debate: Models, methods, and findings.* Erlbaum.

Wampold, B. E., Baldwin, S. A., Holtforth, M. G., & Imel, Z. E. (2017). *What characterizes effective therapists?*. In L. G. Castonguay & C. E. Hill (Eds.), *How and why are some therapists better than others? Understanding therapist effects* (pp. 37–53). American Psychological Association.

Willig, C. (2008). *Introducing qualitative research in psychotherapy: Adventures in theory and method* (2nd ed.). Open University Press.

Winnicott, D. W. (2005). *Playing and reality* (2nd ed.). Routledge.

Wrathall, M. (2019). The task of thinking in a technological age. In A. J. Wendland, C. Merwin, & C. Hadjioannou (Eds.), *Heidegger on technology*. Routledge.

OPEN ACCESS

Travelling in time: Using interpretative phenomenological analysis (IPA) to examine temporal aspects of the personal experience of issues in health and well-being*

Jonathan A. Smith

ABSTRACT

This paper describes a model for thinking of how participants make sense of temporal aspects of their lived experience. The paper argues for the valuable input that interpretative phenomenological analysis (IPA) can make to exploring this experiential timeline. After a brief introduction to IPA as an experiential research methodology, I will describe the growing interest in longitudinal research among qualitative researchers and outline recent thinking on this by leading researcher Bren Neale. I will then point to the distinctive contribution IPA can make to understanding personal experience of time and change. I will present a taxonomy of my IPA research engaging with it and illustrate each study type with research I have been involved in. During the paper we will see the way in which there are indeed two time-travelers involved in this process: researcher and the participant.

Introduction

In this paper I outline a model for thinking about how participants make sense of temporal aspects of their lived experience. This is conceptualized as the experiential timeline which affords an understanding of participants' dynamic sense-making through time, for example, participants in the present making comparisons with where they have come from in the past and imagining where they will be going in the future. The value of the experiential timeline, however, is how it points to the multiple ways in which this temporal domain can be experientially encountered. I will argue that

---

*An earlier version of this paper was given in an invited Keynote address at the Qualitative Research in Mental Health Conference (QRMH9), Budapest, August 2023.

particular features of interpretative phenomenological analysis (IPA) as an experiential qualitative methodology make it a valuable approach to facilitate this examination of temporal experience and I will show how I myself have conducted research in this way. An important inspiration for developing this experiential timeline was reading Bren Neale's 2021 book which offers an important integrative understanding of the development of qualitative longitudinal research. Reading her thoughtful book led me to reflect back on my own research biography and the different styles and designs of qualitative research I had employed. What I am presenting in this paper is the synthesis that has arisen from this thinking and rethinking.

The primary focus of this model is the participant navigating through their life course. What becomes clear when thinking about the experiential timeline, however, is that there are in fact two time-travelers involved in this process: the participant and the researcher. Sometimes the researcher is travelling alongside, and closely in step with, the participant in the temporal domain, but sometimes their trajectories can become creatively uncoupled. Thinking about it, there are actually three different people embarking on this temporal journey as you the reader are invited as a third person to join the time travelling!

Key features of interpretative phenomenological analysis (IPA)

Interpretative phenomenological analysis (IPA) (Smith et al., 2022) is an approach dedicated to the detailed exploration of personal meaning and lived experience. IPA aims to explore how participants are making sense of their personal and social world, to ascertain the meanings that particular experiences, events, and states hold for participants. IPA has now become widely established and is now used to address a wide range of experiential research issues, much of it in health and well- being.

IPA is phenomenological in that it is concerned with a detailed understanding of the participant's lived experience, attempting to understand it, as far as possible, as it shows itself and in its own terms rather than as defined by prior hypotheses or prejudices (Moran, 2000). IPA also emphasizes this project requires an interpretative endeavour on the part of the researcher who is trying to make sense of the participants trying to make sense of their world (Heidegger, 1962/1927). The final important theoretical underpinning for IPA is idiography. IPA is interested in the detailed examination of particular cases, in understanding how particular people have experienced particular events before it begins to look for patterns of convergence and divergence across cases.

A maturing vision of qualitative longitudinal research

There is growing interest in qualitative longitudinal research (QLR), reflected in Neale's (2021) important book which provides an excellent introduction to, and conceptualization of, this area. Neale thinks of QLR as a disparate set of activities only recently consolidated into something approaching a coherent movement. Consonant with the perspective of IPA, Neale stresses the subjective personal experience of time, arguing QLR is concerned with: 'the complex intertwining of "fixed" clock time and "fluid" experiential time and the need to work across these dualities to achieve a more holistic understanding of social processes' (p. 63–4). And Neale valuably asserts the need for ecological validity in research methods concerned with temporal experience: 'If the social world is fluid then we need fluid modes of inquiry to investigate and understand it' (p. 35).

One of Neale's particularly insightful points is to do with the direction of travel in QLR. We tend to think of longitudinal research as being prospective- following people forward through time but Neale links this closely with the retrospective gaze, looking back:

> In its purest form, longitudinal research is prospective. It follows the same people in real time capturing changes & continuities as they occur ... A retrospective approach explores dynamic processes through hindsight, a gaze backwards in time from the vantage point of the present. In QL research, the temporal gaze is directed both back and forward in time, oscillating between the two. (Neale p. 5)

Therefore, one can consider an integrated vision for QLR which involves movements in both directions on the biographical timeline:

Prospective look forward ————————→
←———————— *Retrospective look back*

IPA as useful for exploring time, process and change in personal experience

IPA can make a distinctive and significant contribution to research examining temporal experience. IPA is first and foremost concerned with the detailed examination of personal lived experience. As it is the case that human experience occurs and unfolds temporally, it is valuable to see how IPA methodology can be harnessed to offer a lens on this process of change and continuity over time. It is IPA's commitment to examining the detailed verbal accounts obtained from participants that attunes it to the complex project of considering temporal experience. This is also facilitated by IPA's commitment to first examining each participant case in its own terms- thereby exploring indications of temporal process in each individual case before looking for patterns of convergence and divergence across case.

Thinking about the different ways in which time has been captured in work that I have done leads me to articulate the idea of the experiential timeline:

Past < > Present < > Future

In this model, experiential life is considered mobile and moving dynamically along this experiential timeline. In its most straightforward form, life unfolds linearly and prospectively as the individual lives their life forward. At each point along that timeline, however, the individual can stop and reflect on the process that is occurring and can do this in either direction. Thus, at any moment in the present, the person can look backwards and generate a past as experientially understood and can look forward and imagine *possible futures*.

The IPA researcher also moves along this experiential timeline. There is a growing corpus of IPA research which is longitudinal in the conventional sense, whereby the researcher joins the participant at time points along a chronological trajectory and collects data to help construct a detailed analytic account of that unfolding chronology (Farr & Nizza, 2019). Then working synchronically during that process, the researcher can be witness to the participant's moments of reflection backwards and forwards and build this into the analytic narrative. However, it is also possible for the researcher to step aside from the participant's explicit temporal exploration and examine the process from a different angle or with a different lens. For example, while the participant may be closely engaged in a contemplation of the future, the researcher may be examining links between this and information available about the participant's past.

Taxonomy: IPA and personal experience over time

The thinking I have done around this dynamic experiential timeline model has led me to conceptualize the following taxonomy of my longitudinal IPA research:

Foundational work

- Naturalistic prospective (change explicit)
- Naturalistic retrospective (change implicit)

Recent work

- Impact of intervention: prospective (change explicit)
- Impact of intervention: retrospective (change implicit)

You will see here there is an emphasis on change. This follows from an elemental model of human development and an emphasis on recognizing that humans develop and therefore change across the life course. Of course, that process is more nuanced and temporal experience can be seen as involving a mix of change and continuity. However, it is the change that is more usually of interest and concern and the continuity is more easily conceptualized when seen in the context of change and potential change.

My early work involved detailed studies of participants' temporal experience and some of this was longitudinal in the conventional sense of following people prospectively through time. However, thinking along similar lines to Neale, it is also the case that other research I conducted can be considered longitudinal, in exploring how participants moved back and forth along the experiential timeline between present and past.

More recently, I have been involved in several mixed-methods longitudinal studies examining the effect of interventions. Again, in some of this work the IPA analysis has been prospective and in some it has been retrospective.

I think each of the temporal designs in the taxonomy makes a useful and distinctive contribution to our understanding of lived experience and I would now like to offer illustrations of each of them in practice.

Naturalistic prospective (change explicit)

I will give a brief summary of my early work in this category. While pioneering at the time, the work is longitudinal as generally recognized and I wish to give more attention in this paper to the designs which are more distinctive.

In this study I followed a small number of women through pregnancy and the transition to motherhood. The study explored important features of their personal experience of this transition: concerns, relationships etc. I conducted interviews with each woman at 3, 6–7, 9 months pregnant and then at 5 months after birth. The women kept diaries in between visits where they recorded their own thoughts on the process they were undergoing. The main findings of the study were that the women move from uncertainty/anxiety in the early phase of pregnancy, through social assimilation and preparation for what is to come in the middle phase, to some psychological integration after the birth. A particularly distinctive feature of the study was how women drew on relationships with significant others (partners, friends, and neighbours also going through pregnancy) to learn about, prepare for, and 'rehearse' becoming a mother. See Smith (1999) for more details of the study.

Naturalistic retrospective (change implicit)

I have been involved in several studies on the impact of severe chronic pain. Interestingly, much of the participants' concern is with psychologically damaging aspects of pain- with the way in which the pain is having a debilitating impact on their sense of self. Here is one woman talking about her pain:

> I can't help it even though I don't like it. It's the mean me, my mean head all sour & horrible. I can't cope with that bit, I cope with the pain better. (Helen)

For Helen it is not the physical pain itself which is so disruptive and distressing- rather the most significant impact of the pain is in how it is affecting the way she sees herself.

In these studies, participants who had had pain for a number of years were interviewed once, about the impact of the pain in the present. However, during the encounter, the participants took the opportunity afforded by the interview to spontaneously make comparison and contrasts between their present and past selves.

Here then we can see participants travelling along the experiential time-line from present to the past and the researcher in turn follows that process. However, this does not represent just a unilinear retrospective look back at the past, it is an active and dynamic conversation connecting present and past.

One of the primary features of the interviews is how the participants are engaged in a battle to preserve a good self against the onslaught of the physical pain:

> Like you said, I'm a nice person, but then I'm not, am I? And there's other stuff, if you knew you'd be disgusted. I can't help it even though I don't like it. It's the mean me, my mean head all sour and horrible (Helen)

Several participants make a contrast between the self now (bad and impaired) with their self before the impact of pain (good and strong):

> I am a nice person but the pain takes over & sucks it all out & leaves me miserable. If you didn't know me you'd think I was a miserable cow so *maybe* I was a nice person & now I'm a cow. (Lynette)

This battle is dynamic and different participants speak differently in terms of where they currently stand in this battle. An even more interesting perspective is offered by Linda when she describes the impact of pain:

> I'm only 50 & I should be doing this, that & the other cos they say life begins at 40 but I can't. I just think I'm the fittest because there are 3 girls, I'm the middle one & I thought well I'm the fittest & I used to work like a horse & I thought I was the strongest & then all of a sudden it's just been cut down & I can't do half of what I used to do (Linda)

Linda says a lot in this passage. At the first and most obvious level, she is articulating the multiple ways her deterioration is marked and this can be seen in multiple upward social comparisons. She is doing less well than each of: societal age-related expectations, her siblings, how she was in the past.

However, if we look more closely at exactly what she says, the picture is more complex. In fact, she starts with an assertion of supremacy in the present 'I just think I'm the fittest'. This then undergoes a temporal modification as she shifts tense: 'I thought well I'm the fittest'. It appears Linda is, at one and the same time, saying directly contradictory things: *I am strong now; I am weak now; I was strong in the past.*

So where is the real self located? I would argue that the apparent contradiction is apposite and that Linda's real self can be dynamically positioned on the experiential timeline somewhere between past and present. At one level, Linda recognizes that she is now seriously debilitated compared to how she was when she was younger. However, just like the other women, she is also desperately trying to hang onto the younger 'better' self. And part of the way she does that is by asserting to others and to herself that the apparent present self is not the core Linda, that the real Linda is still that previously established superhuman self with the strength of a horse.

We can see the participants at different points on the trajectory of a moral battle between trying to preserve the old good self versus succumbing to being a different unworthy person, as a result of the intrusive debilitating impact of severe physical pain. We witness in these accounts two connected temporal processes, two related but significantly different movements on the experiential timeline:

1) a retrospective mournful look back to the old self **Past < Present**
2) an attempt at pulling that old self into the present **Past < > Present**

In thinking about that question of where the true self is located, Giddens (1991) writes:

> Self-identity is . . . the self as reflexively understood by the person in terms of her or his biography. Identity here still presumes continuity across time &

> space: but self-identity is such continuity as interpreted reflexively by the agent. (Giddens, 1991, p. 53)

For Giddens, biography is not primarily an account unfolding prospectively but rather the biography as reflected upon, and so conceived by, the participant in the present. An important additional point to make is that the veracity of the participant's account of the past is not at stake because what is important is not what actually happened in the past but the record of that past as perceived by the participant in the present. For more on these studies on pain, see Osborn and Smith (1998) and Smith and Osborn (2007).

Focusing on the temporal processual features of personal experience connects IPA with the important theoretical perspective of narrative enquiry which is concerned with examining the various ways in which participants' accounts are constructed temporally. Bruner (1993) argued for the importance of narrative as a major component of human thinking and sense-making. See Andrews et al. (2013) for a valuable introduction to the narrative way of thinking.

Here, I briefly consider connections with narrative research on health and illness. A classic paper by Williams (1984) shows illness causing participants to reflect on and construct or reconstruct biographical accounts as part of making sense of what has happened. More recently Homma et al. (2016) examine the impact of attending a peer-support group on participants' perception of their Fibromyalgia pain. The authors describe various reconstructive narratives participants produce. In a particularly striking one, participants reforge a connection with their previous self as they change from seeing pain as despoiling their lives to seeing the existence of pain as evidence that they are indeed still alive.

This demonstrates the vitality of the narrative conceptualization. In my study, Linda attempts to overcome the debilitating impact of pain on herself by highlighting her continuity with a superstrong self in the past. Homma's participants tackle the problem differently and, through input from the peer-support group, reconstruct the nature of the pain itself from being a threat to life to being a signifier of life. However, while the content of the narrative constructions is different, the underlying process is the same. Clearly, the endeavours of IPA and narrative can overlap and illuminate each other, and this can be useful in the future research examining temporal experience and identity.

Impact of therapeutic intervention: Prospective (change explicit)

The studies presented so far have been naturalistic in that they have examined the temporal process in lives proceeding without a major intervention from outside. Recently, I have become involved in studies evaluating explicit therapeutic interventions. First, we will consider a design where the IPA component is prospective.

I am currently part of a team working on a convergent, parallel, mixed-methods study. This is a fully fledged longitudinal study in the traditional sense. The study examines the impact of a modified CBT intervention for families with children with epilepsy and associated mental health issues. Quantitative and qualitative data is collected from the families before the therapy and 6 months later in order to assess change.

The main trial was successful as families in the intervention arm show a significantly greater reduction in relevant mental health symptoms compared to the control group (see Bennett et al., 2024). In the qualitative arm of the study, IPA data was collected from a purposively sampled subset of 25 families in the CBT arm. We interviewed parents (and where possible young people) on their understanding of epilepsy, mental health, and the intervention at base line and 6 months later.

This is an innovative study in that while more mixed-methods research including qualitative data is conducted now, within health and psychological sciences research, it is still unusual for the qualitative arm to be longitudinal and, even where it is, most studies are concerned with asking about whether participants were satisfied with the intervention therapy. This study by contrast uses the qualitative arm to examine psychological change over time and as a result of therapy.

Analysis proceeded idiographically as normal for IPA. We looked at the pattern of change and continuity across the two interviews for each case. Only when this had been completed for each individual family, did we move cross-case and look for patterns of change in the whole sample. We are currently mid-analysis but I can present here some preliminary data.

In this first extract, a young woman (aged 15 yrs) and her mother are talking about the impact of fear of potential epileptic episodes on her social life:

Time 1: Before CBT	**Time 2: 6 months later**
Young woman: I don't want (epilepsy) to happen when I'm out because, especially if I'm out with the friends who don't really know full well, I think that makes me panic a bit as well.	*Mother*: Last week she was out with her friends on Friday. And she's making those plans herself so definitely doing more. *Young woman*: And it's like, I'm having fun and I'm spending time with my friends, and it's like my mind's so focused and stuck on what I'm doing now and how I am in the moment, I don't even have any time to think about it.

At Time 1 before the intervention the young woman's social life is severely restricted by her fear of an epilepsy occurrence when she is out with her friends who won't understand what is happening. Six months later, following the intervention, she is proactively organizing social events and has learnt the ability to focus attention on what is *actually* happening in the present so that she is not distracted by the fear of something that *might* happen.

In the second extract from the study below, we can see a change in the way the mother describes her reactions to her son (aged 9):

Time 1: Before CBT	**Time 2: 6 months later**
He hates going to school, absolutely hates it, I know part of it is separating from me, but I do know as well, he says to me all the time, "Mum, what if I have a seizure?"	I used to almost ignore a situation on a Saturday & Sunday I wouldn't talk to him about school because he would get really upset and I wouldn't want to ruin that time. But actually, I've learnt to probably talk about it more to, I suppose, normalize it, which then it isn't so alien to him.

We see how the mother is describing a change in her strategy. Her approach before the intervention was to ignore the presenting problem even when the son was explicitly pressing her, but she has learnt that it is better to engage with her son and discuss the problem in advance.

We see evidence for considerable change in how participants conceptualize their understanding of the problem and how to manage it. This is consistent with the quantitative findings but goes further in enabling us to see the process of change in action. For more on this study see Nizza et al. (2024).

I will here briefly mention another fertile methodological development that is helpful in experiential longitudinal research. The last 15 years or so has witnessed increased employment of visual methods as part of an expanded qualitative paradigm. See Reavey (2011) for a valuable overview of this movement. My colleagues and I have been incorporating visual methods within IPA designs (see e.g. Shinebourne & Smith, 2011). In Nizza et al. (2023), we incorporate visual images within a longitudinal IPA study by comparing participants' pictorial representations of their pain before and after a pain management intervention and this adds a powerful element to the examination of personal change.

Impact of therapeutic intervention: Retrospective (change implicit)

In this study I led the qualitative arm in a mixed-methods four-year evaluation of multi systemic therapy (MST) for families with adolescent with antisocial behavior. MST is an intensive therapeutic intervention where the therapist works closely and intensively with the family for a short period of time. In the main quantitative trial, the researchers followed the families prospectively for four years following the MST to evaluate the long-term impact. Quantitative measures considered the effect of the intervention for those receiving the MST in contrast to a control group which received management as usual (MAU).

The qualitative arm was added at the four-year evaluation and conducted with a subset of MST & MAU participants. In this arm then, there was only one interview with each participant, and we asked the young people detailed questions about their lives now- their relationships, family, work, and their plans for the future.

A detailed, inductive IPA analysis led to conceptualization of participants as either *mature* or *stuck* in the current process of transition to adulthood. This is related to Erikson (1980) and Marcia's (1980) models of navigating the transition from adolescence to adulthood and participants who were considered *mature* can be considered to be broadly consonant with Marcia's achieved status while participants who were *stuck* are akin to the diffused or foreclosure statuses.

After conducting a detailed analysis of each transcript in its own terms, we compared those in the MST arm with those in MAU. If there were differences between groups, we might be able to infer some effect of the MST intervention years earlier. And indeed there was a very clear difference, with the MST young men tending to be *mature*, the MAU young men tending to be *stuck*.

We were quite surprised to see the difference because, for those who had had MST, it seemed like a distant trace in the past. It had been four years earlier, the young men had complex lives and often couldn't even recall the therapist who had conducted the MST. And yet, because participants in the two arms (MST v MAU) were closely matched, having MST or not is the only difference between the two groups at baseline that can account for the difference 4 years later. The full study is reported in Conroy et al. (2023).

Let's look at a small amount of the qualitative data in more detail to get a better sense of how this difference plays out. Here are two extracts from young men who had had MST and were considered to show a mature outlook:

> **MST mature** If I want something, I'll go work for it. I'm working to build up my own label. If I wanted to go out, release a CD under my label, I could. Put it on iTunes and it will come up. That has come from me. (Hal)

> He knows I'm always there for him and he knows that he's always there for me it's like a 50/50 relationship, it's like a male & female relationship without all the other stuff. It's just the closeness. (Adrian)

Hal's extract is brimming with agency. He has a clear vocational plan and has already begun to implement it. He is clearly achieving success in his chosen creative field. Adrian demonstrates a different sort of maturity. When talking about his personal relationships he describes the qualities he finds in a close male friendship and has a sophisticated understanding of the qualities inherent in an intimate relationship and an awareness that he has been able to create a relationship with a male friend which, while platonic, offers many of the features of a sexual relationship but without the romantic connotations.

Now by contrast let's see how the young people who had not received MST talk about their lives:

> **MAU stuck** I suppose it is, looking up a bit. Well, not so much looking up because I haven't done 'em, but, start, looking for a job doing a normal job. All I want is a job, that's it. (Tim)

> I'm gonna stay out of relationships they end up getting me in trouble they get too attached I just pick the wrong ones who have got issues. (Ian)

Tim hesitantly considers the possibility of finding work in the future. However, he has no expectation of achieving a job that would give him satisfaction. And Ian has a pretty bleak view of relationships. His account lacks efficacy. He does not consider he can make good choices when it comes to relationships and now intends to avoid them.

The difference between the young men who had had MST and those who had not is clear in the qualitative data even though the only difference between the groups is whether they had had MST 4 years before. As suggested earlier, this result is even more powerful in that most of the MST group participants didn't remember the therapist.

We would suggest we may be witnessing a latent process. The MST earlier in adolescence may have sewn a seed to help the young men to develop maturity to navigate the adolescent-adult transition. It seems clear something is happening, but it appears to have become so internalized for the young men themselves that they cannot articulate it.

Thinking about our experiential timeline, what is the direction of time travel here? Well actually here we see an interesting separation. In this case, the young men are primarily talking about the present and the future:

Present < > Future

When they do talk about the past, the young men who had MST do not make connections between it and the present. In this way, they are very different to the participants in the pain research we met earlier who make lots of connections between the past and the present. In this MST study, it is we as the researchers who do the time travel between present and past and make links between what is being talked about in the present (and regarding the future) and what we know of what happened to them in their past:

Past < > Present < > Future

Conclusion

In this paper, I have introduced the idea of the experiential timeline as a conceptual aid for the increasing numbers of IPA researchers conducting longitudinal research. This has, in part, been inspired by Bren Neale's important conceptualization of qualitative longitudinal research as a dynamic multi-faceted form of inquiry which has a temporal component including both prospective and retrospective movements.

In the different studies presented, we have seen a complex dynamic process of personal experience across time. Using IPA, we see a detailed picture of how particular individuals navigate temporally through a phenomenon. And we have examined the range of ways participants and researchers move along the experiential timeline:

Past < > Present < > Future

It is still early days for this type of IPA work, but I think the prospect offers great promise for enhancing our understanding of the dynamics of the human experience. I would encourage more qualitative scholars in general, and IPA researchers in particular, to do research which involves moving in varied ways along that experiential timeline. The potential canvas is large and exciting because the experiential timeline has multiple dynamic qualities. Participants are prospectively engaging in a series of activities at a range of temporal paces as they go about their lives and create paths into the future. At one and the same time, they can be recursively looking back to a number of different time points in the past, reflecting upon and creatively reworking various aspects of the biographical trace in the light of subsequent events and the imperatives of the present.

Doing such research is difficult and complex.[1] One faces a proliferation of data, complex analytic design issues and subsequent decisions on presentation strategy. However, the complexity and richness of individual temporal lived experience call for research which is sufficiently agile to do justice to that complexity and richness. I hope in this paper to have given some pointers to the distinctive qualities of what can be achieved by research attempting to take on this challenge.

Notes

1. One of the reviewers of this paper suggested these temporal methodological developments in IPA may warrant a consideration of the interplay between induction and abduction (Neale 2021) in such research. I would like to acknowledge this insightful contribution from the reviewer. There is not space to develop this further in this paper, but it could indeed offer valuable leverage for conceptual development in the future.

Acknowledgement

I would like to acknowledge the important contribution of the different collaborators I have worked with on the empirical studies cited in this paper. These collaborative endeavours provided the ground work that enabled me to move towards constructing the model outlined.

Disclosure statement

No potential conflict of interest was reported by the author(s).

References

Andrews, M., Squire, C., & Tamboukou, M. (Eds.) (2013). *Doing narrative research* (2nd ed.). Sage.

Bennett, S. D., Cross, J. H., Chowdhury, K., Ford, T., Heyman, I., Coughtrey, A. E., Dalrymple, E., Byford, S., Chorpita, B., Fonagy, P., Moss-Morris, R., Reilly, C., Smith, J. A., Stephenson, T., Varadkar, S., Blackstone, J., Quartly, H., Hughes, T., Lewins, A., & Shafran, R. (2024). Clinical effectiveness of the psychological therapy mental health intervention for children with epilepsy in addition to usual care compared with assessment-enhanced usual care alone: A multicentre, randomised controlled clinical trial in the UK. *Lancet*, *403*(10433), 1255–1266. https://doi.org/10.1016/S0140-6736(23)02791-5

Bruner, J. (1993). *Acts of meaning*. Harvard University Press.

Conroy, D., Smith, J. A., Butler, S., Byford, S., Cottrell, D., Kraam, A., Fonagy, P., Ellison, R., Simes, E., & Anokhina, A. (2023). The impact of multi-systemic therapy at long-term follow-up: An experiential study. *Journal of Adolescent Research*, *38*(5), 842–875. https://doi.org/10.1177/07435584211025323

Erikson, E. (1980). *Identity and the life-cycle*. Norton.

Farr, J. & Nizza, I. (2019). Longitudinal interpretative phenomenological analysis (LIPA): A review of studies & methodological considerations. *Qualitative Research in Psychology*, *16*(6), 199–217. https://doi.org/10.1080/14780887.2018.1540677

Giddens, A. (1991). *Modernity and self-identity: Self and society in the late modern age*. Polity Press.

Heidegger, M. (1927/1962). *Being and time*. Blackwell.

Homma, M., Yamazaki, Y., Ishikawa, I., & Kiuchi, T. (2016). 'This really explains my case': reconstruction of Japanese people with fibromyalgia meeting peers. *Health Sociology Review*, *25*(1), 62–77. https://doi.org/10.1080/14461242.2015.1098559

Marcia, J. E. (1980). Identity in adolescence. In J. Adelson (Ed.), *Handbook of adolescent psychology* (pp. 159–187). Wiley.
Moran, D. (2000). *Introduction to phenomenology*. Routledge.
Neale, B, (2021). *The craft of qualitative longitudinal research*. Sage.
Nizza, I. E., Smith, J. A., Bennett, S. D., Chorpita, B., Cross, H., Heyman, I., Moss-Morris, R., Blackstone, J., Coughtrey, A. E., Dalrymple, E., Shah, M., D'oelsnitz, A., MICE Study Group, & Shafran, R. (2024). Examining change in the mental health of young people with epilepsy following a successful psychological intervention. *Clinical Child Psychology and Psychiatry*. https://doi.org/10.1177/13591045241272781.
Nizza, I., Smith, J. A., & Kirkham, J. (2023). Picturing oneself over time: a multimodal interpretative phenomenological analysis of pain management trajectories. *European Journal of Pain, 28*, 741–753. https://doi.org/10.1002/ejp.2214
Osborn, M. & Smith, J. A. (1998). The personal experience of chronic benign lower back pain: An interpretative phenomenological analysis. *British Journal of Health Psych, 3*(1), 65–83. https://doi.org/10.1111/j.2044-8287.1998.tb00556.x
Reavey, P. (Ed.). (2011). *Visual methods in psychology*. Routledge.
Shinebourne, P. & Smith, J. A. (2011). Images of addiction and recovery: An interpretative phenomenological analysis of the experience of addiction and recovery as expressed in visual images. *Drugs: Education, Prevention & Policy, 18*(5), 313–322. https://doi.org/10.3109/09687637.2010.514621
Smith, J. A. (1999). Identity development during transition to motherhood: An interpretative phenomenological analysis. *Journal of Reproductive and Infant Psychology, 17*(3), 281–300. https://doi.org/10.1080/02646839908404595
Smith, J. A., Flowers, P., & Larkin, M. (2022). *Interpretative phenomenological analysis* (2nd ed.). Sage.
Smith, J. A. & Osborn, M. (2007). Pain as an assault on the self: An interpretative phenomenological analysis. *Psych & Health, 22*(5), 517–534. https://doi.org/10.1080/14768320600941756
Williams, G. (1984). The genesis of chronic illness: Narrative re-construction. *Sociology of Health and Illness, 6*(2), 175–200. https://doi.org/10.1111/1467-9566.ep10778250

Uncertainty and existential thinking

Tamás Ullmann

ABSTRACT
The main question of the study is whether our existential problems are changing historically and, if so, what is specific to our era. The paper first distinguishes three main types of existential problems (external, internal and structural), secondly presents the historical dimension of existential experiences. In the third step, it argues that not only do existential experiences change with age, but most probably the form of the subject is exposed to historical transformation. The final part of the paper analyses the uncertainty of our present existential condition from the perspective of the concept of the contemporary subject. I try to argue throughout the paper that a clearly articulated set of concepts of existential thinking can be useful for qualitative psychological research.

In recent decades, we have seen a renewed interest in existential issues. There has been considerable research on existential feelings (Fuchs et al., 2013; Ratcliff, 2012), on the relationship between existentialism and psychotherapy (Yalom, 1980), on the possible links between philosophy of mind and existentialism (Nagel, 1986; Wolf, 2010) and on existential and psychological problems within modern society (Ehrenberg, 1998; Han, 2017). I would like to contribute to this renewed interest by placing existentialist themes in a historical and phenomenological dimension. In the first step I will propose a typology of existential feelings, in the second step I will put this into a historical dimension, in the third step I will relate existential feelings to the basic structure of the subject, and finally I will try to sketch the basic existential state of the present age.

My starting point is a seemingly self-contradictory proposition: existential problems are eternal, but they are not always the same. In other words the finite, fragile and threatened nature of our existence constantly generates existential crises, but depending on culture and historical time, these existential uncertainties are different. Consequently, a demanding qualitative psychological approach needs to know what the real existential problems of the present time and of the contemporary subjects are (if there are no eternal templates of these problems).

At this point I would like to radicalise the existential questioning and make the following two key statements:

(1) There are always existential problems, but it does not follow that they are always the same. It seems that the issues are only apparently the same, but in fact the problems take quite different forms because of the cultural and historical context.
(2) Indeed, an even more radical idea seems defensible to me: not only do our existential problems change from age to age, but even the human subject that experiences and tries to solve them does not remain the same. What kind of existential problems we may have depends very strongly on the „form of subjectivity" characteristic in a given historical period.

I will speak about existential uncertainty from this radicalised historical point of view.

Typology of existential problems

One of the most important contemporary existentialist theories, that of Irvine D. Yalom, gives a list of existential problems. His classical book, *Existential Psychotherapy* emphasizes a basic existential conflict: „neither a conflict with suppressed instictual strivings [Freud] nor one with internalized significant adults [neofreudian, interpersonal approach], but instead a conflict that flows from the individual's confrontation with the givens of existence. And I mean by 'givens' of existence certain ultimate concerns, certain intrinsic properties that are a part, and an inescapable part, of the human being's existence in the world" (Yalom, 1980, p. 8). The book deals with four ultimate concerns: death, freedom, isolation and meaninglessness. Yalom sees them as „inescapable parts" of all human existence: that means they are eternal problems for human beings. In no way do I wish to criticize Yalom's great ideas, but rather to add a dimension of historicity to them, in order to see more clearly the qualitative differences in existential feelings.

If we do not start from the concept of basic psychological conflict, but from the experience of uncertainty, we arrive at a somewhat different typology. Existential problems, which are related to uncertainty, can be grouped in the following way: external, internal and structural. I do not mean to imply that these correspond to successive historical periods in some sort of chronological order, although a parallel could be drawn between the archaic, premodern and modern periods. We can say that in archaic societies, it is the external existential problems that are more prominent, in pre-modern cultures the internal problems are already emerging, and in modernity structural problems become predominant.

The *external* existential problems are those that threaten human existence from outside: death, ageing, misery, disease, epidemic, war. These are eternal themes of the vulnerability of human existence that appear in the earliest cultures: think of the Buddha's confrontation with illness, old age, death, which awakened him and directed his contemplation towards the meaning of existence, or Gilgamesh's search for a way to avoid death, or Ulysses' journey to the underworld. The problems arise from the external conditions of life, that is, they threaten man from „outside". But nothing proves that this external threat is not just some outdated, archaic condition more than our anxieties about climate change or the shocking idea of the possibility of a third world war.

The second group of existential problems stems from factors that are no longer external but, so to speak, *internal* to human life: the question of the meaning of life, love, loneliness, grief, loss of home. The inner existential questions are all somehow related to the meaning and to the wholeness of life. These questions appear long before modernity, think of the therapeutic philosophical schools of late antiquity, the Cynics, the Stoics and the Epicureans, all of which were thinking about the conditions of a happy and meaningful life.

Finally, existential uncertainty concerning the foundations of existence seems to be a typically modern phenomenon. That is what I would call *structural* dimension of existential problems. Here, the subject's external vulnerability is no longer the issue, nor is the subject's internal wholeness of life, but the stability and position of the subject as subject in general. The very foundations of the subject's existence are called into question. A fundamental feeling of the modern age is that everything that is stable can falter and the meaning of anything can be questioned. I would therefore include in the third group of problems the existential feelings of uncertainty concerning the foundations: depersonalisation, loss of the world, loss of reality, loss of meaning, emptiness, anxiety, boredom, disgust, the absurdity of existence, etc (see Colombetti & Ratcliff, 2012).

So historical changes do affect existential problems and there are no unchanging and eternal existential experiences. For example, anxiety, disgust and boredom are typically modern existential experiences. Nevertheless, it can be said that in our modern age we can talk about external existential problems (climate change, war, epidemics) and also about internal issues (loneliness, the meaning of life). In archaic or premodern times, however, we can hardly talk about structural existential problems affecting the very foundations of the subject.

Now let's jump ahead and examine this variability over a smaller period of time, over the last 200–250 years. I argue that the period of modernity is not homogeneous in the sense that we have the same existential problems.

Historicity of existential problems

In the last two or three centuries of modernity, sociologists, historians and critical social philosophers generally distinguish three distinct periods (Fraser & Jaeggi, 2018). The first is the period of classical bourgeois culture from the 19th century onwards. In fact, most classical existentialist authors represent the thinking and cultural logic of this period. The fundamental experience of the classical bourgeoisie is the fundamental experience of modernity itself: all the worldviews, values and religions that were thought to be stable have lost their defining character. The spiritual, existential stability of human existence has been lost. To put it the most succint Nietzschean way: "God is dead". And the loss of stability has led to an uncertainty which, in the case of a somewhat sensitive spirit, can easily lead to existential crisis. The concepts that Kierkegaard, for example, devel-ops to able to describe personal and individual human existence are all products of this experience of fundametal uncertainty: anxiety, despair, resignation, choice, sin, loss of innocence, etc. This is also the main theme of XIXth century novels: how the individual can find his way in a state of existential uncertainty and cultural transformation.

The second existential era lasts from the beginning of the 20th century until the '68 revolts. This period is usually referred to as the era of Fordist capitalism, when mass production, uniformised and mass consumption, mass culture dominated life-world. The disciplinary power (Foucault, 1977) of this time creates uniformised and conformised forms of existence based on consumption (best example: the suburban middle class culture of 1950s-60s America). The fundamental existential question of this unifor-mised and conformised way of life is how can we live our own lives? How do we become individuals? What does it mean to be autonomous? The hippies of the 1960s were not rebelling against exploitation, but against their parents' conformist approach to life. They did not want a fairer distribution of wealth, but they had a desire for meaning beyond the consumption of the products of mass culture. Alienation from reality (disgust, absurdity, boredom) is the central theme of this period (think, for example, of Antonioni's existentialist films and their suffering, brooding, anxious heroes). The ideal to be achieved in this period, that is, authentic life for a uniformised and conformist subject is expressed in the form of an autonomous, individual existence, mainly in the form of aesthetic freedom.

The postmodern era, which began in the 1970s, marks another shift. Authentic freedom, individuality and autonomy, previously desired, are no longer a mere aspiration, but given possibilities, even a requirement for everyone. What sociologists and critical philosophers have called the era of neoliberal capitalism is nothing else than the emergence of a new cultural logic (Jameson, 1991). This cultural logic says that one should not be the same as everyone else and that one should not build a life based on disciplined work, but that one should enjoy life, be autonomous and individual. The central slogan of this era is self-realisation and fulfilment of individuality. Whereas the previous era required normal workers and consumers, the current era increases consumption by creating individual, self-actualising subjects. For such a subject, the existential crisis comes no longer from the inability to be different from others. It comes from the fact that everything is given to us to be ourselves, to fulfil ourselves and to find pleasure in life, but somehow we fail to do so. Everything that people have ever wanted (freedom, prosperity, security, travel) is given to postmodern subjects, yet they fail. This failure leads to depression and burnout. In the past, people struggled for authentic autonomy and freedom of self-expression, but now it is given for everyone. The question is: how can we be ourselves in these circumstances? The desire for self-realisation should come from within, but if it comes from outside as a requirement, than it is very difficult to meet this requirement. This is a classic double bind situation. If enjoyment is not spontaneous but an obligation, then it is actually very difficult to meet this requirement.

The period of modernity thus creates different existential situations and confronts people with different existential problems. We are anxious, but not in the same way as Kierkegaard, we are bored, but not in the same way as Heidegger, existence seems absurd, but not in the same way as for Camus. The era of classical bourgeois culture, the welfare era of mass production and mass consumption and, finally, postmodern individualism, pose quite different existential problems. Uncertainty over the death of God and the decline of culture, uncertainty over the acquisition of attainable goods, and uncertainty over the invention and fulfilment of the individual self – these are three markedly different types of uncertainty, with three different types of anxiety.

Transformation of the subject

After sketching the historical dimension, we can now go one step further: it seems that it is not just that the human subject is always the same, but faces different existential problems depending on the historical period. This would be a plausible idea, by the way, and the philosophical concept of the modern subject, which defines the horizon of philosophies of consciousness from Descartes to Husserl, actually suggests this. But the formula is more complicated: not only can we say that existential problems transformed (and the subject remains), but we can say as well that the structure or form of the subject itself takes a different shape.

For the structure and functioning of our subject is perhaps not as self-evidently given as Descartes' cogito argument would have us believe. According to Descartes, the only certainty we have is that if we think, then we most certainly exist – everything else is uncertain. It follows that the inner sphere in which we appear to ourselves as self-consciousness, as soul, as subject, is an ultimate, evidentially given primordiality. Something that we cannot even imagine could be otherwise. In the 20th century, however, it is mainly this kind of certainty that has faltered: as Freud put it, the self is no more master of its own house. In other words, a multiplicity of unconscious modes of operation determine and control the structure of the self. The unconscious, however, takes many forms: we can speak not only of personal unconscious, but also of social unconscious, which is formed in the normalising system of our intersubjective network of relationships. The social environment affects not only the subject's 'surface', his social shell, but also the way in which the subject relates to himself and concieves himself. The subject is not in contact with an archaic soul, but through patterns of self-knowledge he or she connects with him- or herself and *becomes* a certain kind of subject. All societies act on their subjects, but modern society no longer acts on its subjects only from the outside, through the word of power, but also from within, through micro-channels. This is what Michel Foucault calls the specificity of modern power: it does not act from the outside, through coercion, but from the inside, through discipline, control and normalisation (Foucault, 1977). Social normality and the expectations that follow from it have a much stronger effect on the subject than the theatrical and ostentatious manifestations of political power. This anonymous, subconscious influence is not on our conscious thinking, but on the deepest structural elements of our subject: how and what we desire, how we see the world, and how we see ourselves (Ehrenberg, 1998).

Simply put: social 'normality' in any society creates the dominant 'subject form'. Dominant here does not mean that it dominates over others, but that it is the most prevalent form of subject formation under the given circumstances and that it is well suited to those circumstances. Again, I will try to illustrate this claim with examples by ditinguishing three forms of modern subjectivity.

In the late 19th century, at the time when Freud developed his theory of psychoanalysis and his view of man, the repressed, neurotic subject was the dominant form of subjectivity. The bourgeois culture operated according to very strict moral rules and repressed all instinctual drives. Freud's theory describes the human being in terms of this experience of the mechanism of sexual repression (Oedipus triangle, superego, forbidden desires, fantasy, etc.).

The American middle class of the 1950s existed and functioned on the basis of a very different form of subject. At its heart was consumption and material gain. This kind of uniformised, conformised, normalised life found it difficult to tolerate difference. Everyone dressed more or less similarly, lived in similar suburban houses, went to work in the same way, the household was run by the woman (who was not working), etc. It was not difficult for the next generation to rebel against such a standardised, consumption-oriented, uniform life.

From the 1970s onwards, a change in lifestyle appeares and reveals a deep transformation of the logic of society as a whole. What is needed are no longer disciplined and consumption-oriented individuals who can be well integrated into the world of work in factories, offices, banks and bureaux, but individuals who keep production alive by conceiving their whole lives in terms of consumption. The postmodern form of subjectivity has dominated the Western world since the 1980s (Jameson, 1991). The life of this subject is not centred on the repression of desires (as in the Freudian model) or on the living out of desires through consumption (as in the 50-ies and 60-ties), but on the command of pleasure. The social unconscious commands the Freudian subject as follows: 'You must not act out your desires! the instincts must be fought against!', whereas the imperative of contemporary social unconscious is the following: 'Be youself! Enjoy! If you don't enjoy, you are a loser!'. The difference between the two kinds of imperatives expresses clearly the difference between two cultural logics.

The existential condition of our times

Among many other factors, perhaps the analysis of the structure of the (post) modern subject offers the best characterisation of the existential condition of our time. Instead of an exhaustive description, I will give only a few characteristics of the form of subject that characterises us.

Characteristics of the new subjectivity

According to a contemporary German social philosophical movement (Wertkritik – critique of value), we must not only criticise the way capitalism works and reject the extremely unfair forms of distribution that the newer, neoliberal capitalism has created, but we must also realise that this new cultural and economic logic penetrates to the very depths of our subject. In fact, we should reject the very form of subjectivity that the contemporary world of life has created in us (Jappe, 2023). According to Wertkritik, this form of subject has three basic characteristics: narcissistic, competitive and infantile (e.g. the Freudian subject is disciplined, rational and neurotic).

The contemporary subject is narcissistic, because it seeks to show and to admire itself in every situation, rather than to cultivate or transforme its inner sphere. Facebook as a phenomenon would hardly have been as successful a century ago: communication and contact have been always important part of our lives, but the constant and compulsive display and public representation of self is only part of the life of the newest subject form. In the absence of stable social and cultural values, the subject finds ultimate value in itself – that is the logic of narcissism. It loves itself, admires itself, is anxious for itself and tries to build up itself through representations (photos, images, videos, comments, experiences, social contacts, etc.).

Postmodern subject is not only narcissistic, but deeply competitive: it does not think of itself as part of a community, but as an isolated individual. The modern competitive subject is an extreme version of the process of individuation. Common existence is only a virtual given, the traditional family has lost its cohesive force, and he or she feels stable only when he or she achieves a visible result in comparison with others. Modern subject needs others, but only to show him or herself and to prove him or herself better.

Finally, the contemporary subject is infantile in the sense that no one is interested in the long-term mastery of desires and the rational acquisition of corresponding goods, but only in the immediate gratification of desires. Not only does modern subject want everything and immediately he or she desires, but the socio-cultural logic calls him or her to desire as much as possible, and even more. The prevailing view is that only the full and complete realisation of one's desires leads to fulfilment and happiness.

The contemporary concept of happiness fits perfectly into this logic. The notion of happiness we take for granted has nothing to do with community values or moral goodness or virtuous living. Happiness is clearly seen as the creation of individual well-being and prosperity. The notion of happiness propagated by our culture is the goal vision of an extremely individualistic, introverted, depoliticised subject. In other words, it is not the natural, eternal conception of happiness, but a schema that follows from contemporary cultural logic (Cabanas & Illouz, 2018).

The structure of the unconscious

According to Freud's late model, in our unconscious, both the super-ego and the ideal ego are opposed to the ego and the Id. However, the super-ego and the ideal ego have a very different relationship to the ego. As a consequence, the cultural logic based on them is also very different.

The most important unconscious factor in the earlier form of subjectivity based on repression was the superego, through which the various prohibitive commands were enforced, which curbed instinctual drives. The superego was linked to the position of an authoritative father (a position that could be held by anyone, not just the father) and its basic function was prohibition. This in turn produced repression and neurosis. The unconscious of the contemporary subject, on the other hand, is not centred on the superego, but on the ideal ego (Idealich) (hence its fundamental narcissism). The super-ego forbids, represses, denies, restrains (it says: stop!), while the ideal ego constantly seduces and stimulates (it says: Try it! Go ahead! Enjoy!). The super-ego produced disciplined subjects (who were essentially neurotic, but at least had clearcut rules to conform to and rebel against). The ideal ego, on the other hand, presents an ideal that is very difficult to achieve. And if we fail, we cannot blame our failure on the forbidding father or anyone else who denies our desires, we only have ourselves to blame: then comes psychological breakdown, burnout and depression.

One of the main sources of our incertainty is that we are prisoners of the expectations of the ideal ego. The super-ego is forbidding, it is completely negative, but it has clear rules. The ideal ego does not forbid anything, it only calls for pleasure. This paradoxical double bind, however, puts the subject in a situation of total uncertainty. I would express this with another analogy: if we cannot process the stimulus, that is, if we cannot transform raw sensation into experience, we are left with a multitude of chaotic stimuli. If I must enjoy life before I know how to live it well, how to integrate enjoyment into a meaningful life, then either total confusion ensues, or a mad pursuit of row pleasure. The result will be either a confused, insecure, passive subject, or an aggressive, pleasure-oriented, all-consuming individual.

Subjectivity in power relations

In contemporary social philosophy, there is much talk about latent power in society. Some talk about disciplinary power (Foucault), some about controlling power (Deleuze), some about bio-power (Agamben), some about permissive power (Han). These forms of power are all different from visible political power, and appear rather as invisible normalising forces operating on unconscious level. Latent power relations shape the functioning of the subject in different ways.

The new form of subject is intrinsically linked to the functioning of the power in question. Disciplinary power produces repressed and submitted subjects, permissive power produces self-actualizing, performance-obsessed subjects. The contemporary form of cultural logic or social power no longer acts on our bodies, no longer disciplines our bodies, but acts on our psyche, stimulating us by encoding our unconscious desires. This is what Byung Chul Han calls psycho-power and psychopolitics (Han, 2017). Psychopolitics is not only about mapping the desires of the subject and inducing him to indulge in hundreds of consumer goods, but also about encoding these desires and pushing subjects towards desires that make them more narcissistic, more competitive, more consumer-oriented. Consumption is no longer just about objects, tools, real estate, but much more about experiences, and experiences that can be presented immediately (f.ex. in Facebook). An important tool for the subject's self-optimisation is psychological therapy, training, lifestyle counselling, coaching, etc. Anything that enables the subject to function better, that is, to realise itself better is welcome.

Positive psychology is one of the most important theory and method in this social (and market) segment. Flow, mindfulness, resilience, resonance, meditation are buzzwords that seek to improve the state of the subject through a variety of sophisticated practices. They optimize the subject. Optimizing the state of the subject, however, is a very ambiguous idea. The central question is whether the otherwise very attractive, realistic, pragmatic insights of positive psychology can be considered part of general psychopolitics (optimising the subject in order to better integrate it into production and especially into consumption) or whether positive psychology helps us to break the spell of psychopolitics and free us from its influence. In other words, do the efforts of contemporary positive psychology help us to break free from the constraints of the normalised subject (narcissism, competition, infantilism) or, on the contrary, do they optimise and normalise the subject, enabling it to participate fully again in the process of self-exploitation? It is because of these ambiguities that some authors have coined the terms psycho-bourgeois, happiness industry and happycratie (Cabanas & Illouz, 2018).

Authentic life

As the existential problems change historically, so too does the conception of authentic life itself. Not only the problems change, but also the possible solutions. For Kierkegaard, the choice of choice and ultimately faith was the authentic way, Heidegger conceived of authentic life as a kind of heroic, reflective solitude, Sartre saw in the creation of art the authentic way out of anxiety, and Camus in the clear-headed endurance of life's absurdity.

I think that, for example, Heidegger's concept of authenticity can no longer be applied to the existential problems of our time without further ado. Why? Because, in Heidegger's time, authenticity was the way of a few, let us say of a sophisticated spiritual elite. Now, however, all are required to realise themselves, to find their authentic selfhood. How can we be authentic in an age in which almost every fashion product is sold with the advertising slogan: 'if you buy this, you will be yourself'? The slogan of a Hungarian drug chain expresses the spirit of the times succinctly and to the point: 'I shop here, I am myself here'.

The idea of authenticity is no longer linked to moral or intellectual excellence, artistic creation or political commitment. Authenticity is simply no longer linked to a brave, free, risk-taking, creative life. Nowadays, authenticity is nothing other than a well-functioning, optimised, balanced self. The pure emptiness of individual well-being.

It would be very interesting to take stock of contemporary proposals for authentic living (none of which correspond to the ideas of classical existentialism): aesthetic self-creation (Foucault) the flow (Csikszentmihalyi, 1990), flourishing (Seligman, 2011), the mindfulness proposed in the wind, Hartmut Rosa's concept of resonance (Rosa, 2021), Byung Chul Han's proposal for slowing down life, meditative idleness, gardening (Han, 2015). No one talks any more about determination, facing fate, artistic creation or active social responsibility. We have been given the opportunity to choose ourselves, but this free, authentic choice of self is very difficult to give substance to.

The modern subject is exposed to external, internal and structural existential uncertainty at the same time. Not only is it made precarious by economic crises, war, epidemics and climate change, but it is also deprived of the values that sustain a meaningful life. And finally, it is trained into a form of subjectivity that forces it to constantly compete and prove itself. The only certain point for the individual in a world deprived of values, constantly changing and threatening, is nothing else than its own subjectivity. No wonder that such extreme uncertainty leads to an epidemic of psychological problems. Mere happiness is no longer enough; in addition to psychological well-being, we need to find some objective meaning to life.

Disclosure statement

No potential conflict of interest was reported by the author(s).

Funding

This work was supported by the Hungarian Scientific Research Council under Grant number K 138745.

References

Cabanas, E., & Illouz, E. (2018). *Happycratie. Comment l'industrie du bonheur a pris le contrôle de nos vie?*. Premier parallèle.

Colombetti, G., & Ratcliffe, M. (2012). Bodily feeling in depersonalisation: A phenomenological account. *Emotion Review*, *4*(2), 145–150. https://doi.org/10.1177/1754073911430131

Csikszentmihalyi, M. (1990). *Flow: The psychology of optimal experience*. Harper & Row.

Ehrenberg, A. (1998). *La fatigue d'être soi. Dépression et société*. Odile Jacob.

Foucault, M. (1977). *Discipline and punish. The birth of the prison*. Random House.

Fraser, N., & Jaeggi, R. (2018). *Capitalism: A conversation in critical theory*. Verso.

Fuchs, T. (2013). The phenomenology of affectivity. In K. W. M. Fulford et alii (Ed.), *The oxford handbook of philosophy and psychiatry* (pp. 612–631). Oxford University Press.

Han, B. C. (2015). *Burnout society*. Stanford University Press.

Han, B. C. (2017). *Psychopolitics: Neoliberalism and new technologies of power*. Verso.

Jameson, F. (1991). *Postmodernism, or the cultural logic of late capitalism*. Duke University Press.

Jappe, A. (2023). *The adventures of the commodity: For a critique of value (Critical theory and the critique of society)*. Bloomsbury Academic.

Nagel, Thomas. (1986). *The view from nowhere*. Oxford University Press.

Ratcliff, M. (2012). The phenomenology of existential feeling. In S. Marienberg & J. Fingerhut (Eds.), *Feelings of being alive* (pp. 23–54). de Gruyter.

Rosa, H. (2021). *Resonance: A sociology of our relationship tot he world*. Polity Books.

Seligman, M. (2011). *Flourish: A virionary new understanding of happiness and well-being*. Free Press.

Wolf, S. (2010). *Meaning in life and why it matters*. Princeton, Princeton University Press.

Yalom, I. D. (1980). *Existential psychotherapy*. Basic Books.

Using medical records in qualitative research: Advantages and limitations

Antonina Bryniarska

ABSTRACT
Cooperation between professionals, adolescent patients with anorexia nervosa and their parents is essential for the treatment outcome. This is why it has been studied using qualitative research, however, such research has mainly concentrated on self-report methods. In this paper, the methodological approach of using medical reports of stationaryhospitalisation in a child psychiatry ward is described. BothConsensual Qualitative Research (CQR) and Comparative Case Study (CCS) methodologies were used to obtain a multidimensional and in-depth picture of cooperation in such difficult circumstances. In this study, the procedure is meticulously and incrementally illustrated, presenting the context of the study, characteristics of the collected data, analysis process, and research team, which is particularly relevant in qualitative methods.Advantages and limitations of such an approach ale also discussed, based on our experience. Finally, the work's clinical value is commented, proving that using both CQR and CCS provides some important clinical implications for specialists.

Introduction

Methods for exploring collaboration between parents and health professionals

Anorexia nervosa in children and adolescents, due to its egosyntonic nature (Couturier & Lock, 2006) and the highest mortality rate of all mental disorders (Tylec et al., 2013), remains a special group of disorders when it comes to the need for collaboration between patients, professionals and patients' parents. More research on this type of trialogue has emerged in recent years (Jespers, 2022; Johns et al., 2019), but many questions remain unanswered.

Qualitative research makes it possible to explore the 'how' and 'why' questions, broadening the context and deepening the understanding of the participants' internal psychological processes, hence it is readily used in research on the complex mechanisms underlying eating disorders (Walker & Lloyd, 2011). One commonly-used qualitative research method is to conduct semi-structured in-depth interviews, which might also be noticed in the field of collaboration between the three sides of the trialogue in eating disorder treatment. Richmond et al. (2020) highlighted the importance of hearing from adolescents, their primary caregivers, as well as their multidisciplinary clinicians. They examined each of the parties forming the trialogue to gain insight into how each defined recovery. He surveyed 24 people with a range of eating disorders, their parents and professionals, using in-depth, semi-structured, qualitative interviews. The same in-depth interview method was used to explore the experiences of health professionals caring for patients with AN (Reid et al., 2010). The parental experiences in regard to interactions with clinicians treating their children with eating disorders were explored more broadly by interviews conducted with willing parents (McMaster et al., 2004).

Another way to obtain qualitative clinical data is to organise a focus group to answer the research questions posed by researchers. Saria et al. (2019) conducted five focus groups with nurses and parents of critically ill children, while Mitrofan et al. (2019) used this method to survey the care experiences of young people with eating disorders and their parents. Both of these methods, in-depth interviews and focus groups, have also been used to explore patients' perspectives on the process of their treatment regarding eating disorders (Sampson et al., 2015).

In their meta-analysis on the relationship between family functioning and the outcome of eating disorders, Holtom-Viesel and Allan (2014) emphasize the need for further qualitative research beyond self-reporting. Such attempts were made, for example, by presenting clinical data in the form of family therapy sessions to explore parental involvement in eating disorder treatment (Balottin et al., 2018; Reyes-Rodriguez et al., 2019). However, the authors of this paper have not encountered a report analysing the interface between professionals, patients and their parents in inpatient treatment using clinical data.

In terms of how the data was analysed, the methods used in the publications discussed above were thematic analysis (Braun & Clarke, 2021), content analysis (Elo et al., 2014), or similar qualitative analyses that allowed a few key themes to be highlighted. One study on the parents' perspective (Walker & Lloyd, 2011) used Consensual Qualitative Research (C. E. Hill et al., 2005).

Aim of research

International recommendations on AN clearly emphasise the importance of parental involvement in the treatment process (NICE, 2020), and our clinical experience has shown the importance of collaboration between professionals and parents of minors. Parental involvement in the form of outpatient family therapy is widely described in the literature (Simic & Eisler, 2019), but less is known about what such cooperation should look like in the treatment of the most severe course of the disease, which takes place in inpatient wards. Hence, our area of interest was the collaboration between professionals and parents of adolescent patients with a diagnosis of anorexia nervosa during inpatient hospitalisation (Bryniarska et al., 2024).

We were interested in gaining an in-depth understanding of the phenomena described, so we decided to use qualitative methods. In the absence of studies on inpatient hospitalisation based on medical data, we decided to use this kind of authentic data, taken from a system for reporting medical events. As the authors of these records are professionals working in an inpatient ward, the fact that the analysis of such mediated, indirect material would be more complex, requiring care and caution, had to be taken into account.

Our premise was to look simultaneously at the experiences of parents, patients and staff. The epistemological nature of the data enabled us to answer the question of how staff perceive their interventions and the reactions of parents or patients to the proposed treatment.

In summary, the aim of this methodological paper is to describe the advantages and limitations of using medical records in qualitative research methods in a clinical population study using data in the form of medical records. To do this, we describe our methodological approach in detail: the qualitative methods, the context of the study, the characteristics of the collected data, the analysis process and the research team, which is particularly relevant in qualitative methods. We were also interested in the extent to which such a research approach produces results that can be useful in clinical work, giving some precise clinical implications.

Methods

In this paper, we follow the standards for reporting qualitative research (O'Brien et al., 2014).

Qualitative approach

Our basic premise was the exploratory nature of our study. Therefore, we decided to use a qualitative method without any initial concrete assumptions, i.e. consensual analysis. With the continuation of exploratory work, the need to dive even deeper into the data arose and it was decided to use a case comparison to supplement this project; this is how the second method was selected. The choice of methodology reflected qualitative thinking along a funnel: from a more general to the most detailed description possible. The latter was obtained by meticulously comparing the cases. Due to the parallelism of the approaches, each subsection will describe them separately: their theoretical assumptions, our analysis, and the results.

Consensual Qualitative Research (CQR)

One of the qualitative methods invented for research in the field of psychology and psychotherapy is the multi-stage Consensual Qualitative Research (CQR) approach. It is based on grounded theory, resigning the primary researchers' assumptions and using the bottom-up approach (Strauss & Corbin, 1994). It enables the in-depth exploration of the experiences, attitudes, and beliefs of individuals (Hill & Knox, 2021; C. E. Hill et al., 2005).

The name of this approach highlights the importance of achieving consensus among researchers regarding the data. This is usually done with several intermediate steps, with multiple returns to the raw data and continuation of the discussion. The data for CQR involves words or narratives rather than numbers (C. E. Hill & S. Knox, 2021).

Comparative Case Study (CCS)

An additional part of the study, broadening the treatment process of two patients was analysed through the Comparative Case Study (CCS) methodology. This approach allows the generation of not only a rich description, but also an especially in-depth, contextual understanding (Campbell, 2010). Unlike CQR, this method has rarely been used for psychological or psychotherapeutic research, and has been more frequently used in the social sciences, including the field of law, which is why we would like to detail this methodology below.

There are five conditions of CCS to be a relevant methodology and all are met in our research design: a) we question the 'how' and 'why' of the hospitalisation intervention, focusing on outcomes for a process. This is a situation where b) no other intervention (treatment) could be implemented and c) the context is crucial in understanding the success or failure of the intervention. Furthermore, regarding data, d) there is a possibility of iterative data collection and e) experimental designs are impossible due to practical or ethical reasons (Goodrick, 2014).

Context of the study

The study context is an inpatient ward for patients under 14 years old, the Psychiatry Ward of St. Louis Regional Specialized Children's Hospital in Cracow. We used real, clinical data derived from the AMMS (Asseco Medical Management Solutions) program, which maintains medical records in this particular hospital. The data of all patients with a diagnosis of anorexia nervosa (F50.0 according to ICD-11) hospitalised in this ward between 2017 and 2020 was initially included in the study. We obtained the data of 37 patients, but according to the particular research question there were 36, 32 or 2 cases analysed. All data was anonymised and all necessary consents were collected: from Head of Ward, Hospital Directors and [anonymization] Bioethics Committee number [anonymization]. More details can be found in (Bryniarska et al., 2024). The parents described and compared in the comparative study also provided their signed consent.

Data collection

The authors of the clinical data were the medical personnel working in the Child Psychiatry Ward. There were 10 medical doctors (2 psychiatry specialists and 8 psychiatry residents), and 9 nurses, with all of them providing daily reports. Additionally, there were four psychotherapists; one with psychoanalytic training with family intervention experience and three undergoing comprehensive psychodynamic-systemic training, who put notes regarding individual and family consultations. The latter were of particular interest in this study: family meetings were the key moments for cooperation and were attended by the therapeutic team, parents and sometimes also the patient. The therapeutic team of a particular patient always consisted of an attending psychiatrist and a psychotherapist. During each family meeting, a psychotherapist took manual notes and afterwards made official notes in the medical incident reporting system. Therapists use these records in clinical team meetings, during case supervisions, for their own therapeutic work, and to accurately record the treatment process. These notes are important as part of the medical documentation, showing the course of hospitalisation, the procedures and interventions applied during treatment, but also the description of the patient's medical history, the child's previous development and the current difficulties of both patients and their families. It is worth mentioning that there may also be constraints on producing relevant medical notes, such as fatigue, mental strain on therapists, time pressure, too many patients to care for, and emotional response to parental behaviour, etc. The credibility of the study (Giacomini et al., 2000) stems also from the fact that the notes were made by the same people, the staff employed in the present ward at a specific time.

In CQR analysis, family consultation notes were used, while in CCS analysis five groups of data regarding particular patients were provided, each one in a separate file: medical reports, nursing reports, epicrises, individual psychological observations, and family psychological observations. The authors were: psychiatrists, nurses, again psychiatrists, and the two last data sets were prepared by psychologists, all of them medical personnel on the ward.

Researchers' characteristics and reflexivity

The qualitative analysis of this study was conducted by three clinicians, psychotherapists, working together in an ambulatory context. The research team met Hill's recommendations for CQR (2005): diverse levels of experience, and all members familiar to each other from prior clinical and scientific work with a common approach, here: systemic thinking. The most experienced member, in both scientific and clinical work, in this study took on the role of judge-supervisor of this analysis.

As qualitative researchers, we should be aware of being part of the social world that we study (Palaganas et al., 2017). This is why the social background of research members is important: all of them are middle-class medical workers, aged between 30 and 60, heterosexual, clinicians working mostly with families. According to the significance of 'reflexivity' in qualitative research, it should be emphasised how our 'social background, location and assumptions affect the research practice' (Hesse-Biber, 2012). In our opinion, a particularly relevant fact is the personal link to the analysed material. Two younger researchers were former employees of the ward and the 3rd was unfamiliar with this context.

Therefore, from the beginning of the study, we were aware of the potential risks of our experiences influencing the analysis process. These were related to emotional involvement, familiarity with the authors of the notes, our own professional and private past experiences in this ward or familiarity with some of the patients. In the course of the analysis, it also became apparent that the researchers' emotions were aroused by the assumptions and approaches of the work in relation to the treatment of eating disorders. If stronger emotional reactions arose, we reflected on this each time and discussed it in depth, including the supervisor in this process, who was devoid of this implication. *Epistemological reflexivity* (Palaganas et al., 2017) appeared to be crucial for the reliability of the study.

Data analysis

CQR analysis

The consensual analysis of the material was conducted by three researchers: two of them provided the initial parts of the work and then the third author, as an expert, supervised it. At every stage, the final conclusion was achieved by recurrent discussions among the research members (Walker & Lloyd, 2011). In line with CQR, a five-step process was followed when analysing the data, as described below (C. E. Hill et al., 2005).

(1) Developing domains: this stage started from exploratory familiarisation with individual cases; each researcher became acquainted with some records of parental meetings, trying to reflect the provisional names of domains. Later, the team discussed the categories and the names of the domains and subdomains were modified while continuing analysis of further material. The process was based on the data, but also contained the theoretical background of researchers, a systemic approach, as being atheoretical is impossible (Braun & Clarke, 2021). Finally, the eight most general domains were distinguished: 1) individual predispositions and development, 2) context of disease, 3) peer context, 4) current functioning during hospitalisation, 5) somatic complaints, 6) follow-up treatment plan, 7) interventions of personnel, and 8) family context. According to the research questions, emphasis was placed on the last two domains. The family context was analysed in depth in the first paper (Bryniarska et al., 2024), while the interventions were described profoundly in the second manuscript (Authors, 2023, accepted for publication).

(2) Constructing core ideas: two researchers familiarised themselves with the raw data and related domains, by organising them into core ideas (C. E. Hill et al., 2005). The main core idea was a division between families with beneficial cooperation and those struggling with cooperation. These emerged from the data that we analysed in more detail, which were the domains 'family context' and 'interventions'.

(3) Cross analysis: all data was coded by assignment to particular categories, which led to the next stage, cross-analysis. Using tables, we coded each case, which enabled us to provide the frequency of domain occurrence.

This stage required the most strenuous consensus-building efforts as sometimes researchers did not initially agree with each other. One particular example is the citation 'father massages daughter's abdomen to decongest her bowels, describing her as a "dried up teenager"'. One researcher coded it as a non-efficient understanding of the AN mechanisms limiting it to some medical, somatic terms, while the other researcher coded this part as adaptive change in family functioning related to AN. Both researchers tried to explore the phrase in the broader context of this patient's documentation, but a consensus was still not achieved. As a last step, a supervisor was included in the discussion and it was finally decided among the team that the medical context is crucial, hence the parent's behaviour was understood as a willingness to provide relief.

(1) Auditing: the supervisor's role was to check whether the raw material was in the correct domain and if their names were appropriate. Additionally, two external, independent researchers were invited to reflect on whether the wording captured the essence of the material. Finally, one of those independent researchers, with years of experience working with qualitative methods, proposed some improvements in the final wording of some subdomains regarding the interventions of personnel, indicating the mediated nature of the data. This was also discussed until a final consensus was reached.
(2) Stability check: due to the great volume of the qualitative material, the stability check was made on part of the data, concerning those aspects that were most relevant to us. This material was reviewed with no new domains or subdomains considered necessary, hence stability was proven.

CCS analysis

The Comparative Case Study design consists of six steps, which is described as follows (Goodrick, 2014). First, clarify the Key Evaluation Questions (KEQs) and purpose of the study to decide whether this is an appropriate design. Second, identify initial propositions or theories to focus on. Third, define the type of cases that will be included and how the case study process will be conducted. Fourth, identify how evidence will be collected, analysed and synthesised within and across cases, and implement the study. Later, consider alternative explanations for the outcomes and, finally, report findings.

According to the steps described above, we proceeded as follows. Initially, the purpose of our study was to explore the parental understanding of their child during the psychiatric inpatient hospitalisation. More specifically, we tried to investigate how parents perceive their child's mental states during that time and we also aimed to describe how personnel can react to support them in crucial moments. Hence, we considered CSS as an appropriate method. We concentrated on the systemic approach and the importance of cooperation between family members and professionals (Johns et al., 2019). Then, the cases were chosen from a deliberate sample (Kaarbo et al., 1999), in regard to similarities in symptomatology and the treatment course.

According to the case study process, we analysed data from the beginning till the end of hospitalisation, which is why we chose those patients that finished the treatment on time. Then, all the excerpts that referred to the topic were chosen. Thanks to the diverse sources of material, we traced the time perspective, i.e. which intervention followed which event. The alternatives to explanations regarding the relationship with parents, such as the influence of peers or health conditions of family members, were taken into consideration. However, no such variability over time or impact on the course of symptoms has been proven in this area. The findings were reported separately for each case, presenting one essential event selected carefully, when parents' understanding was limited and staff responded adequately.

Data processing

Family consultation data was downloaded from the medical system and copied into an anonymised text document, for each patient separately. For CQR, the data of each patient was categorised and then, in cross analysis, an MS Excel table was created with a summary of patients and their corresponding categories. In this file, the cases were divided into those 'cooperating' and 'struggling with cooperation'. In CCS, not only were therapists' notes analysed, but also those of doctors and nurses, hence different sources in parallel were studied. Researchers tried to deconstruct events from all of the notes, reflecting a subjective perspective of each specialist.

We recognise that the medical records are created by the treatment team, hence their interpretation is included. The parts of the meeting they chose to describe and how they did it depended on them. Additionally, during the analysis we created our categories not only on the semantic meaning of an excerpt, but we also used our perception and understanding to interpret the narratives of the staff discourse. Our aim was to be as close to the data as possible, however, we are fully aware of our subjective and mediating role, hence an interpretative level of analysis was used. In such a way, the results of the analysis are categories showing the staff's view, not only simple reporting of events during hospitalisation. To sum up the mediated role of the data, the medical personnel focused on something while writing the notes, in the discourse they had chosen, they made an interpretation of what was said and done, and the researchers made an interpretative analysis of the professionals' interpretation of events. It is crucial to be aware of this mediated nature of medical records while analysing the results.

Sampling strategy

The clinical was structured narratively in a reflexive way by one of the specialists. The first part of the study focused on family meeting notes by psychotherapists, with the notes between 2 and 37 sentences long, usually about half a page from one meeting. The average number of records for a patient is 5 family consultations per hospitalisation, a total of 162 notes from 162 family meetings were analysed. When eight domains in CQR were distinguished and two essential domains were chosen from them, each note from family consultations was studied again in accordance with the chosen domain: family context or interventions. Each passage corresponding to one of the categories was included. All patients were analysed in this way, and only then was it decided that no further sampling was necessary.

Examples of such notes from family consultations description can be seen below: 'Meeting with Ana's parents, attended by a medical doctor and psychologist. Ana's current functioning according to the parents was discussed, the course of day walks and the planned pass. The hypothesis of the connection between Ana's illness and the conflict between the desire to be a child and growing up was discussed. In this context, the experience of older children entering adolescence was discussed, and in the course of the conversation on this topic, the image of a lack of strong difficulties emerged, but also a lack of space for rebellion and having one's own opinion'. The second note from family consultations contains more descriptive statements about the family context (with some quotations from a patient), as much as specialists' interventions showing their perspective and interpretations presented to family members. 'The observed pattern of denial in both Ana's and the family's behaviour was discussed with the parents. Postponing the confrontation of difficulties or task-based thinking, "proving/presenting" strength and the absence of difficulties (shedding responsibility) were discussed. We talk about the girl's strong ambivalence towards the recovery process "I can put on weight but so that it is not visible". We address Ana's reported sense of unfairness in her treatment – she believes she is being "polite and trying" at the same time as not receiving the expected results. The emotions that arise for her are flooding through, making no room for failure in the task-based approach. The team discusses observations of Olga's exhaustion in interactions based on her anticipatory need to provide and mask problems. Themes of trust and parental decision-making in the perspective of strong pressures from the child are addressed'.

The typical structure of a note contains information regarding: who attended, what the themes of the meeting were, what the interventions were and the professional's subjective perception of parental response.

Additionally, in CCS, the excerpts were chosen from each specialist's notes when regarding the parental understanding of the child's emotions and then how the personnel intervened upon it. Here, a wider range of data was used, including the records of psychiatrists and nurses, but these notes were shorter, usually about two to five lines, and longer only in the case of an incident. The notes consist of patient evaluation on admission, one report from a doctor and two reports from a nurse daily, five notes from family consultations in both cases, and 13 or 22 individual consultations. A total of 585 records were analysed, and the excerpts regarding the understanding of the child were chosen and then analysed in detail. Each record had between one and a dozen sentences.

An example of a shorter medical observation is: 'The patient did not require intervention. Somatic complaints were not reported, meals were eaten. She slept at night'. A longer excerpt considering the emotional state, one of nursing observation, states: 'The girl is in a changeable mood, at first cheerful, talkative, after a while in a lowered mood, crying. In conversation with the nurse she said that it was due to self-loathing and self-hatred. After the conversation she gradually calmed down, returned to her friends, in their company, she was cheerful, smiling. She fell asleep after 9 pm'.

Results

The results of this study are presented in three manuscripts: two of them on the results of CQR (one published in 2022 and one awaiting publication) and one on the results of CCS (also accepted for publication), hence, the aim of this paper is not to present all the results. It was decided to present one fragment from each type of analysis in order to prove the usefulness of these methods. Each example also contains raw data to present the coded material.

Results of the CQR analysis

A domain derived from the data was parental *Emotional attitude toward hospitalisation*, regarding the reactions and emotions of parents toward inward treatment, as perceived by therapeutic teams during the hospitalisation. In the CQR analysis, five categories of this domain emerged [Table 1]. 1) *Sense of the ward's harmfulness* refers to the negative influence the ward might have on patients. Parental anxiety was provoked, among others, by declines in mood ('mother requests an additional meeting because of fear of daughter's depression, which parents link to hospitalisation'), destructive peer influence ('parents discern self-harm attempts as imitating other patients – ward's harmfulness'), or pharmacotherapy ('mother's concern for side effects of medication'). 2) *Ambivalence toward treatment* presents parental internal conflicts, e.g. loyalty to child's request or doctor's recommendations: 'father feels anxiety when his daughter is tense while eating, but stays passive' or 'mother is worried about length of hospitalisation, she would like to discharge daughter, but she doesn't due to fear of disease'. 3) *Discrepancy between parents* impacting decisions on treatment: 'disparity

Table 1. Results of the CQR analysis.

Core idea	Category	Defining features	Frequency (% of sample)
Reactions and emotions toward hospitalization	Sense of the ward's harmfulness	High anxiety	6 (19.4)
		Perceiving children's reactions as evoked by the ward	
	Ambivalence toward treatment	Internal conflict of a parent	10 (32.3)
		Contradictory pursuits	
	Discrepancy between parents	Different understanding of problem and its solution in the parental dyad	5 (16.1)
	Difficulties in accepting child's emotions	Parents emotional reactions to anger, sadness or irritation of their child	7 (22.6)
	Longing for a child	Difficulties caused by separation	4 (12.9)

Source: Bryniarska et. al., 2024.

among parents in daughter's food restriction – mother agreed out of fear, father was opposed'. 4) *Difficulties in accepting child's emotions*: anger ('parents' need to avoid daughter's resentment'), sadness ('parental anxiety regarding her decline in mood'), or irritability and tension ('parents' anxiety about daughter's mental state – mother requests something for the nerves"). *5) Longing due to separation*: 'mother is not doing well with daughter's absence—she misses her, cries a lot'. For more details see: Bryniarska et al. (2024).

Results of the CCS analysis

Part of the CCS results was the description of a situation when it seemed to the therapeutic teams that the parents lost the ability to understand their child's experiences during the hospitalisation and we tried to reconstruct from the different medical records (nurses observations, doctors' daily reports and therapists' official notes), how it was conducted by medical personnel to support parents' understanding of their child. We will present below a direct citation from a manuscript which is a short description of the interventions in one case, while the other case and more results might be found in Authors (accepted for publication, 2023).

Victoria

The patient, during individual psychotherapy sessions, spoke of her 'fear of expectations and pressure from the family. [...] The family pressures her to "try harder", by achieving the weight required for hospital discharge. Victoria, on the other hand, resists by talking about her lack of readiness for such rapid growth'.

The following day, the parent's behaviour highlighting the child's concerns could be observed. The physician on duty noted that the girl 'was being fed by her mother during the visit, most likely to get her body weight to the next stage'. The nurses intervened immediately: 'it was pointed out to the mother that this was too much in too short a time'.

A family meeting was held the following day with the focus on parental understanding. The intervention was conducted through several logical steps. The girl's feelings of pressure were discussed with her parents ('she perceives her efforts so far as insufficient'). Then, the patient's 'ambivalence about contesting her own needs with the desire to please others' was intervened upon. In relation to this, special attention was paid to an incident from the previous day, when the mother overfed her daughter during a visit. In this context, 'the impact of their own expectations on the relationship with their daughter was discussed with the parents'. At the end of the meeting, the patient was also invited to join. She spoke of her anxiety regarding outpatient treatment, which 'will make her angry, and she equates the expression of anger with the loss of family relationships – especially with her father'. (. . .) Three weeks later, in an individual conversation with a psychotherapist, the patient talked about a greater sense of self-awareness and autonomy: 'Victoria [. . .] refers to the treatment process – she presents the changes she notices in herself. She talks about being bolder, and able to be close to someone, at the same time putting a limit to her privacy, and being able to express her emotions without fear of losing her loved ones'. (Authors, accepted for publication, 2023)

Discussion

Qualitative research provides an in-depth understanding of the problem, the mechanisms and internal experiences of patients, their families, and the medical personnel caring for them, hence they are well suited for psychiatric research (Janusz et al., 2019). This is important because of the fact that 'medicine is not only a mechanistic and quantitative science, but also an interpretative art' (Giacomini et al., 2000). The long, narrative descriptions contained in the cited medical records made qualitative analysis possible, although the process was fraught with some challenges. Both the benefits and limitations of using medical data for qualitative research will be presented below.

Advantages of such methodology

Through the use of medical records, we had access to unique clinical data that includes the perspective of diverse personnel: therapists, doctors and nurses. This enabled us to distinguish categories considering cooperation and interventions using CQR analysis, on the one hand, and to track hospitalisation in a way that is both processual (using dates and times of medical records) and multidimensional, in CCS. The reports have also the value of frequent use of citations, meaning that staff quote the exact passage of a parent's or patient's statement.

In this study, we learn about the staff's perspective on the process of inpatient hospitalisation of patients with eating disorders. Another advantage of such a research model is that we avoided the self-report bias (Bauhoff & Michalos, 2014) by using data that professionals at the time of writing did not know would be subjected to scientific study. This also prevented the impact of self-description on the qualitative data (Holtom-Viesel & Allan, 2014). In addition, the authorship of the documentation is doubly beneficial: these are the same people, i.e. the staff employed in the ward at the time described, and simultaneously thanks to the number of authors, we obtain a greater level of objectivity.

Since the data was heavily immersed in the clinical context, involving patients with a specific psychiatric diagnosis, concerned with the context of inpatient treatment, and the researchers are also clinicians, the material is of great clinical relevance. Moreover, the use of qualitative methods made it possible to obtain results that can be very useful for those working in a clinical context, primarily psychotherapists and psychiatrists, but also other specialists, nurses, nutritionists, and social workers.

CQR methodology provides explanations and descriptions of parental experiences and professionals' interventions. Thanks to a specific procedure, this method allows the data to be processed using core ideas, domains and precise categories, which enables a description of the studied population, also by reporting them in tables containing quantities of each category apart. In our study, CQR also allowed us to distinguish two contrasting groups and then to compare them in the following parts of research (Bryniarska et al., 2024). CCS, on the other hand, allowed the dynamics of cooperation to be presented in a microanalytic way. Our study proved the differences between a cooperating family and one struggling with collaboration in understanding the child. Moreover, when a critical moment appeared in both cases, CCS enabled us to show the process of specialists intervening and helping the parents to overcome their predicament (Authors, accepted for publication, 2023).

Limitations of such methodology

A frequent objection to qualitative methods is the small number of respondents, which makes it impossible to generalise conclusions for the whole population. This is why it could be considered to combine the qualitative and quantitative research (Razafsha et al., 2012). There is also the argument that this type of study is immersed in a very specific context, here: an inpatient child psychiatry unit of 14 year olds, in Poland, working in a specific model. However, certain mechanisms of action or functioning, the way the family experiences things etc., will be similar in different contexts (Coelho et al., 2021).

Some might also question the neutrality of the researchers, who should not be involved in the described phenomenon. It has been proven that we co-create the narrative, we influence it, which also applies to the relationship between professionals and patients (Andersen, 1992). Qualitative researchers see the solution to this difficulty in the concept of reflexivity and self-awareness, which guards against the unconscious influence of one's own beliefs or past experiences on the perception and understanding of the phenomenon under study (Reay, 2007). As therapists, clinicians and qualitative researchers, we have consistently tried to return with reflection to the topics, considering our own distortions (Palaganas et al., 2017). Inviting external researchers, who were neither involved in this research project nor in the work in the described inpatient ward, was also intended to increase objectivity.

The above argument also applies in the context of the authors of the records. The specificity of this study was the use of medical data, which does not provide us with direct access in response to particular questions, but only mediated access. In fact, we get to know the perception of the staff, which may be distorted by their own sensitivity and perception of specific patients. In this case, the researchers also drew on their clinical and therapeutic experience to be cautious of this type of distortion in the narratives. A reader should be aware of the reflective and subjective characteristics of each note, which means that only mediated access to someone's experience is available here.

It is also worth mentioning that compiling such a large amount of data from the medical system is a time-consuming and complicated process. Not only was the raw data voluminous, but this type of data analysis is a labour-intensive process, requiring the same data to be revisited repeatedly.

Conclusions

The design of this whole scientific project was incremental. Firstly, all the data was gathered and in the first analysis the general domains appeared. Then, we delved into two branches to deepen the analysis with subdomains along with their quantities. On the basis of one subdomain, the respondents were divided into two groups: one with beneficial cooperation and one struggling with cooperation. This division was consistently applied in the subsequent stages of the study. All of this analysis was conducted using CQR by determining domains, subdomains and then describing specific categories.

The final step was based on a micro process, which involved tracing the hospitalisation of two cases. One from each of the comparison groups was selected and the data source was expanded, it was not limited to therapists' records, but also other professionals' notes were included. An attempt was made to trace how this collaboration is co-created. To this end, CCS was used.

Qualitative research is a well-established method to study internal experiences. An important aspect is the need for team collaboration. The analysis of CQR and CCS with such challenging, clinical material could not be conducted alone. It is also beneficial when researchers have experience in both clinical contexts and qualitative research. An essential task for researchers is also having an aware, reflexive position, which helps to increase the transparency of analysis and has the potential to minimise the impact of bias (Palaganas et al., 2017; Reay, 2007). These need to be triggered individually, but also raised during data work sessions, among team members.

In conclusion, the qualitative study of medical data has its limitations, such as the influence of the researcher as well as the author of the medical reports, the small sample size of the subjects, etc., but provides an opportunity for a unique attempt to show the complexity in the course of treatment. With regard to the mediated nature of the data, we could reflect that this methodology enables an attempt to trace the dynamic process of co-creation: staff interventions, parental responses, and consideration of the child's perspective, which would be difficult to obtain in any other way. And if the aim was specifically to explore collaboration, these methods seem aptly used.

Disclosure statement

No potential conflict of interest was reported by the author(s).

ORCID

Antonina Bryniarska http://orcid.org/0000-0003-3941-6962

References

Andersen, T. (1992). Relationship, language and pre-understanding in the reflecting processes. *Australian and New Zealand Journal of Family Therapy, 13*(2), 87–91. https://doi.org/10.1002/j.1467-8438.1992.tb00896.x

Balottin, L., Mannarini, S., Mensi, M. M., Chiappedi, M., & Balottin, U. (2018). Are family relations connected to the quality of the outcome in adolescent anorexia nervosa? An observational study with the Lausanne Trilogue Play. *Clinical Psychology and Psychotherapy, 25*(6), 785–796. https://doi.org/10.1002/cpp.2314

Bauhoff, S. (2014). *Self-report bias in estimating cross-sectional and treatment effects bt - encyclopedia of quality of life and well-being research* (A. C. Michalos, Ed.) Springer Netherlands. https://doi.org/10.1007/978-94-007-0753-5_4046

Braun, V., & Clarke, V. (2021). One size fits all? What counts as quality practice in (reflexive) thematic analysis? *Qualitative Research in Psychology, 18*(3), 328–352. https://doi.org/10.1080/14780887.2020.1769238

Bryniarska, A., Wojszel, B., Popiołek, L., & Józefik, B. (2024). Young adolescents with anorexia nervosa—the cooperation between parents and medical personnel in stationary Treatment. *The American Journal of Family Therapy, 52*(2), 160–175. https://doi.org/10.1080/01926187.2022.2071356

Campbell, S. (2010). Comparative case study. In A. J. Mills, G. Eurepos, & E. Wiebe (Eds.), *Encyclopedia of case study research* (pp. 174–176). SAGE.

Coelho, J. S., Suen, J., Marshall, S., Burns, A., Lam, P. Y., & Geller, J. (2021). Parental experiences with their child's eating disorder treatment journey. *Journal of Eating Disorders, 9*(1), 1–14. https://doi.org/10.1186/s40337-021-00449-x

Couturier, J., & Lock, J. (2006). Denial and minimization in adolescents with Anorexia Nervosa. *International Journal of Eating Disorders, September*, 27–30. https://doi.org/10.1002/eat

Elo, S., Kääriäinen, M., Kanste, O., Pölkki, T., Utriainen, K., & Kyngäs, H. (2014). Qualitative content analysis. *SAGE Open, 4*(1), 215824401452263. https://doi.org/10.1177/2158244014522633

Giacomini, M. K., Cook, D. J., & Guyatt, G. H. (2000). Users' guides to the medical literature: XXIII. Qualitative research in health care B. What are the results and flow do they help me care for my patients? *Jama, 284*(4), 478–482. https://doi.org/10.1001/jama.284.4.478

Goodrick, D. (2014). Comparative case studies. *Methodological briefs: Impact evaluation 9.*

Hesse-Biber, S. (2012). *Handbook of feminist research: Theory and praxis* (2nd ed.). https://doi.org/10.4135/9781483384740

Hill, C. E., & Knox, S. (2021). Conceptual foundations of consensual qualitative research. *Essentials of Consensual Qualitative Research*, 3–10. https://doi.org/10.1037/0000215-001

Hill, C., & Knox, S. (2021). *Essentials of consensual qualitative research*. American Psychological Association. https://doi.org/10.1037/0000215-000

Hill, C. E., Thompson, B. J., Hess, S. A., Knox, S., Williams, E. N., & Ladany, N. (2005). Consensual qualitative research: An update. *Journal of Counseling Psychology, 52*(2), 196–205. https://doi.org/10.1037/0022-0167.52.2.196

Holtom-Viesel, A., & Allan, S. (2014). A systematic review of the literature on family functioning across all eating disorder diagnoses in comparison to control families. *Clinical Psychology Review, 34*(1), 29–43. https://doi.org/10.1016/j.cpr.2013.10.005

Janusz, B., Czapkiewicz, K., Wolska, M., Bierzyński, K., Müldner-Nieckowski, Ł., & Furgał, M. (2019). Guidelines for constructing clinical case studies in psychotherapy. *Psychoterapia*, *191*(4), 41–56. https://doi.org/10.12740/PT/115884

Jespers, A. (2022). Child and adolescent psychiatric units: From working for parents to working with parents. *11th Conference of The European Family Therapy Association*, 7–10 September 2022, Ljubljana.

Johns, G., Taylor, B., John, A., & Tan, J. (2019). Current eating disorder healthcare services – the perspectives and experiences of individuals with eating disorders, their families and health professionals: Systematic review and thematic synthesis. *British Journal of Psychiatry Open*, *5*(4), 1–10. https://doi.org/10.1192/bjo.2019.48

Kaarbo, J., Bingol, H. B., & Collier, D. (1999). A practical guide to the comparative case study method in political psychology related papers conflict management strategies in mergers and acquisitions: A comparative case study of I. *Political Psychology*, *20*(2), 369–391. https://doi.org/10.1111/0162-895X.00149

McMaster, R., Beale, B., Hillege, S., & Nagy, S. (2004). The parent experience of eating disorders: Interactions with health professionals. *International Journal of Mental Health Nursing*, *13*(1), 67–73. https://doi.org/10.1111/j.1447-0349.2004.00310.x

Mitrofan, O., Petkova, H., Janssens, A., Kelly, J., Edwards, E., Nicholls, D., McNicholas, F., Simic, M., Eisler, I., Ford, T., & Byford, S. (2019). Care experiences of young people with eating disorders and their parents: Qualitative study. *British Journal of Psychiatry Open*, *5*(1), 1–8. https://doi.org/10.1192/bjo.2018.78

National Institute for Health and Care Excellence. (2020). *Eating disorders: Recognition and treatment*. NG69. NICE Guidelines. Retrieved October 01, 2023, from https://www.nice.org.uk/guidance/ng69

O'Brien, B. C., Harris, I. B., Beckman, T. J., Reed, D. A., & Cook, D. A. (2014). Standards for reporting qualitative research: A synthesis of recommendations. *Academic Medicine*, *89*(9), 1245–1251. https://doi.org/10.1097/ACM.0000000000000388

Palaganas, E. C., Sanchez, M. C., Molintas, M. V. P., & Caricativo, R. D. (2017). Reflexivity in qualitative research: A journey of learning. *The Qualitative Report*, *22*(2), 426–438. https://doi.org/10.46743/2160-3715/2017.2552

Razafsha, M., Behforuzi, H., Azari, H., Zhang, Z., Wang, K. K., Kobeissy, F. H., & Gold, M. S. (2012). Qualitative versus quantitative methods in psychiatric research. *Methods in Molecular Biology* (Clifton, N.J.), *829*, 49–62. https://doi.org/10.1007/978-1-61779-458-2_3

Reay, D. (2007). Future directions in difference research: Recognizing and responding to difference. In S. N. Hesse-Biber (Ed.), *Handbook of feminist research: Theory and praxis* (pp. 605–612). Thousand Oaks.

Reid, M., Williams, S., & Hammersley, R. (2010). Managing eating disorder patients in primary care in the UK: A qualitative study. *Eating Disorders*, *18*(1), 1–9. https://doi.org/10.1080/10640260903439441

Reyes-Rodriguez, M. L., Watson, H. J., Barrio, C., Baucom, D. H., Silva, Y., Luna-Reyes, K. L., & Bulik, C. M. (2019). Family involvement in eating disorder treatment among latinas. *Eating Disorders*, *27*(2), 205–229. https://doi.org/10.1080/10640266.2019.1586219

Richmond, T. K., Woolverton, G. A., Mammel, K., Ornstein, R. M., Spalding, A., Woods, E. R., & Forman, S. F. (2020). How do you define recovery? A qualitative study of patients with eating disorders, their parents, and clinicians. *International Journal of Eating Disorders*, *53*(8), 1209–1218. https://doi.org/10.1002/eat.23294

Sampson, R., Cooper, J., Barbour, R., Polson, R., & Wilson, P. (2015). Patients' perspectives on the medical primary–secondary care interface: Systematic review and synthesis of qualitative research. *British Medical Journal Open*, *5*(10), e008708. https://doi.org/10.1136/bmjopen-2015-008708

Saria, V. F., Mselle, L. T., & Siceloff, B. A. (2019). Parents and nurses telling their stories: The perceived needs of parents caring for critically ill children at the Kilimanjaro Christian Medical Centre in Tanzania. *BMC Nursing*, *18*(1), 1–8. https://doi.org/10.1186/s12912-019-0381-8

Simic, M., & Eisler, I. (2019). Maudsley family therapy for eating disorders. In J. L. Lebow, A. L. Chambers, & D. C. Breunlin (Eds.), *Encyclopedia of couple and family therapy*. https://doi.org/10.1007/978-3-319-49425-8_168

Strauss, A., & Corbin, J. (1994). Grounded theory methodology: An overview. In: N. K. Denzin & Y. S. Lincoln (Eds.), *Handbook of qualitative research* (pp. 273–285). Sage Publications, Inc.

Tylec, A., Olajossy, M., Dubas-Ślemp, H., & Spychalska, K. (2013). Możliwość czy przymus leczenia? Anoreksja psychiczna - Uregulowania prawne. Opis przypadku. *Psychiatria Polska*, *47*(3), 531–539.

Walker, S., & Lloyd, C. (2011). Barriers and attitudes health professionals working in eating disorders experience. *International Journal of Therapy and Rehabilitation*, *18*(7), 383–390. https://doi.org/10.12968/ijtr.2011.18.7.3837219

Developing reflexivity and self-compassion in group psychotherapy: A dialogical and narrative approach

Maria Viou and Eugenie Georgaca

ABSTRACT

In this paper, we apply dialogical concepts to understand the development of self-reflexivity and self-compassion during psychotherapy. Specifically, we present a study that mapped clients' voices and explored their changes in group psychotherapy. Thematic narrative analysis was used to study 20 two-hour group therapy sessions of a systemic informed approach. The analysis involved mapping of the voices of each group member, categorizing them as compassionate and/or reflexive and a sequential depiction of the group voices through timelines. The last step of the analysis included studying the development of self-reflexive and self-compassionate voices through time. It showed an important change, not on the number of clients' self-reflexive voices that appeared during psychotherapy, but mostly on the quality of the self-reflexive voices in favor of voices that were both self-reflexive and self-compassionate. This change seems to take place as a result of the internalization and "rehearsal" of more kind and compassionate voices that appear in the group dialogues. Hence, this study suggests that, in parallel with focusing on the presence and amount of the reflexive processes that occur in psychotherapy, psychotherapy research should also focus on the changes in the quality of these processes, and particularly the development of self-compassion in psychotherapy.

Background

Reflexivity and self-compassion in psychotherapy

Reflexivity is part of human metacognition, concerning the capability of a person to think about thought (Flavell, 1979). It also entails personal perception and awareness about the process of thinking (Kuhn & Dean, 2004). In psychotherapy the therapeutic mechanisms that are linked to change involve clients' reflexivity about relationships, emotions, beliefs and experiences, showing that reflexive engagement is an important part of psychotherapy (Levitt et al., 2006). Also, psychotherapy can be seen as offering clients an opportunity to develop the capacity for self-reflexivity (Lysaker et al., 2011). Clients' self-reflection has been linked to positive therapeutic results and therapeutic change (Angus et al., 1999; Laitila et al., 2005), as people with higher levels of self-reflection are more likely to be more adaptive (Dimaggio et al., 2010).

From a narrative approach, the development of clients' reflexive stance towards their acts, beliefs, needs, experiences and values is an important part of psychotherapy, as it enables processing and self-organization of emotions and experiences and reconstruction of meanings and perspectives on situations, allowing the development of a cohesive personal narrative (Angus et al., 1999; L. S. Greenberg, 2002; L. Greenberg & Angus, 2004). Hence, reflexivity in psychotherapy is important for the development of new and alternative views and understandings both of the self and others (Angus & McLeod, 2004).

Self-compassion is another quality whose development has been considered essential and desired in psychotherapy over the last years and is linked with positive outcomes (Gilbert, 2000, 2005, 2009; Gilbert et al., 2006; Neff, 2003b, 2003b). Self-compassion refers to kindness and acceptance towards the self, understanding the difficulties as part of common humanity and mindful awareness and acceptance of all kinds of emotions and thoughts (Neff, 2003b). However, compassion is not only about empathy; an essential component of compassion is the motivation to act (Gilbert, 2009). Research has highlighted the importance of self-compassion for mental health. The development of a less critical and more compassionate stance towards the self has been suggested as important and helpful in many psychotherapy approaches (Androutsopoulou, 2013, 2015; Androutsopoulou & Viou, 2019; Eicher et al., 2013; Gilbert & Procter, 2006; Leary et al., 2007; Mayhew & Gilbert, 2008; Pauley & McPherson, 2010; Viou & Georgaca, 2020, 2021, 2023b).

Dialogical self theory

Various therapeutic approaches have suggested an understanding of the self as dialogical and polyphonic (Angus & McLeod, 2004; Avdi, 2012; Bromberg,

2004; Cooper, 2004; H. J. M. Hermans, 2004a, 2004b; Schwartz, 2013). Our research is mostly influenced by Dialogical Self Theory (DST) (H. J. M. Hermans, 2004a; 2012; H. J. M. Hermans & Dimaggio, 2004; H. M. J. Hermans & Gieser, 2012; 2006), according to which the self comprises of different aspects, that are in a dialogical relationship with one another. When referring to aspects of the self, the terms I-positions and voices have both been used, often interchangeably, in dialogical research (Bertau, 2007; H. J. M. Hermans & Kempen, 1993). Here we focus on the concept of voices; we adopt the view that I-positions may be endowed with voices (H. J. M. Hermans, 1996), and thus we see voices as expressions of I-positions. Correspondingly, we consider that a person's position repertoire (M, 2006) can be elucidated through mapping their voice repertoire (Androutsopoulou, 2015).

These I-positions can move in space and in time (H. J. M. Hermans, 2004a). The self can include not only the internal domain of the self (e.g. I as a child), but also external positions (e.g. my mother, my therapist). Hence, according to H. J. M. Hermans (2001), social positions and collective voices are not only outside but also inside the individual self. This process of internalizing external voices seems to start from early on, from the voice of the mother (Bertau, 2004, 2012), and continues throughout life (Bertau & Karsten, 2018), whereby the voices of significant others can be experienced as inner voices and become positions of the self. However, internalization is not a linear process of adopting others' voices. Rather, the psyche, the cultural, social and interpersonal domains are all part of a continuous interaction. In other words, the self and its positions are continuously formed and performed in social and cultural contexts (Georgaca, 2001; Viou & Georgaca, 2023a). In psychotherapy, the encouragement of inner dialogue between the different aspects of the self is considered essential (H. J. M. Hermans, 2004a, 2004b) and therapeutic change can be understood as the emergence of a flexible dialogue between voices (Avdi & Georgaca, 2009).

Reflexivity and self-compassion in dialogical approaches

In the dialogical perspective, self-reflection is understood as a voice that occurs when someone comments on a memory, a thought, an action and/or an emotion of the self. Through self-reflection, the speaker becomes an observer and a dialogue between two voices takes place. For example, Leiman (2004) mentions that, when a client makes a comment on her appearance, she takes a distance and positions herself by the evaluative comment she makes. Reflexive voices can be strict and judgmental towards the self or they can be more self-compassionate (Leiman, 2002; Viou & Georgaca, 2020, 2023b).

Compassion has not been thoroughly studied in dialogical approaches. It is most often theorized as a distinct reflexive voice (compassionate voice) or I-position (I as compassionate), and specifically as a meta-position or a promoter position (H. J. M. Hermans & Hermans-Konopka, 2010; Viou & Georgaca, 2021). A meta-position is a position of the self that understands and comments on the links between the different I-positions (H. J. M. Hermans, 2004a). Given that self-compassion is a reflexive stance adopted by an I-position toward one or more I-positions, compassionate I-positions are closely linked to meta-positions (Viou & Georgaca, 2021). Promoter positions are I-positions that play a role in the composition of the self, through enabling the self to develop (H. J. M. Hermans & Hermans-Konopka, 2010). According to Konopka et al. (2018), I-as compassionate is an example of a promoter position, since it enhances integration of new and existing positions, supporting in this way a sense of cohesion.

Our previous work on the multiple reflexive voices of the self and their expression in the psychotherapy context has revealed a range of voices, some being kinder and more compassionate toward the self (e.g. an assertive voice), while others being stricter and more critical to the self (e.g. a guilty voice) (Viou & Georgaca, 2020, 2023b). In this paper, we suggest that compassion is not a distinct voice that can be identified in the self as a meta-position or a promoter position but should be seen as a quality of the voices that constitute the self and specifically a quality of the reflexive voices that are identified in the therapeutic process.

Aim of the study

This paper is part of a wider project that aims to explore and map the development of the clients' voices during long-term group psychotherapy from a dialogical perspective. As mentioned above, the development of self-reflexive voices is deemed necessary in psychotherapy. However, less is being said about the process of developing self-reflection in psychotherapy and the quality of these reflexive voices. The aim of this paper is, thus, to highlight the changes that take place during psychotherapy in the emergence and quality of self-reflexive voices.

Method

This research project consisted of tracking the development of therapy clients' voices during the course of group psychotherapy of a systemic informed approach (Viou & Georgaca, 2023b).

Participants & group setting

Study participants were members of an existing psychotherapy group. There were four Greek women, whose ages varied between 22–40 years old. The group was coordinated by two female psychotherapists with 8–10 years of practice. The therapists follow a specific therapy perspective, the SANE model, which combines four dimensions i.e. systemic, attachment, narrative/dialogic and encephalon/neurosciences (Androutsopoulou et al., 2021).

In this model, sessions are held on a weekly basis and last two hours. The format of the group consists of group members' uninterrupted narrative, talking about issues preoccupying them during the week, with some exploratory questions made by the therapists, followed by the feedback of other group members and finally the interventions made by the two psychotherapists. In this paper, we will refer to the clients' long uninterrupted storytelling as 'client monologues' in order to distinguish them from the dialogue between the group members and the therapists' interventions, which we name 'group dialogue'.

The group was already working for a year before the beginning of this study. Three group members (Nadia, Vera, Olga) had been in this particular group for approximately one year and one member (Marina) for one month. They all had attended individual psychotherapy for at least six months before entering the group. Participants are referred to by pseudonyms.

Analysis

Analysis was applied to 20 two-hour group therapy sessions conducted over two years. We selected two consecutive sessions every two months to include at least one monologue of each of the four group members. The sessions were audio recorded with the participants' informed consent and transcribed by the first author. The themes that emerged from the analysis, together with selected extracts, were translated into English for publication purposes. The analysis includes two distinct but interrelated levels.

The ***first level*** of analysis entailed ***mapping the voices*** that appeared in the group therapy material. Client voices were identified and described using thematic narrative analysis (Riessman, 2008). Thematic narrative analysis is a type of narrative analysis that focuses on the content of narratives. Systematically organizing the content of narratives allowed us to identify patterns and portray them as narrative themes (Floersch et al., 2010) and to discover common thematic features across narratives (Riessman, 2008). Given the diversity of the ways of doing narrative research and analysis of narratives (Parks, 2023), thematic narrative analysis was selected, as it is considered an important approach for studying autobiographies (Lieblich et al., 1998). In our view, all autobiographical narratives, including psychotherapy transcripts, are stories aiming to make sense of peoples' lives, experiences and identities (Androutsopoulou, 2015; Bruner, 2004; Emerson & Frosh, 2009).

Based on our theoretical perspective, we assume that the themes emerging from the analysis correspond to client voices, as they are higher-level constructs, constituting constellations of similarly themed individual expressions. The analysis closely followed the guidelines and steps of thematic analysis (Braun & Clarke, 2006). We performed the analysis separately for the client monologues and the group dialogues, ending up with two thematic maps respectively, representing all the themes/voices of the clients and therapists in the material.

After completing the thematic analysis of the client monologues, we recorded the frequency of each voice, as a marker of their dominance in the client's self. We also grouped the voices according to their qualities as self-reflexive (SR)/non-self-reflexive (NSR) and self-compassionate (SC)/non-self-compassionate (NSC). Given that, to our knowledge, there is not one single structured method to evaluate compassion and reflexivity, we followed criteria based on the definition of these two terms (Gilbert, 2005, 2009, 2014; Leiman, 2004; Neff, 2003b). Specifically, each voice was examined in terms of the four elements of compassion: 1) kindness 2) accepting difficulties as part of human nature 3) awareness of all thoughts and emotions and 4) taking responsibility to act (Gilbert, 2009; Neff, 2003b). We grouped the first three elements of compassion in one category (SC1), as they are all related to empathy, and we considered the fourth element as a second distinct category related to assertiveness (SC2). Also, each voice that appears when the speaker expresses an evaluative stance towards some aspect of their self was considered self-reflexive (Leiman, 2004).

We then proceeded to the ***second level*** of analysis, a ***sequential organization and tracking of the voices***. We constructed timelines of the voices, as they appeared in the therapeutic session, while marking the speaker and their quality in terms of self-reflexivity and self-compassion. This allowed us to identify specific sequences of voices, study dialogical patterns in the group process and explore the development of voices in time.

The analysis was conducted by the first author and was cross-checked by the second author. Through collaborative discussion, consensus was reached on all instances of differing views. Triangulation by a third researcher was also applied to increase depth of the analysis (Flick, 2004).

Ethics

Participants were informed of the confidentiality procedures, and they all read and signed an informed consent form in three stages for the wider project: in the beginning, mid-way through and at the end of the project (McLeod, 2001). This study was approved by the research ethics committee of the School of Psychology of the Aristotle University of Thessaloniki.

Findings

Mapping and categorization of voices in the monologues

The first step in the process involved mapping the voices of each group member in the client monologues. In Table 1 we present three commonly detected voices in the client monologues, for demonstration purposes. We present the name of the voice in the left-hand column, its description in the middle column and an example of the voice in the right-hand column.

We constructed a table (Table 2) that includes all 22 voices tracked in the client monologues, organized according to their quality, with an indication of the frequency of their appearance as a marker of their dominance in the client's self.

We noticed that all self-compassionate voices are self-reflexive. Since self-compassion refers to the self in a kind way, we were not expecting to find any voice of a group member towards the self that was self-compassionate but not self-reflexive. However, not all self-reflexive voices are self-compassionate. For example, the self-understanding voice expressed by all group members is a self-reflexive (SR) and a self-compassionate voice (SC), but the guilty voice, i.e. a voice that expresses guilt towards the self, is a self-reflexive (SR) but not a self-compassionate (NSC) voice.

Our analysis highlights the richness of the group members' discourse. It showed that many group members had identical voices but also voices that differed. Furthermore, each member had different combinations of SR/NSR and SC/NSC voices. Also, all narrators have similar number of voices identified but differed in the number of instances of voices both in total and in each category. This difference might be related to the dominance of each voice per member, to the number of monologues of each member and to the length and richness of their narratives. For example, Nadia was absent many times for

Table 1. Examples of voices in the client monologues.

Voice	Description	Examples
Assertive SR/SC2	Tries to differentiate from other people, expresses healthy anger and asserts one's rights	*"I know I have the skills and I am confident that I will succeed even if I don't have her approval" (Vera)*
Self-understanding SR/SC1	Understands motive, actions, thoughts and emotions regarding the self, the self becomes an ally	*"I did not decide what to do based on guilt as I used to do. I understand now it was the child in me that was screaming, needing love and care" (Nadia)*
Guilty SR/NSC	Strict voice, takes on responsibility for everything	*"I told her that, if something ever happened to her, I would be the one having spoken to her in a bad way . . . if something happened, it would be my fault" (Marina)*

Table 2. Presentation of all the voices identified in the client monologues across all sessions, their dominance and quality.

Voice quality	Voice	Marina	Nadia	Vera	Olga
NSR-NSC	Overwhelmed	10	28	20	28
	Judgmental voices of others	7	2	1	
	Pleasing others	28	1		1
	Being numb	8	3		
	Theorizing			2	
	Non-trusting			3	
	Withdrawn			3	
	Voice of must				2
	Understanding others	33	11	6	7
	Number of voices	*5*	*5*	*6*	*4*
	Number of instances	*86*	*45*	*35*	*38*
SR-NSC	Self-blaming	15	13	19	43
	Gulty	23	10	17	10
	Self-devaluing	35	6	3	11
	Hopeless	1	6	5	8
	Number of voices	*4*	*4*	*4*	*4*
	Number of instances	*74*	*35*	*44*	*72*
Number of NSC voices		*9*	*9*	*10*	*8*
Number of NSC instances of voices		*160*	*80*	*79*	*110*
SR-SC1	Self-understanding	56	37	51	77
	Self-supporting	19	6	15	40
	Self-soothing	1	3	9	13
	Self-protecting	1	3	2	1
	Hopeful	18	5	21	11
	Emotional	27	9	9	
	Spotting exceptions				8
	Number of voices	*5*	*5*	*5*	*5*
	Number of instances	*66*	*26*	*52*	*74*
SR-SC2	Assertive	62	37	51	77
	Assuming agency	4	3	1	4
	Number of voices	*2*	*2*	*2*	*2*
	Number of instances	*66*	*40*	*52*	*81*
Number of SC voices		*7*	*7*	*7*	*7*
Number of instances of SC voices		*128*	*66*	*104*	*158*
Number of voices per narrator		17	17	18	16
Number of instances of voices per narrator		**280**	**154**	**210**	**302**

health reasons, so she had few recorded monologues. Olga was characterized by a quick alternation between voices, while Vera narrated a story often based only on one dominant voice.

We also noticed specific patterns in each category of voices. In the first category, i.e. NSR-NSC, the overwhelmed voice is a voice that appeared in all group members' monologues. This might be because it is common in therapy to start a narration describing difficulties in regulating emotions. On the other hand, the instances of the other voices of each group member depended on their dominant voices. For example, in the same category, Marina had 28 instances of the pleasing others voice and 33 instances of the understanding others voice, which is related to her difficulty in differentiating herself from others. In the SR and NSC category we identified many instances of voices, highlighting that many voices that are self-reflexive are not self-compassionate. More specifically, the self-blaming voice and the guilty voice are mostly common across all group members, while the self-devaluing voice is mostly dominant in the narratives of Marina and is related to her personal history and difficulties. In the categories that are both SR and SC (1&2) the self-understanding voice is the most dominant voice in the narratives of the group members. However, the dominance of the self-understanding voice for each group member differed. Also, the SC1 category is expressed with many different voices and instances of voices while the SC2 includes only two voices, the assertive voice, which is expressed more often, and the assuming agency voice, which appeared more rarely.

The same processes were applied to the clients' and therapists' voices tracked in the group dialogues. The 10 voices identified in the group dialogues are presented in Table 3.

Most voices were non-self-reflexive and compassionate towards the group members. Finding mostly non-self-reflexive voices was expected, as the feedback was directed to others and not to the self. The abundance of compassionate voices is noteworthy, as it indicates that clients mainly use compassionate voices when addressing other group members; this was taken into account in subsequent analytical steps.

Sequential organization and tracking of the voices

The sequential analysis of the data allowed us to study the development of the group members' voices, and specifically of the self-reflexive and self-compassionate voices, in time during psychotherapy. To do this, we focused on the development of voices through time in the clients' monologues. We counted the number of voices of every group member for each category per session. We present eight graphs, two for each client, that depict the development of the self-reflexive and non-self-reflexive voices (Graphs 1, 3, 5, 7) and of the self-compassionate voices (both SC1 and SC2) and non-self-compassionate voices

Table 3. Presentation of all the voices of clients and therapists identified in the group dialogue and their quality.

Voice quality	Voice	Marina	Nadia	Vera	Olga	Therapist1	Therapist2
NSR-C	Supporting	✓	✓	✓	✓	✓	✓
	Understanding	✓	✓	✓	✓	✓	✓
	Spotting exceptions	✓	✓	✓	✓	✓	✓
	Protecting		✓	✓	✓	✓	✓
	Challenging		✓			✓	✓
	Justifying	✓		✓	✓	✓	✓
	Hopeful		✓	✓		✓	✓
	Furious		✓				
	Overwhelmed		✓	✓			
SR-C	Self-reflexive	✓	✓	✓	✓	✓	

(Graphs 2, 4, 6, 8) per session. The horizontal axis portrays the number of sessions that were analyzed and the vertical axis the number of voices identified. The different categories of voices are captured with different colors.

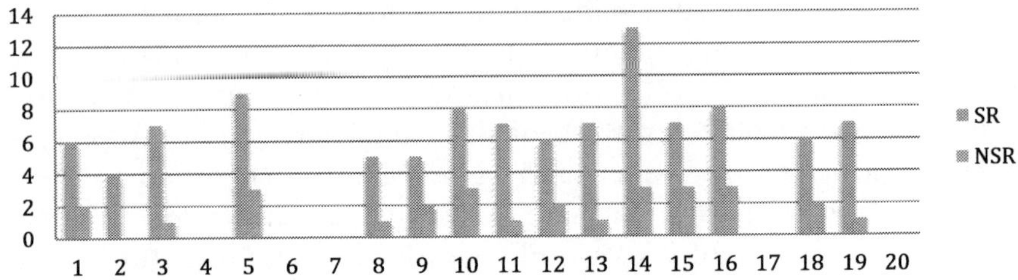

Graph 1. Development of Vera's self-reflexive and non-self-reflexive voices during psychotherapy.

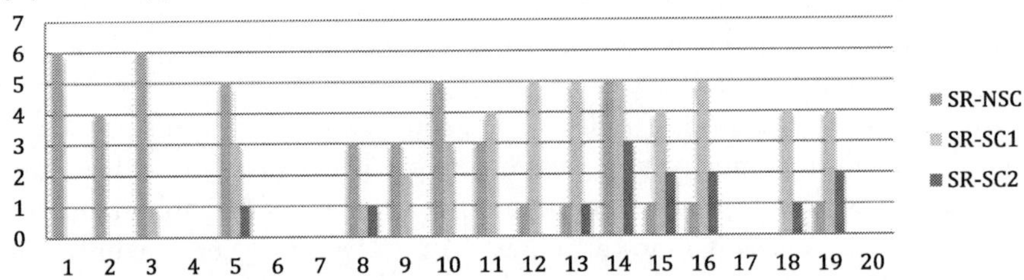

Graph 2. Development of Vera's self-compassionate and non-self-compassionate voices during psychotherapy.

Graph 1 depicts the development of Vera's self-reflexive and non-self-reflexive voices during group psychotherapy. We did not notice important changes in the total number of self-reflexive and non-self-reflexive voices in time. What we noticed (Graph 2) was a significant decrease of non-self-compassionate voices (SR-NSC) and also a significant increase of self-compassionate voices (SR-SC1 & SR-SC2). In the beginning of the recorded sessions, Vera's monologues were mostly populated by SR-NSC voices, such as the self-blaming voice and the guilty voice. SR-SC voices started to develop in time, from session 3, especially the more empathic voices (SR-SC1), such as the self-understanding voice. More assertive voices (SR-SC2) appeared later in the sessions [session 5]. In the final sessions [sessions 15–20], few SR-NSC voices were identified but several NSR-NSC voices remained, especially the voices related to the difficulty of self-regulating emotions, such as the overwhelmed voice.

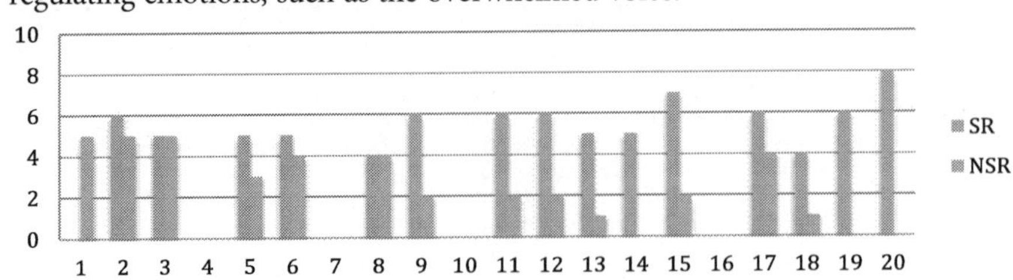

Graph 3. Development of Marina's self-reflexive and non-self-reflexive voices during psychotherapy.

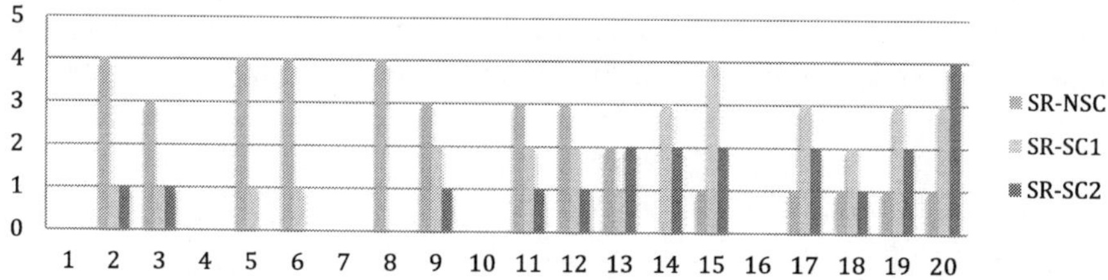

Graph 4. Development of Marina's self-compassionate and non-self-compassionate voices during psychotherapy.

In Marina's case we identified an increase in the total number of self-reflexive voices and a decrease in the total number of non-self-reflexive voices (Graph 3). Initially her monologues were mostly populated with non-self-reflexive and non-self-compassionate voices, such as the overwhelmed voice (NSR-NSC), but also, as we can see in Graph 4, by self-reflexive but non-self-compassionate voices, such as the self-devaluing voice (SR-NSC) and the pleasing others voice (SR-NSC). Through time, and especially after session 9, more empathic self-compassionate voices (SR-SC1) appeared, such as the self-understanding, the self-supporting and the hopeful voice, as well as assertive self-compassionate voices (SR-SC2), such as the assertive voice and the voice assuming agency. Also, there was a noticeable decrease of SR-NSC voices.

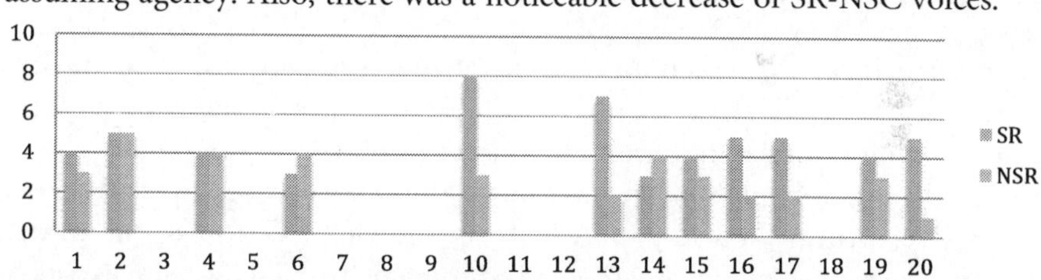

Graph 5. Development of Nadia's self-reflexive and non-self-reflexive voices during psychotherapy.

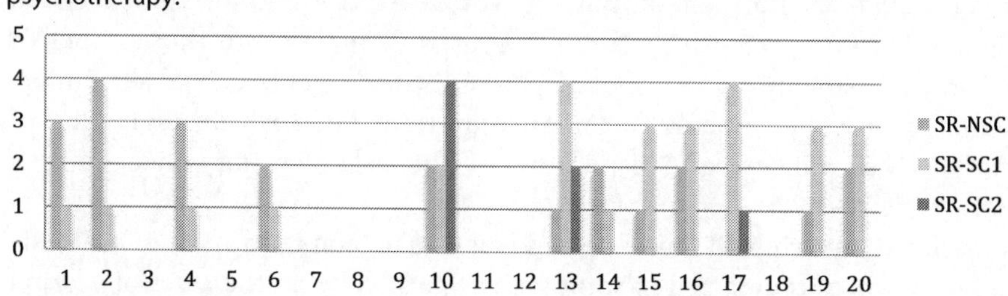

Graph 6. Development of Nadia's self-compassionate and non-self-compassionate voices during psychotherapy.

In Nadia's monologues, we also identified a slight increase in the total number of self-reflexive voices and a slight decrease in the total number of non-self-reflexive voices (Graph 5). We also noticed, as depicted in Graph 6, a gradual decrease of the SR-NSC voices, such as the self-blaming voice, with a parallel increase of the SR-SC1 voices, such as the self-understanding voice and the hopeful voice. The sudden increase of the assertive voice (SR-SC2) that appeared in session 10 can be attributed to life events and was not sustained.

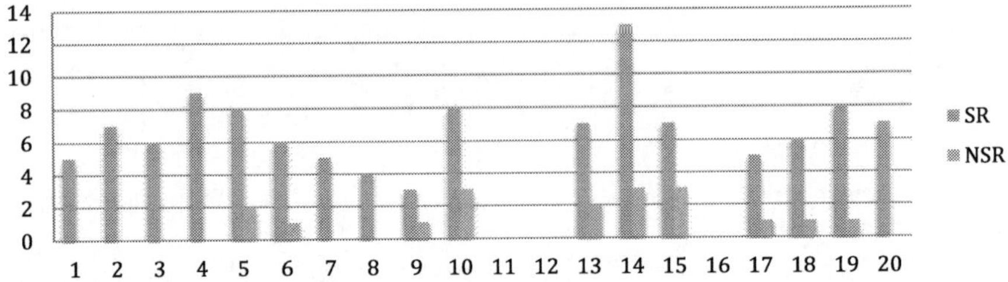

Graph 7. Development of Olga's self-reflexive and non-self-reflexive voices during psychotherapy.

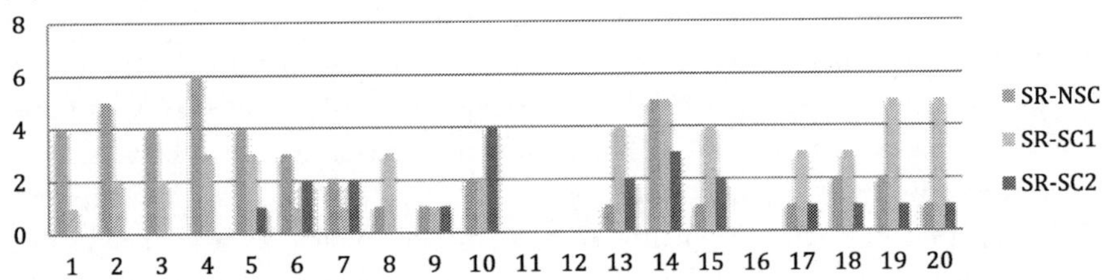

Graph 8. Development of Olga's self-compassionate and non-self-compassionate voices during psychotherapy.

In Olga's case, as seen in Graph 7, the monologues were mostly populated by self-reflexive voices and few non-self-reflexive voices, that remained stable in time. The increase of some NSR-NSC voices during the monologues in the middle of the recorded sessions [sessions 10–15] were connected to life events. As shown in Graph 8, the initial sessions [sessions 1–4] were mostly populated by SR-NSC voices, such as the self-blaming, self-devaluing and hopeless voice, and a few SR-SC1 voices, such as the self-supporting voice. At the end of the recorded sessions [sessions 15–20], there is a noticeable increase in the number of self-compassionate voices, mostly SR-SC1 voices, such as the self-understanding and the hopeful voice. An important decrease through time of the SR-NSC voices, and especially of the self-blaming voice, is also noticeable.

When comparing all four clients, a small change in the appearance of self-reflexive voices is detected in some cases. Specifically, in the cases of Marina and Nadia whose monologues in the initial sessions were populated mostly by non-self-reflexive voices, we see a noticeable decrease of the non-self-reflexive voices and a slight increase in the self-reflexive voices. In the cases of Vera and Olga there was no significant change in the total number of self-reflexive-voices in time, as their monologues were mostly populated by self-reflexive voices from the initial sessions.

It is evident that all group members already had self-reflexive voices in their voice repertoire. However, most of these self-reflexive voices were critical towards the self and not self-compassionate. An important change in the quality of the self-reflexive voices seemed to take place. As depicted in the four graphs (2,4,6,8) that depict the development of self-compassion, in all group members there was a decrease of the number of self-reflexive but not self-compassionate voices, such as the guilty voice and the self-blaming voice, and an increase of the self-reflexive voices that are self-compassionate, such as the self-understanding voice and the assertive voice. Finally, the assertive self-compassionate voices (SR-SC2) seem to emerge later in the sessions, while the empathic self-compassionate voices (SR-SC1) can be identified earlier.

In our previous work we examined the mechanism that takes place in psychotherapy leading to this gradual change in the quality of the voices that populate the group members' narratives, partly explaining the changes identified above. According to our findings, the shifting dominance of voices in favor of self-compassionate voices happens gradually through the internalization of compassionate voices of the therapists and the other group members. It seems that, after being rehearsed in the context of the group dialogue, self-compassionate voices are internalized by the speaker who cultivates them even further and they become the dominant voices of the group members, enriching the inner dialogue and providing an inner response to the previously non-self-compassionate dominant voices. Details about this process of gradual internalization of self-compassionate voices can be found in Viou and Georgaca (2023a).

Discussion

Our analysis revealed a variety of voices that can be tracked in the clients' monologues and group dialogues, which portray the group members' voice repertoires. Some of the clients' voices were common and some of the voices differed. Voices had different degrees of dominance in each clients' narratives, and that seemed to change in time.

Voices vary in their degree of reflexivity and compassion. From our data it is evident that all self-reflexive voices increased slightly in time during psychotherapy while the number of non-self-reflexive voices decreased, especially in the cases where the monologues were initially populated mostly by them. However, this change was minor. Most clients seemed to express several self-reflexive voices from the beginning of the recorded sessions. This would be expected, as psychotherapy itself is an invitation to speak about oneself.

Furthermore, our findings indicate that not all voices that are self-reflexive are also self-compassionate. There are different aspects of reflexivity expressed in the group members' voices (see also Leiman, 2004). For example, many voices that are reflexive, such as the self-blaming voice and the guilty voice, are not compassionate but critical and judgmental towards the self. An important change that we identified was not a change in the number of self-reflexive voices, but a significant change in the quality of these voices. Specifically, we identified an important increase in the number of the voices that were both self-reflexive and self-compassionate. It is noteworthy that self-compassionate voices related to empathy and kindness (SR-SC1) appeared earlier and were more varied, compared to self-compassionate voices that focused on assertiveness and action (SR-SC2). This might indicate that accepting and being kind to oneself is a prerequisite for assuming agency and pursuing change. This is also one of the fundamental assumptions in psychotherapy, and the trend identified might reflect the prioritization of self-understanding in the process of psychotherapy. These findings suggest that, while focusing on the presence and amount of the reflexive processes that occur in psychotherapy (see for example, Angus & McLeod, 2004; Dimaggio et al., 2010), psychotherapy research and practice should also focus on the quality of these processes, and specifically the development of self-compassion in the course of therapy, and the therapeutic processes that might facilitate it.

Through analysing the sequences of voices and tracking their development in the course of the therapy, we documented that compassionate voices articulated by clients and therapists in the group interaction are gradually expressed by clients in their monologues (Viou & Georgaca, 2023a). This indicates a process of internalization, whereby voices of others expressed in interpersonal interaction become voices of the self, changing and hopefully enriching one's voice repertoire. However, this is not a linear process of gradual interiorization but a dynamic process, whereby the self is performed in interactional settings through the collective rehearsing and mutual exchange of voices; thus, the importance of helpful and empowering voices being cultivated in interpersonal and, in our case, therapeutic contexts in order to become possible for them to be incorporated in individual members' self.

Given that we take voices to be expressions of I-positions and the frequency of voices to reflect the dominance of the corresponding I-positions in the clients' self, we may assume that the increase of self-compassionate voices detected in our material indicates that I-positions that are compassionate become stronger, more central and more dominant in the clients' self; at least they become more readily available for use to express, experience and understand one's self. The few new voices that appeared in later sessions might indicate the existence of silenced I-positions that were at last endowed with a voice (Bertau, 2007). Alternatively, they might reflect the creation of a new I-position, that was not previously available to the self.

In sum, this empirical study highlights the function of therapy for the reorganization of the client's self through the development of helpful inner voices. It specifically revealed the ways in which the number and quality of the self-reflexive voices change during therapy through the interaction with the helpful, compassionate voices of the group members, enriching all clients' voice repertoire.

Limitations & future research

The fact that one of the authors was also a therapist in the specific therapeutic group most probably had an impact on the way the material was processed and analyzed. However, the negotiation between the two main researchers at all stages of the process and the triangulation by another researcher provided balance and enriched the analysis.

Moreover, the analysis was conducted in one specific group of a specific psychotherapeutic approach. As in all cases of limited volume of material, further analysis is needed to enhance our understanding of the changes that take place in the voices of clients in psychotherapy in terms of self-reflection and self-compassion, through analyzing more groups and therapeutic approaches.

Concluding remarks

In our study we examine clients' voices as an expression of their self. We try to identify how voices change in the therapeutic exchanges between group members and therapists and we assume that a change in the appearance and frequency of voices depicts an inner change in the self. We understand this change of dominance of voices as a process of internalization of external voices. It seems that, after being rehearsed in the context of the group dialogue, compassionate voices are internalized by the speaker strengthening their own self-compassionate voices. This process of reorganization of voices and strengthening of helpful and self-compassionate voices takes place to some extent through the gradual internalization of compassionate voices of others that occur in the therapeutic dialogue.

In terms of dialogical self theory, our study demonstrates the process of acquiring and internalizing others' voices, whereby the social voices of actual others become inner voices of the self, providing empirical support for the thesis that voices are not only personal but also social in nature (Bertau, 2012; Georgaca, 2001; H. J. M. Hermans, 2001; Viou & Georgaca, 2023a). In terms of psychotherapeutic research, our study highlights the importance of self-compassion and showcases a way of empirically tracking the development of clients' self-compassionate voices, with implications for psychotherapy research and practice.

Disclosure statement

No potential conflict of interest was reported by the author(s).

References

Androutsopoulou, A. (2013). The use of early recollections as a narrative aid in psychotherapy. *Counselling Psychology Quarterly*, *26*(3–4), 313–329. https://doi.org/10.1080/09515070.2013.814086

Androutsopoulou, A. (2015). Moments of meaning: Identifying inner voices in the autobiographical texts of mark. *Qualitative Psychology*, *2*(2), 130–146. https://doi.org/10.1037/qup0000028

Androutsopoulou, A., Bafiti, T., & Kalarritis, G. (2021). "From mind to culture": Developing a treatment plan manual for the enriched systemic psychotherapy model SANE-system attachment narrative encephalon®. In M. Mariotti, G. Saba, & P. Stratton (Eds.), *Handbook of systemic approaches to psychotherapy manuals, European family therapy association series* (pp. 571–591). Springer. https://doi.org/10.1007/978-3-030-73640-8_31.

Androutsopoulou, A., & Viou, M. (2019). The guided imagery therapy activity "Inner dialogue-child adult meeting" (ID-CAM): Steps and applications. *Journal of Creativity in Mental Health*, *14*(3), 343–356. https://doi.org/10.1080/15401383.2019.1624993

Angus, L., Levitt, H., & Hardtke, K. (1999). Narrative processes coding system: Research applications and implications for psychotherapy practice. *Journal of Clinical Psychology*, *55*(10), 1255–1270. https://doi.org/10.1002/(SICI)1097-4679(199910)55:10<1255:AID-JCLP7>3.0.CO;2-F

Angus, L., & McLeod, J. (2004). Toward an integrative framework for understanding the role of narrative in the psychotherapy process. In L. Angus & J. McLeod (Eds.), *The handbook of narrative and psychotherapy practice, theory and research* (pp. 367–374). Sage.

Avdi, E. (2012). Exploring the contribution of subject positioning to studying therapy as a dialogical enterprise. *International Journal for Dialogical Science*, *6*(1), 61–79.

Avdi, E., & Georgaca, E. (2009). Narrative and discursive approaches to the analysis of subjectivity in psychotherapy. *Social and Personality Psychology Compass*, *3*(5), 654–670. https://doi.org/10.1111/j.1751-9004.2009.00196.x

Bertau, M.-C. (2004). Developmental origins of the dialogical self: Some significant moments. In H. J. M. Hermans & G. Dimaggio (Eds.), *The dialogical self in psychotherapy* (pp. 29–42). Brunner-Routledge.

Bertau, M.-C. (2007). On the notion of voice: An exploration from a psycholinguistic perspective with developmental implications. *International Journal for Dialogical Science*, *2*(1), 133–161.

Bertau, M.-C. (2012). Developmental origins of the dialogical self: Early childhood years. In H. J. M. Hermans & T. Gieser (Eds.), *Handbook of dialogical self theory* (pp. 64–81). Cambridge University Press.

Bertau, M.-C., & Karsten, A. (2018). Reconsidering interiorization: Self moving across language spacetimes. *New Ideas in Psychology*, *49*, 7–17. https://doi.org/10.1016/j.newideapsych.2017.12.001

Braun, V., & Clarke, V. (2006). Using thematic analysis in psychology. *Qualitative Research in Psychology*, *3*(2), 77–101. https://doi.org/10.1191/1478088706qp063oa

Bromberg, P. M. (2004). Standing in the spaces: The multiplicity of self in psychoanalytic relationship. In H. J. M. Hermans & G. Dimaggio (Eds.), *The dialogical self in psychotherapy* (pp. 138–151). Brunner-Routledge.

Bruner, J. S. (2004). The narrative creation of self. In L. A. Angus & J. McLeod (Eds.), *The handbook of narrative and psychotherapy* (pp. 2–14). Sage. https://doi.org/10.4135/9781412973496.d3.

Cooper, M. (2004). Encountering self-otherness: 'I-I' and 'I-me' modes of self-relating. In H. J. M. Hermans & G. Dimaggio (Eds.), *The dialogical self in psychotherapy* (pp. 60–73). Brunner-Routledge.

Dimaggio, G., Hermans, H. J. M., & Lysaker, P. H. (2010). Health and adaptation in a multiple self: The role of absence of dialogue and poor metacognition in clinical populations. *Theory & Psychology*, *20*(3), 379–399. https://doi.org/10.1177/0959354310363319

Eicher, A. C., Davis, L. W., & Lysaker, P. H. (2013). Self-compassion: A novel link with symptoms in schizophrenia? *The Journal of Nervous and Mental Disease*, *201* (5), 389–393. https://doi.org/10.1097/NMD.0b013e31828e10fa

Emerson, P., & Frosh, S. (2009). *Critical narrative analysis in psychology: A guide to practice*. Palgrave/Macmillan.

Flavell, J. H. (1979). Metacognition and cognitive monitoring: A new area of cognitive–developmental inquiry. *American Psychologist*, *34*(10), 906–911. https://doi.org/10.1037/0003-066X.34.10.906

Flick, U. (2004). Triangulation in qualitative research. In U. Flick, E. Kardorff, & I. Steinke (Eds.), *A companion to qualitative research* (pp. 178–183). Sage.

Floersch, J., Longhofer, J. L., Kranke, D., & Townsend, L. (2010). Integrating thematic, grounded theory and narrative analysis: A case study of adolescent psychotropic treatment. *Qualitative Social Work*, *9*(3), 407–425. https://doi.org/10.1177/1473325010362330

Georgaca, E. (2001). Voices of the self in psychotherapy: A qualitative analysis. *British Journal of Medical Psychology*, *74*(2), 223–236. https://doi.org/10.1348/000711201160939

Gilbert, P. (2000). Social mentalities: Internal "social" conflict and the role of inner warmth and compassion in cognitive therapy. In P. Gilbert & K. G. Bailey (Eds.), *Genes on the couch: Explorations in evolutionary psychotherapy* (pp. 118–150). Brunner-Routledge.

Gilbert, P. (2005). *Compassion: Conceptualizations, research and use in psychotherapy*. Routledge.

Gilbert, P. (2009). *The compassionate mind*. Robinson.

Gilbert, P. (2014). The origins and nature of compassion focused therapy. *British Journal of Clinical Psychology*, *53*(1), 6–41. https://doi.org/10.1111/bjc.12043

Gilbert, P., Durrant, R., & McEwan, K. (2006). Investigating relationships between perfectionism, forms and functions of self-criticism, and sensitivity to put-down. *Personality and Individual Differences*, *41*, 1299–1308. https://doi.org/10.1016/j.paid.2006.05.004

Gilbert, P., & Procter, S. (2006). Compassionate mind training for people with high shame and self-criticism: A pilot study of a group therapy approach. *Clinical Psychology & Psychotherapy*, *13*(6), 353–379. https://doi.org/10.1002/cpp.507

Greenberg, L. S. (2002). *Emotion-focused therapy: Coaching clients to work through their feelings.* American Psychological Association.

Greenberg, L., & Angus, L. (2004). The contributions of emotion processes to narrative change in psychotherapy: A dialectical constructivist approach. In L. Angus & J. McLeod (Eds.), *Handbook of narrative psychotherapy: Practice, theory, and research* (pp. 331–349). Sage.

Hermans, H. J. M. (1996). Voicing the self: From information processing to dialogical interchange. *Psychological Bulletin, 119*(1), 31–50. https://doi.org/10.1037/0033-2909.119.1.31

Hermans, H. J. M. (2001). The dialogical self: Toward a theory of personal and cultural positioning. *Culture & Psychology, 7*(3), 243–281. https://doi.org/10.1177/1354067X0173001

Hermans, H. J. M. (2004a). The dialogical self: Between exchange and power. In H. J. M. Hermans & G. Dimaggio (Eds.), *The dialogical self in psychotherapy* (pp. 3–28). Brunner-Routledge.

Hermans, H. J. M. (2004b). Innovation of self-narratives: A dialogical approach. In L. E. Angus & J. McLeod (Eds.), *The handbook of narrative and psychotherapy* (pp. 174–192). Sage.

Hermans, H. J. M. (2012). *Between dreaming and recognition seeking: The emergence of dialogical self theory.* University Press of America.

Hermans, H. J. M., & Dimaggio, G. (2004). The dialogical self in psychotherapy: Introduction. In H. J. M. Hermans & G. Dimaggio (Eds.), *The dialogical self in psychotherapy* (pp. 1–10). Brunner-Routledge.

Hermans, H. M. J., & Gieser, T. (2012). Introductory chapter: History, main tenets, and core concepts of dialogical self theory. In H. J. M. Hermans & T. Gieser (Eds.), *Handbook of dialogical self theory* (pp. 1–22). Cambridge University Press. https://doi.org/10.1177/1354067X0173001.

Hermans, H. J. M., & Hermans-Konopka, A. (2010). *Dialogical self theory: Positioning and counter-positioning in a globalizing society.* Cambridge University Press.

Hermans, H. J. M., & Kempen, H. J. G. (1993). *The dialogical self: Meaning as movement.* Academic Press.

Konopka, A., Neimeyer, R. A., & Jacobs-Lentz, J. (2018). Composing the self: Toward the dialogical reconstruction of self-identity. *Journal of Constructivist Psychology, 31*(3), 308–320. https://doi.org/10.1080/10720537.2017.1350609

Kuhn, D., & Dean, D., Jr. (2004). Metacognition: A bridge between cognitive psychology and educational practice. *Theory into Practice, 43*(4), 268–273. https://doi.org/10.1207/s15430421tip4304_4

Laitila, A., Aaltonen, J., Wahlström, J., & Lynne, A. (2005). Narrative process modes as a bridging concept for the theory, research and clinical practice of systemic therapy. *Journal of Family Therapy, 27*(3), 202–216. https://doi.org/10.1111/j.1467-6427.2005.00312.x

Leary, M. R., Tate, E. B., Adams, C. E., Allen, A. B., & Hancock, J. (2007). Self-compassion and reactions to unpleasant self-relevant events: The implications of treating oneself kindly. *Journal of Personality and Social Psychology, 92*(5), 887–904. https://doi.org/10.1037/0022-3514.92.5.887

Leiman, M. (2002). Toward semiotic dialogism. *Theory & Psychology, 12*(2), 221–235. https://doi.org/10.1177/0959354302012002631

Leiman, M. (2004). Dialogical sequence analysis. In H. J. M. Hermans & G. Dimaggio (Eds.), *The dialogical self in psychotherapy* (pp. 255–270). Brunner/Routledge.

Levitt, H., Butler, M., & Hill, T. (2006). What clients find helpful in psychotherapy: Developing principles for facilitating moment-to-moment change. *Journal of Counseling Psychology*, *53*(3), 314–324. https://doi.org/10.1037/0022-0167.53.3.314

Lieblich, A., Tuval-Maschiach, R., & Zilber, T. (1998). *Narrative research: Reading, analysis and interpretation*. Sage.

Lysaker, P. H., Buck, K. D., Carcione, A., Procacci, M., Salvatore, G., Nicolò, G., & Dimaggio, G. (2011). Addressing metacognitive capacity for self reflection in the psychotherapy for schizophrenia: A conceptual model of the key tasks and processes. *Psychology & Psychotherapy: Theory, Research & Practice*, *84*(1), 58–69. https://doi.org/10.1348/147608310X520436

M, H. H. J. (2006). The self as a theatre of voices: Disorganization and reorganizations of a position repertoire. *Journal of Constructivist Psychology*, *19*(2), 147–169. https://doi.org/10.1080/10720530500508779

Mayhew, S. L., & Gilbert, P. (2008). Compassionate mind training with people who hear malevolent voices: A case series report. *Clinical Psychology & Psychotherapy*, *15*(2), 113–138. https://doi.org/10.1002/cpp.566

McLeod, J. (2001). *Qualitative research in counselling and psychotherapy*. Sage.

Neff, K. D. (2003a). The development and validation of a scale to measure self-compassion. *Self and Identity*, *2*(3), 223–250. https://doi.org/10.1080/15298860309027

Neff, K. D. (2003b). Self-compassion: An alternative conceptualization of a healthy attitude toward oneself. *Self and Identity*, *2*(2), 85–102. https://doi.org/10.1080/15298860309032

Parks, P. (2023). Story circles: A new method of narrative research. *American Journal of Qualitative Research*, *7*(1), 58–72. https://doi.org/10.29333/ajqr/12844

Pauley, G., & McPherson, S. (2010). The experience and meaning of compassion and self-compassion for individuals with depression or anxiety. *Psychology & Psychotherapy: Theory, Research & Practice*, *83*(2), 129–143. https://doi.org/10.1348/147608309X471000

Riessman, C. K. (2008). *Narrative methods for the human sciences*. Sage.

Schwartz, R. C. (2013). Moving from acceptance toward transformation with internal family systems therapy (IFS). *Journal of Clinical Psychology*, *69*(8), 805–816. https://doi.org/10.1002/jclp.22016

Viou, M., & Georgaca, E. (2020). Compassionate voices of clients and therapists in systemic group psychotherapy: A narrative study. *Journal of Constructivist Psychology*, *33*(4), 422–440. https://doi.org/10.1080/10720537.2019.1679302

Viou, M., & Georgaca, E. (2021). Enriching our inner dialogue": An activity to explore compassionate voices. *Journal of Constructivist Psychology*, *34*(2), 207–217. https://doi.org/10.1080/10720537.2020.1717150

Viou, M., & Georgaca, E. (2023a). "Their voice becomes my voice": Understanding the development of the dialogical self through the internalization of voices in group psychotherapy. *Theory & Psychology*, *33*(4), 577–596. https://doi.org/10.1177/09593543231176254

Viou, M., & Georgaca, E. (2023b). Tracking change in group psychotherapy: Systematic methodological steps to record the development of clients' voices. In E. Tseliou, C. Demuth, E. Georgaca, & B. Gough (Eds.), *International routledge handbook of innovative qualitative research in psychology* (pp. 215–228). Routledge.

Exploring the grief journey of bereaved spouses: Insights into the impact of sedation within palliative care

Livia Sani, Yasmine Chemrouk, Rozenn Le Berre, Marthe Ducos, Delphine Peyrat-Apicella and Marie-Frédérique Bacqué

ABSTRACT
Despite being the most susceptible to psychopathological consequences, bereaved cancer spouses remain a vastly understudied group. Addressing this gap, a dedicated French research team comprising clinical psychologists, philosophers, and physicians is conducting an ongoing study focused on the emotional and affective complexities experienced by bereaved spouses after the loss of a loved one due to oncological diseases within the realm of palliative care and Continuous Deep Sedation until Death (CDSD). The preliminary data presented below concern the analysis of nine semi-directed interviews analyzed using ALCESTE software, a tool for statistical analysis of textual data based on word co-occurrences. Analysis and comparison of the thematic categories that emerged showed that social support, deep loneliness, and the preservation of memories emerged as central elements of the marital bereavement experience. In addition, the study highlights the critical role of comprehensive palliative care in France and the delicate nature of sedation experiences, revealing intense emotions such as helplessness and anger. Clear communication and active family participation in end-of-life decisions emerged as crucial factors in alleviating the grieving process in spouses. These findings provide valuable insights for healthcare professionals and counselors and underscore the critical need for further research focused on sedation.

Introduction

Palliative care, an integral component of healthcare for individuals with severe or incurable illnesses, aims to enhance the quality of life and alleviate suffering for both patients and their families (WHO, 2020). This multidisciplinary approach team involved professionals from various disciplines, including doctors, nurses, support workers, psychologists, paramedics, pharmacists, physiotherapists, and volunteers.

Within the realm of palliative care, Continuous Deep Sedation until Death (CDSD) emerges as a practice employed in cases of extreme suffering (Bruinsma et al., 2014; Lucchi et al., 2023), involving the administration of sedative medications to induce deep unconsciousness until the patient's passing (Bruinsma et al., 2014).

The terminology surrounding CDSD varies in international literature, with the use of different terms such as continuous sedation, Palliative Sedation (PS), terminal sedation, continuous PS therapy, continuous deep sedation, and slow euthanasia (Papavasiliou et al., 2014; Rietjens et al., 2006; Rys et al., 2012; Ten Have & Welie, 2014), however, in this article, we will adopt the term CDSD, following the model of the French law Claeys-Leonetti of 2016 (LOI n° 2016–87, 2016), which regulates sedation in the authors' home country, France (Mesnage et al., 2020).

The use of CDSD presents unique challenges and ethical considerations, such as in the context of cancer care, which constitutes approximately 34% of diagnoses in palliative care (WHO, 2020), and whose treatment pathway and end-of-life care involves myriad physical, emotional and psychological struggles for cancer patients. Unlike other terminal conditions, cancer is often characterized by unpredictable symptom trajectories, varying levels of pain and suffering, and the potential for rapid deterioration. Consequently, the decision to employ CDSD in cancer care requires careful consideration of the patient's unique circumstances, treatment goals, and preferences, as well as the potential impact on family members and caregivers.

Research has shown that caregivers of sedated patients often express a high degree of satisfaction and appreciation for the treatment, particularly for its effectiveness in symptom relief (Morita et al., 2004). However, Bruinsma et al. (2014) highlight a crucial issue regarding the communication and information surrounding sedation, noting that while CDSD may provide a sense of peaceful death, the lack of clear communication from healthcare professionals can lead to unsatisfactory experiences for caregivers (Bruinsma et al., 2014). Similarly, Shen et al. (2018) observed varying concerns among family members of sedated patients in specialized palliative and critical care settings (Shen et al., 2018). Their study revealed that in palliative care units, the use of CDSD was associated with higher levels of grief among family members, suggesting potential emotional repercussions of the sedation process.

Despite these challenges, limited attention has been directed towards understanding the experiences of spouses who have lost their partners to cancer in such circumstances (Sani et al., 2023). This oversight appears paradoxical, given that bereaved spouses, across various contexts, are the individuals most exposed to a significant risk of developing complications, such as anxiety disorders, depression (Garrouste-Orgeas et al., 2019), and prolonged grief (Fernández-Alcántara & Zech, 2017; Prigerson et al., 2009).

To bridge this gap, this study aims to delve into the narratives of bereaved spouses and explore the multifaceted dimensions of their grief within the context of palliative care and CDSD. Specifically, we seek to understand how the use of sedative practices influences the bereavement experiences of spouses who have lost their partners to cancer and to identify potential areas for improvement in support and care provision.

This study, conducted within the framework of the AFTERSEDATIO research project, employs a mixed longitudinal approach involving questionnaires and semi-structured interviews administered at three, six, and twelve months following the loss of a spouse with an oncological disease in palliative care. By comprehensively examining the experiences of bereaved spouses over time, we aim to provide a nuanced understanding of the challenges and needs they face throughout the grieving process.

To drive our investigation, we pose the following research question: How do bereaved spouses experience and cope with the loss of their partners within the context of palliative care and CDSD?

By elucidating the nuanced experiences and needs of bereaved spouses, we aim to inform healthcare practices and support services, ultimately enhancing the quality of care provided to individuals navigating the complexities of bereavement following the loss of a spouse to cancer within the context of CDSD.

Materials and methods

The data presented below represents preliminary results obtained as part of the research project called AFTERSEDATIO. This project, conducted in France, is structured as a mixed longitudinal study that involves the administration of questionnaires and semi-structured interviews at three (T0), six (T1), and twelve months (T3) following the loss of a spouse with an oncological disease in palliative care. The primary objective of this study is to analyze the experiences and potential psychological consequences of bereaved partners following the experience of palliative care and continuous deep sedation until death.

The research team involved in this investigation has a diverse professional composition, including experts in clinical psychology, philosophy, and medicine.

This study adheres to ethical guidelines outlined in the Declaration of Helsinki and has received approval from the Ethics Committee of the [Details omitted to comply with anonymization rules].

All participants provided informed consent prior to their involvement in the study.

Participants

As shown in Table 1, the participants included 6 women (66.7%), 3 men (33.3%), with an average age of 63.9 years old (43–82), and, in most cases, living alone (77.7%) following the decease. The deceased spouses were predominantly men (66.7%), with an average age at the time of decease of 67.9 years old (49–78), and most of them (88.9%) had received a diagnosis of

Table 1. Sociodemographic data of participants and deceased.

	n (%)
Gender	
Participants	
Women	6 (66.7)
Men	3 (33.3)
Deceased	
Men	6 (66.7)
Women	3 (33.3)
Age (mean (SD); min-max))	
Participants	63.9 (12.5; 43–82)
Deceased	67.9 (9.35; 49–78)
Education level of participants	
Master's degree	3 (33.3)
High school	2 (22.3)
Bachelor's degree	1 (11.1)
Professional certificate	1 (11.1)
Professional diploma	1 (11.1)
NA*	1 (11.1)
Job Status	
Retirement	6 (66.7)
Part-time	1 (11.1)
Full-time	1 (11.1)
Homemaker	1 (11.1)
Who the participants live with	
Alone	7 (77.7)
With family	2 (22.3)
Where participants live	
Urban areas	7 (77.7)
Rural areas	2 (22.3)
Participants have children	
Yes	9 (100)
No	0 (0)
Age of children (mean (SD))	36.7 (13.9)
Taking medicines before the loss	
Anxiolytics	1 (11.1)
Antidepressants	2 (22.3)
Non	6 (66.7)
Taking medicines after the loss	
Anxiolytics	2 (22.3)
Antidepressants	3 (33.3)
None	4 (44.4)
Type of cancer	
Blood cancer (e.g. lymphoma, leukaemia, myeloma, etc.)	1 (11.1)
Organ cancer (e.g. breast, lung, pancreas, liver, etc.)	8 (88.9)
CDSD	
Yes	5 (55.6)
No	1 (11.1)
NA*	3 (33.3)

*NA = Not Available.

organ cancer (e.g. breast, lung, pancreas, liver, etc.), and 55.6% were sedated until the time of decease (CDSD).

Procedure

Participants were interviewed between September 2022 and March 2023, three months later the loss, that corresponds to T0 of the study AFTERSEDATIO.

The interviews were semi-structured and conducted online via the BBB, the platform of the [Details omitted to comply with anonymization rules], with a mean length of 49 minutes.

Table 2 shows the interview guide used by the first two authors [Details omitted to comply with anonymization rules], who are both researchers and clinical psychologists experts in grief and psycho-oncology.

Data analysis

Interviews were transcribed and then analyzed using ALCESTE (the acronym means: *Analyse Lexicale par Contexte d'un Ensemble de Segments de Texte*), a methodological approach based on a technique first developed in 1979 by Max Reinert at the laboratory of Jean-Paul Benzécri, CNRS, Paris.

ALCESTE is a software that allows quantitative analysis of textual data (Reinert, 1987), that divides the text into Units of Context (UC), which encompass one or more consecutive sentences, and whose segmentation is based on criteria such as punctuation and the number of relevant words.

Using a chi-square-based analysis, starting from these UCs, ALCESTE assesses co-occurrences within the text, i.e. how frequently and where a word appears. Subsequently, it extracts classes of words identified within the text, presented in descending order, starting from the class with the

Table 2. Examples of questions from the guide used to conduct semi-structured interviews.

Categories	Examples of questions
The deceased	*Can you tell me about your spouse?* *How would you describe your spouse?*
The disease	*Can you tell the story of the disease?* *How did you experience it?*
Sedative practices	*Has your spouse been sedated? If so, what type of sedation?* *How did you experience this moment?* *What do you think of the medical team?*
The death	*How did the death happen?* *What were his circumstances?*
Grief reactions and experience	*How did you or are you coping with your grief?* *What are the effects of this death on your life?* *What emotions have you experienced?* *Do you receive support from your loved ones?*

highest co-occurrence frequency and proceeding to the one with the lowest frequency.

Within each class, words (and consequently, sentences selected from the text) are hierarchically organized based on their co-occurrences. Selected sentences may begin or end at any point within a sentence or constitute complete sentences.

Thematic analysis was initially conducted independently by two authors of the study [Details omitted to comply with anonymization rules], who reviewed the phrases extracted from the software and began to identify potential categories. Then, during a consultative procedure, consensus was reached on the themes and categories of each class by comparing the themes obtained individually, and in case of uncertainty or disagreement, the opinion of a third evaluator [Details omitted to comply with anonymization rules] was sought.

Analysis by several independent researchers helped to ensure consistency of interpretations and word classes identified.

Finally, the analysis with ALCESTE was applied in a purposeful and informed manner, considering the specifics of the Units of Context (UCs) and trying to minimize any bias.

Analysis with ALCESTE was considered the best option for several reasons. First, by using ALCESTE, lexical classes and themes can be quickly and easily extracted from a large corpus. Moreover, numerous studies have confirmed its scientific validity in the humanities fields (Geka & Dargentas, 2010; Lahlou, 1998; Metz et al., 2019; Scharnitzky & Kalampalikis, 2007; Truc, 2011).

ALCESTE offers several advantages over traditional qualitative text analysis methods, as its automated approach streamlines the initial processing of large textual datasets, facilitating efficient analysis. While ALCESTE provides a systematic clustering of text, human interpretation remains crucial for deriving meaningful insights, ensuring a balance between automation and expert judgment. This combination of automated processing and human input enhances reproducibility and customization, making ALCESTE a valuable tool for qualitative text analysis across diverse fields.

Results

The ALCESTE analysis has revealed three distinct classes of words within our textual corpus (Table 3), that provide an in-depth overview of the themes

Table 3. Thematic categories were obtained from the ALCESTE analysis.

Class 1	Class 2	Class 3
Social support	Medical treatments	Palliative care
The deceased spouse	Management of the disease by the doctors	Sedation
Loneliness		

that have emerged from the data and play a crucial role in interpreting the overall results. To offer a more concrete illustration of the analysis, below are some examples of selected sentences analyzed through ALCESTE that represent the first among the 5–6 sentences with the highest chi-square.

The Class 1 is characterized by the categories of *Social support, The deceased spouse*, and *Loneliness*, while in Class 2, we find the categories of *Medical treatments* and *Management of the disease* by the physicians. This class reflects the crucial role of medicine and medical care in the perception of grief and it shows how the participants have experienced the process of illness and medical treatments in relation to the loss and death of a spouse.

The last class (Class 3) features categories *Palliative Care* and *Sedation*, highlighting medical decisions and interventions made in end-of-life situations.

Class 1 : Social support

> *It does me good to talk to people who have the same story as me, whether they've lost a spouse, a child, or a parent. . . .. [. . .] I have no one to share these moments, these couple moments with. I have friends, but there are things I don't share. The things you say fit depending on who you talk to, but I really want to change my life and turn this page of 2022 that has been particularly difficult.*
>
> *(D.N)*

> *I have another colleague who lost her husband very young, he was only 40, and suddenly this year she lost her husband too. When we can talk together it's nice, but she's very fragile and I think she's kind of running away from me.*
>
> *(Y.D.)*

Class 1: The deceased spouse

> *He was a man of great faith. He was a musician, a great soccer supporter, someone who loved his family very much, who enjoyed seeing his children, his granddaughter, and who was very tender and took good care of me. . .*
>
> *(Y.D.)*

> *She loved her. . . There is a family grave, she loved her grandmother very much who died 2 years ago at the age of 101.*
>
> *(V.M.)*

Class 1: Loneliness

> *We used to be 4 couples who went on vacation together, who did a lot of things together, and now there are 3 couples and then . . . me, all alone.*
>
> *(V.M.)*

> *It's doubly difficult because you live with the person, and we've been married for 39 years and knew each other for 40. It's a lifetime that we've been together, although we've had difficult times. [. . .] It's not like he died at 80, 85. Of course, it's very hard, but in that case the couple has lived through many things before,*

traveling, doing things together.

(S.E)

Class 2 : Medical treatments

He had two blood tests, they gave him intravenous iron twice because the port was not working, and he had another CT scan. . .

(G.K.)

First there was chemotherapy and radiation therapy. After some – I don't know – maybe yes, she started in July, and in September, October, the first checkup was good.

(V.M.)

Class 2: Management of the disease by the doctors

We were told that we needed to make an appointment with a urologist. We did. So, over the next week, everything happened very quickly, with a flurry of medical appointments and medical referrals.

(D.N)

There are some positive memories I don't even remember, what I do remember is: 'the immunotherapy treatment didn't work, your cancer overgrew, the immunotherapy acted like a fertilizer, it spread, you're terminal, there won't be a second dose of immunotherapy'.

(O.A.)

Class 3: Palliative care

On Friday afternoon we arrived at the continuing care unit. They took us to the doctor's office, 8 people, nurses, doctors, psychologists, it was impressive.

(D.N)

We were able to ask all the questions we wanted. We spent hours and hours talking to the doctors. We were able to ask all the questions we wanted. We were looked after very well.

(A.A)

Class 3: Sedation

I was on the phone with a friend of mine, and I saw a private number on the screen, so I said I would hang up right away. It was the hospital calling. Then I got a call from the Dr, who said, 'Mrs., you have to come urgently, his condition is deteriorating, we will sedate him, you have to come'.

(D.N)

They called me at 7 o'clock and when we arrived, it was maybe 9:00 or 9:30, and he was sedated. Did they do it in the middle of the night? Did they do it early in the morning? I didn't ask. . .

(S.E)

Discussion

In the following study, the experiences of spouses who lost their partners due to cancer following palliative care and sedation were explored. The results of the thematic analysis revealed three distinct classes of words within our textual corpus, each shedding light on different aspects of the bereavement experience. These classes provide an in-depth overview of the themes that have emerged from the data and play a crucial role in interpreting the overall results.

Within Class 1 (comprising *Social support, Deceased spouse, Loneliness*), the category *social support* emerges as one of the central themes, confirming what has been highlighted in the literature (Brazil et al., 2010; Fasse et al., 2013; Zech, 2019) and the importance of family support and social networks in the context of spousal grief. The sense of loneliness also emerged as a significant element in the experience of loss that appears to stem from the perception of an irreplaceable void left by the spouse's passing ('We used to be 4 couples who went on vacation together, who did a lot of things together, and now there are 3 couples and then ... me, all alone'. - V.M).

The experience of losing a partner is intertwined with the redefinition of oneself and one's role in society, leading to deep feelings of isolation, disorientation, and identity restructuring (Wehrman, 2023). These results clearly underscore how the psychological dimension is intimately interconnected with the social dimension of spousal grief.

Furthermore, the presence of the *deceased spouse* category (also in Class 1) has highlighted the need to share and reflect on the memories of their spouse and the desire to preserve their memory through storytelling and sharing of stories. This process of sharing seems to play a fundamental role in their grieving process and in maintaining an emotional connection with the deceased.

In Class 2 (Class 2: *Medical treatments, Management of the disease by the doctors*), participants described in detail their experiences with *medical treatments*, reflecting on the challenges and emotional nuances associated with the process of illness and medical care about the loss and death of a spouse. They recounted various treatments and medical procedures, illustrating the complex and emotionally charged journey of illness and medical care ('We were told that we needed to make an appointment with a urologist. We did. So, over the next week, everything happened very quickly, with a flurry of medical appointments and medical referrals'. - D.N).

Class 3, whose categories are *Palliative care and Sedation*, highlights medical decisions and interventions made in end-of-life situations. Participants stressed the importance of comprehensive support during palliative care ('On Friday afternoon we arrived at the continuing care unit.

They took us to the doctor's office, 8 people, nurses, doctors, psychologists, it was impressive'. - D.N), while sedation emerged as a delicate aspect of their experience, often accompanied by feelings of powerlessness and unexpectedness.

The grouping of themes in our study reflects the interconnectedness of various aspects of the bereavement experience among spouses who have lost their partners to cancer, encompassing social support, memories of the deceased, and experiences with medical treatments and palliative care. Recognizing the intertwining nature of emotional, social, and medical factors is crucial for understanding the multifaceted needs of grieving spouses. This holistic perspective guides the development of comprehensive support strategies tailored to address the complexities of loss and bereavement.

Additionally, this study provides fresh insights into less-explored areas, such as the interplay between medical treatments, palliative care, and sedation in the bereavement experience. By elucidating the challenges and emotional nuances associated with these aspects, it contributes to a deeper understanding of the end-of-life journey for both patients and their spouses.

Conclusions

The qualitative analysis of the emotional experiences of grieving spouses has allowed us to uncover the psychological challenges and resources involved.

While medical care is essential, it alone cannot fully address the intense emotional reactions of spouses. This suggests and confirms that storytelling and sharing memories are integral parts of the grieving process (Bacqué & Hanus, 2023), while loneliness is a common challenge for those facing the loss of a spouse (Freak-Poli et al., 2022).

In addition, clear communication and active family participation in decisions related to the Continuous Deep Sedation until Death Sedation are crucial, also to avoid surprises and ensure that choices align with the wishes of patients and their families (Imai et al., 2022).

Moreover, our study prompts reflection on compassionate timing in end-of-life care, a concept equally significant but so far neglected in the literature. The experiences shared by spouses underscore the delicate balance between addressing physical suffering and allowing adequate time for farewells. Incorporating the notion of compassionate timing into practice involves considering the optimal timing of medical interventions alongside the emotional needs of patients and their families. By doing so, healthcare professionals can ensure a more holistic and compassionate approach to end-of-life care, providing both relief from physical pain and meaningful opportunities for saying goodbye.

Therefore, it is imperative to develop comprehensive supportive approaches that integrate psychological and medical care.

These findings can be valuable for healthcare professionals, counselors, and emotional support professionals, guiding them in providing targeted support to people who are going through the pain of losing a spouse due to oncological illness (Sani et al., 2023).

They also highlight the need for policies that prioritize comprehensive end-of-life care and support services for patients and their families.

Future research should focus on longitudinal studies to explore the long-term psychological impact of bereavement and identify effective interventions to promote resilience and well-being among bereaved spouses.

In addition, there is an urgent need to explore the specific effects of sedation on spouses of terminally ill patients. Subsequent studies devoted exclusively to exploring this topic hypothetically would offer a more comprehensive understanding of the challenges and needs of bereaved spouses in the palliative care setting.

In conclusion, although the results of our study may align to some extent with the existing literature, they offer new insights and perspectives that enhance our understanding of the bereavement experience among spouses of cancer patients receiving palliative care and CDSD. By shedding light on new concepts and perspectives and highlighting their implications for future practice and research, our study contributes to the ongoing dialogue on end-of-life care and bereavement support.

Limitations

We emphasize that these are preliminary data, and it will be interesting to evaluate future results, however it should be noted that our study is not without limitations.

Firstly, the relatively small sample of participants may limit the representativeness and generalizability of our results to a larger population. Additionally, the predominance of women (66.7%) could influence the dynamics of grief, introducing potential gender variability. The specificity of the French cultural context in which the study was conducted may limit its generalizability to different cultural contexts.

Finally, the online data collection and the need to select excerpts for analysis could pose some challenges in the representativeness of the data itself.

Acknowledgments

We would like to thank our participants, the French hospitals who are helping us to recruit the bereaved spouses, and [Details omitted to comply with anonymization rules].

Disclosure statement

No potential conflict of interest was reported by the author(s).

Funding

This work was supported by the Institut National Du Cancer [INCA_15908].

Data availability statement

The data that support the findings of this study are available from the author upon reasonable request.

Authorship

All authors contributed to the conception and design of this article. Details omitted to comply with anonymization rules.

References

Bacqué, M.-F., & Hanus, M. (2023). *Le deuil*. Presses Universitaires de France - PUF (9ème édition).

Brazil, K., Bainbridge, D., & Rodriguez, C. (2010). The stress process in palliative cancer care: A qualitative study on informal caregiving and its implication for the delivery of care. The American Journal of Hospice & Palliative Care, 27(2), 111–116. https://doi.org/10.1177/1049909109350176

Bruinsma, S. M., Brown, J., van der Heide, A., Deliens, L., Anquinet, L., Payne, S. A., Seymour, J. E., & Rietjens, J. A. C. (2014). Making sense of continuous sedation in end-of-life care for cancer patients: An interview study with bereaved relatives in three European countries. Supportive Care in Cancer, 22(12), 3243–3252. https://doi.org/10.1007/s00520-014-2344-7

Fasse, L., Sultan, S., & Cecile, F. (2013). Expérience de pré-deuil à l'approche du décès de son conjoint: Une analyse phénoménologique interprétative. Psychologie Française, 58(3), 177–194. https://doi.org/10.1016/j.psfr.2013.02.001

Fernández-Alcántara, M., & Zech, E. (2017). One or multiple complicated Grief(s)? The role of kinship on grief reactions. Clinical Psychological Science, 5(5), 851–857. https://doi.org/10.1177/2167702617707291

Freak-Poli, R., Kung, C. S. J., Ryan, J., Shields, M. A., & Kelley, J. (2022). Social isolation, social support, and loneliness profiles before and after spousal death and the buffering role of financial resources. *The Journals of Gerontology: Series B*, 77 (5), 956–971. https://doi.org/10.1093/geronb/gbac039

Garrouste-Orgeas, M., Flahault, C., Poulain, E., Evin, A., Guirimand, F., Fossez-Diaz, V., Perruchio, S., Verlaine, C., Vanbésien, A., Kaczmarek, W., Birkui de Francqueville, L., De Larivière, E., Bouquet, G., Copel, L., Verliac, V., Marché, V., Mathias, C., Gracia, D., Mhalla, A., & Timsit, J.-F. (2019). The Fami-life study: Protocol of a prospective observational multicenter mixed study of psychological consequences of grieving relatives in French palliative care units on behalf of the family research in palliative care (F.R.I.P.C research network). *BMC Palliative Care, 18*(1), 111. https://doi.org/10.1186/s12904-019-0496-4

Geka, M., & Dargentas, M. (2010). L'apport du logiciel Alceste à l'analyse des représentations sociales: L'exemple de deux études diachroniques. Les cahiers internationaux de psychologie sociale, *Numéro* 85(1), 111–135. https://doi.org/10.3917/cips.085.0111

Imai, K., Morita, T., Mori, M., Yokomichi, N., Yamauchi, T., Miwa, S., Inoue, S., Naito, A. S., Masukawa, K., Kizawa, Y., Tsuneto, S., Shima, Y., Otani, H., & Miyashita, M. (2022). Family experience of palliative sedation therapy: Proportional vs. continuous deep sedation. *Supportive Care in Cancer*, 30(5), 3903–3915. https://doi.org/10.1007/s00520-021-06745-1

Lahlou, S. (1998). *Penser manger*. Presses Universitaires de France. https://doi.org/10.3917/puf.insti.1998.01

Lucchi, E., Milder, M., Dardenne, A., & Bouleuc, C. (2023). Could palliative sedation be seen as unnamed euthanasia?: A survey among healthcare professionals in oncology. *BMC Palliative Care*, 22(1), 97. https://doi.org/10.1186/s12904-023-01219-z

Mesnage, V., Bretonniere, S., Goncalves, T., Begue, A., Bernardin, G., Brette, M.-D., Brillaxis, P., Cadier, A., Drure, V., Foureur, N., Goudot, F.-X., Grimont, E., Hachmaoui, L., Lepeintre, A., Maillard, F., Meyohas, M.-C., Moïsi, L., Parmentier, E., Philippart, F. . . . Fournier, V. (2020). Enquête du centre national des soins palliatifs et de la fin de vie sur la sédation profonde et continue jusqu'au décès (SPCJD) à 3 ans de la loi Claeys-Leonetti. *La Presse Médicale Formation*, 1 (2), 134–140. https://doi.org/10.1016/j.lpmfor.2020.04.010

Metz, C., Calmet, J., & Thevenot, A. (2019). Women subjected to domestic violence: The impossibility of separation. *Psychoanalytic Psychology*, 36(1), 36–43. https://doi.org/10.1037/pap0000186

Morita, T., Ikenaga, M., Adachi, I., Narabayashi, I., Kizawa, Y., Honke, Y., Kohara, H., Mukaiyama, T., Akechi, T., & Uchitomi, Y. (2004). Family experience with palliative sedation therapy for terminally ill cancer patients. *Journal of Pain and Symptom Management*, 28(6), 557–565. https://doi.org/10.1016/j.jpainsymman.2004.03.004

Papavasiliou, E., Payne, S., & Brearley, S. (2014). Current debates on end-of-life sedation: An international expert elicitation study. *Supportive Care in Cancer*, 22 (8), 2141–2149. https://doi.org/10.1007/s00520-014-2200-9

Prigerson, H. G., Horowitz, M. J., Jacobs, S. C., Parkes, C. M., Aslan, M., Goodkin, K., Raphael, B., Marwit, S. J., Wortman, C., Neimeyer, R. A., Bonanno, G., Block, S. D., Kissane, D., Boelen, P., Maercker, A., Litz, B. T., Johnson, J. G., First, M. B., Maciejewski, P. K., & Brayne, C. (2009). Prolonged grief disorder: Psychometric validation of criteria proposed for DSM-V and ICD-11. *PLOS Medicine*, 6(8), e1000121. https://doi.org/10.1371/journal.pmed.1000121

Reinert, P. M. (1987). Classification Descendante Hierarchique et Analvse Lexicale par Contexte—Application au Corpus des Poesies D'A. Rihbaud. *Bulletin of*

Sociological Methodology/Bulletin de Méthodologie Sociologique, 13(1), 53–90. https://doi.org/10.1177/075910638701300107

Rietjens, J. A. C., van Delden, J. J. M., van der Heide, A., Vrakking, A. M., Onwuteaka-Philipsen, B. D., van der Maas, P. J., & van der Wal, G. (2006). Terminal sedation and euthanasia: A comparison of clinical practices. *Archives of Internal Medicine*, 166(7), 749–753. https://doi.org/10.1001/archinte.166.7.749

Rys, S., Deschepper, R., Mortier, F., Deliens, L., Atkinson, D., & Bilsen, J. (2012). The moral difference or equivalence between continuous sedation until death and physician-assisted death: Word games or war games?: A qualitative content analysis of opinion pieces in the indexed medical and nursing literature. *Journal of Bioethical Inquiry*, 9(2), 171–183. https://doi.org/10.1007/s11673-012-9369-8

Sani, L., Chemrouk, Y., Le Berre, R., Peyrat-Apicella, D., & Bacqué, M.-F. (2023). The loss of a spouse following an oncological disease: A scoping review. *Illness, Crisis & Loss*, 10541373231202471. https://doi.org/10.1177/10541373231202471

Scharnitzky, P., & Kalampalikis, N. (2007). Analyse lexicale des sources d'influence dans les jurys d'assises. *Bulletin de psychologie*, Numéro 491(5), 425–432. https://doi.org/10.3917/bupsy.491.0425

Shen, H.-S., Chen, S.-Y., Cheung, D. S. T., Wang, S.-Y., Lee, J. J., & Lin, C.-C. (2018). Differential family experience of palliative sedation therapy in specialized palliative or critical care units. *Journal of Pain and Symptom Management*, 55(6), 1531–1539. https://doi.org/10.1016/j.jpainsymman.2018.02.007

Ten Have, H., & Welie, J. V. M. (2014). Palliative sedation versus euthanasia: An ethical assessment. *Journal of Pain and Symptom Management*, 47(1), 123–136. https://doi.org/10.1016/j.jpainsymman.2013.03.008

Truc, G. (2011). Analyser un corpus illisible? Le logiciel Alceste confronté à des registres de condoléances. *Langage et societe*, 135(1), 29–45. https://doi.org/10.3917/ls.135.0029

Wehrman, E. C. (2023). "I don't even know who I am": Identity reconstruction after the loss of a spouse. *Journal of Social & Personal Relationships*, 40(4), 1250–1276. https://doi.org/10.1177/02654075221127399

WHO. (2020). *Palliative care*. World Health Organization. https://www.who.int/news-room/fact-sheets/detail/palliative-care

Zech, E. (2019). Accompagner les membres d'une famille endeuillée: Avec toujours plus de présence, respect, chaleur, compréhension empathique et authenticité. *Médecine Palliative*, 18(4–5), 239–242. https://doi.org/10.1016/j.medpal.2019.03.003

OPEN ACCESS

"Lost in space and time": Fathers' experiences of preterm birth

Dóra Monostori, Kinga Lampek and Marta B. Erdos

ABSTRACT

This study is a qualitative analysis of fathers' experiences of preterm birth. Preterm birth affects about ten per cent of the families globally. It is a traumatic event, especially when the infant is very preterm. Often, parents are struggling with the experience without any psychological support. Though fathers' role in the child's healthy psychological development has been confirmed by recent studies, the impact of preterm birth on their paternal identity and their needs for support in this emotionally burdening situation has not been studied extensively. We analysed ten interviews using Interpretative Phenomenological Analysis, a method to study sensitive themes to determine the key themes as potential areas of intervention. We could find that these fathers live their lives in extended liminality, characterized by chaos and unpredictability, and are struggling with new, often unusual roles and responsibilities that may completely upset their private life – work balance. The first contact with the child is usually ambivalent and is burdened with grave concerns about the potential harms. Communication at Perinatal Intensive Care Units (PICUs), though seen as supportive, is not tailored to fathers' competencies. Targeted intervention by trained counsellors at PICU could help the fathers overcome these traumatizing experiences.

Introduction

Having a preterm baby significantly influences the quality of life and the socioeconomic status of the family (Baldoni et al., 2021). Preterm birth is a deep loss, a 'psychologically seismic event' (Tedeschi & Calhoun, 2004, p.5.) for both parents, shattering their core beliefs and future visions about their generativity and caretaking roles (Monostori, 2021). Mothers' experiences have been studied more extensively but exploring fathers' birth-related experiences is a recent theme (Arnold et al., 2013; Baldoni et al., 2021, Carson et al., 2015; Ionio et al., 2016). Fathers are expected to provide for the family, run errands and be strong, be a source of support for the mother and the child, though they themselves may need support (Robinson & Robinson, 2022). Paternal experiences concerning perinatal traumas may be suppressed but are deep.

Preterm birth is a common event, affecting about 10% of the families, with the rates between 4–16% across the different countries. According to the estimate by the World Health Organization (World Health Organization, 2023), 13.4 million babies were born preterm in 2020. These infants are born alive before the 37th completed gestational weeks. WHO differentiates between extremely (<28), very (28-<32) and moderate/late (32 - <37) stages. Babies' chances of survival, especially in the first group, depend on the accessibility and the quality of medical care and are only 10% in the low-income countries and about 90% in high-income settings (WHO, 2023). Preterm birth might lead to chronic complications for the child, compromising the quality of their life. Risks of living with certain neurodevelopmental problems (such as cerebral palsy, learning disabilities, visual and hearing impairments etc.) are elevated for those born before the 32nd gestational week (Arnold et al., 2013; Carson et al., 2015; World Health Organization, 2023). This might require long-term adaptation on part of the entire family as the child's self-sufficiency and their capacity for independent living might be limited.

In Hungary, the context of this study, the rate of preterm birth is 8–9%. Infant mortality rate is on the decrease and is currently 3.49, approximating the EU27 average (3.3) (Hungarian Central Statistical Office, 2022). A current challenge is to provide adequate family-centered care for the families struggling with this burdening life situation characterized by loss of control experiences and helplessness (Monostori, 2021). Perinatal Intensive Care Units (PICUs), where preterm babies are treated, are allowed, but not required to employ psychologists, social workers, counsellors, or any other personnel trained to provide psychosocial support for the parents.

Becoming a parent is a deep identity change and may be accompanied by mood disturbances and anxiety (Carson et al., 2015; Genesoni & Tallandini, 2009). Parents should develop new knowledge, skills, and attitudes, responding to their child's developmental needs. Caregiving behavior is influenced by many factors, including parents' mental health, the bond between the couple, the child's physical condition and temperament, the parents' own psychosocial development and intergenerational issues, as well as broad societal and cultural factors (Danis et al., 2020). Preterm birth is an additional risk factor for anxiety and depressive symptoms for both parents

(Candelori et al., 2015, Carson et al., 2015; Ionio et al., 2016, Petersen & Quinlivan, 2021). Mental problems may include posttraumatic stress disorder (PTSD) as a longstanding response to the shock. Abnormal illness behavior, addictions and behavioral disorders may occur. Risks for subsequent divorce are elevated (Baldoni et al., 2021). In their study, Carson et al. (2015) could identify double risks for postpartum psychological disorders (depression, anxiety, and the related somatic symptoms, measured at 9 months after delivery) for the fathers of very and moderately preterm babies, and with very preterm babies, for both parents. In addition to fathers of very preterm babies, young fathers (<30 years) are also vulnerable (Ettenberger et al., 2024).

Preterm birth might occur spontaneously or can be the outcome of an emergency or planned caesarean section in life-threatening conditions for the mother, the infant or both. In Carson et al. (2015) study, 94.1% of fathers were present at birth. In the Hungarian context, fathers are not allowed to witness and participate in the delivery, unless it is judged as a normal one by the medical staff. Babies in life-threatening medical conditions are immediately separated from the parents. Fathers can meet the mother and the baby only after the surgery. However, the father is usually the first one to meet the infant (Baldoni et al. 2021; Hollywood & Hollywood, 2011; Stefana et al., 2022). He is struggling alone with his experiences, radically changing his anticipations that he has cherished about becoming a proud father of a healthy and vigorous baby. He is the one to inform the mother and the other family members about the infant's condition though he is hardly prepared to translate between the medical staff and concerned family members and friends.

In addition, the mother is seen as the primary carer, therefore fathers' contact with the mother and the infant is limited (known as maternal gatekeeping, Baldoni et al., 2021). As the father's role in this traumatizing situation is not seen as central as the mother's, support given to him will quickly diminish – soon after the mother has arrived at PICU. Fathers have a vague role as they are neither patients, nor visitors (Arnold et al., 2013). Further, the workplace usually would not tolerate fathers' long-term absence and their visits may be restricted to the weekends. In Hungary, only 16% of fathers take the ten-day paternity leave available right after the birth of the child (European Parliament, 2023).

Preterm babies look very different, and their parents are not prepared for the first encounter ('like little baby sparrows', Arnold et al., 2013, p. 3.). In addition, fathers in the domestic context usually have few immediate caring responsibilities that would involve occasional immersions in medical contexts. For them, this experience is usually more shocking. The overall PICU environment with life-saving equipment also seems frightening. Seeing all these, parents are afraid that their baby may suffer from chronic and serious conditions or might die. Loss of control experiences lead to anger, sensations of loss, envy, impotence and 'feeling under everyone's eyes (a fish in an aquarium)' (Baldoni et al., 2021, p. 3.). As fathers are prepared to protect the mother and the infant, the frightening environment with all these emotional burdens may lead to defensive behavior (Baldoni et al., 2021). The cases when hard decisions must be made are a source of deep intramarital conflicts. Robinson and Robinson (2022) in their autoethnographic study raise an example when the final parental decision of pulling the plug emerged. The mother saw their baby fighting for his life, but the father could see him slowly deteriorating. Fathers may feel isolated in the crisis of preterm birth but may not ask for help (Baldoni et al., 2021). Their isolation extends to communication with the broad social environment. Cultural traditions to share the experiences of an average, 'normal' childbirth are available, but the complications of preterm birth are hard to describe for concerned others.

Preterm birth may significantly influence the quality of parental bonding. In addition to fathers' protecting roles, also encouraging the child's explorations in the physical and social environment, recent studies have confirmed the importance of father-infant bonding in the child's emotional development. The quality of father-child attachment will influence the child's capacity for emotion regulation and mentalizing (Baldoni et al., 2021; Schaber et al., 2021). Hormonal and neurobiological changes prepare the fathers for providing optimal care. Rising levels of oxytocin enable them to empathize and engage in social activities, a decrease in testosterone and estradiol makes them more sensitive and less aggressive, and the level of prolactin increases in response to the baby's crying to elicit caring and protection (Baldoni et al., 2021).

Materials and methods

Study design

The interviews used in this retrospective study were conducted in 2018 as part of a comprehensive research project on preterm birth, using mainly a quantitative approach (Ethical approval: RKEB, 234/2017-SZTE). 67 semi-structured interviews were conducted with parents whose children had been treated at PICU, 11 fathers and 56 mothers. The interviews were made by students and practitioners (special pedagogues and psychologists working at an early childhood intervention center). The ones conducted by practitioners with substantial counselling skills are eligible for an in-depth analysis.

The duration of these semi-structured interviews ranged between 40–90 minutes, and they were conducted in the homes of the families. The interviews included the following themes:

(1) Pregnancy and delivery: What did the respondents know about preterm delivery? Were there any special antecedent risks/anticipations about preterm birth? How did the delivery happen? What do they

think the causes of preterm birth were? What kind of help could the parents receive during pregnancy and delivery? Were there any prior/subsequent maternal health complications?

(2) Experiences after delivery: How was the respondent informed about the necessity of intensive care? How did they feel about it? What were the first impressions about PICU/meeting the infant for the first time? What professionals did they meet at PICU? Further themes included the help received, positive and negative experiences, feelings about themselves as parents and about their child, opportunities to share their feelings with others, and potential stigmatization.

(3) Services they currently use and access to the necessary services, opinions about peer support, participation in a network of peers, and mentoring (receiving and giving help to families who are struggling with similar problems).

The respondents answered some of the above questions only briefly and used the opportunity to recount their traumatic experiences, devoting most of the time to delivery experiences, actual or perceived risks and worries, impressions about PICU, seeing or touching their child for the first time, the milestones they could discover in the infant's development while at PICU, and their struggles to cope with the stresses. Lasiuk et al. (2013) also noted that respondents in their study welcomed the opportunity to talk about their experiences as they are rarely asked about these.

Considering the life transforming aspects of the experience, we decided to use Interpretative Phenomenological Analysis, a method to study sensitive themes.

Participants

Families were contacted through an early childhood intervention service, and 11 fathers consented to participate in the interview. The majority, 10 of the 11 fathers had preterm babies, and at the time of the interview, they were pre-school children (aged 2–7) with special educational needs (learning disabilities and/or behavioral problems). All the fathers were married to or were living in registered partnership with the mother.

Table 1. is a summary of respondents' demography and the circumstances of birth.

Data analysis

We used IPA to explore how fathers remembered and made sense of their experiences during the past few years. Unique experiences of the family crisis and the related meaning-making processes were central to our analysis,

Table 1. Demographic information and circumstances of birth.

Pseudonym	Age	Education	Completed gestational weeks	Birth	Number of preterm births
Jason	44	secondary	26	singleton	1
Will	32	secondary	35	twins	2
Robert	39	tertiary	26	singleton	1
Aidan	37	secondary	34	triplets	1
Charlie	35	tertiary	28	singleton	1
Zach	30	tertiary	26	twins	1
Siggy	38	secondary	35	twins	1
Noah	38	secondary	32	singleton	1
George	35	secondary	34	singleton	1
Jack	35	secondary	29	singleton	1

utilizing IPA's double hermeneutics (Eatough & Smith, 2013; Rácz et al., 2016). IPA was conducted by the first and third authors. We used researcher and disciplinary triangulation. The first author had a triple perspective as an academic studying this theme and a practitioner as a health visitor, social worker, and grief counsellor working for a foundation that provides services for families with preterm babies. Further, she is an expert by experience as an adoptive mother of a very preterm baby, from his first days up to now, when he has reached early adolescence. The third author's perspectives were formed in her former practitioner roles as a mental health counsellor providing crisis intervention, and currently, an academic studying loss, grief, and posttraumatic growth. Concerning preterm birth, she had lay but very vivid experiences. As a mother of four children, she could realize how stressful it can be to constantly worry for your own child's health and even for their life. These diverse and complementary perspectives, the empathy we could feel, and the continuous dialogue between us during the analysis facilitated translating the respondents' interpretations on their lived experiences into structured comments and themes while maintaining our sensitivity and staying close to the data. Initially, we worked independently, reading, commenting, and re-reading the verbatim transcriptions, searching for the emergent themes first in the individual interviews and then applying cross-case comparisons. As a next step, we shared our notes, and discussed and compared our comments and suggestions for the themes to integrate these into more comprehensive master themes. Occasionally, we returned to the original texts for a more precise interpretation. The hermeneutic cycles between the details and the entire text corpus preceded literature review as suggested by Eatough and Smith (2013). Finally, we compared our findings to those of previous studies reviewed in the Introduction. We left ourselves some time (a couple of days) for reflection between the subsequent cycles. Allowing such a space for thinking over each other's suggestions and consolidating, deepening, and integrating our ideas into a holistic view proved useful in our previous qualitative projects.

Results

Not surprisingly, fathers' experiences were strongly determined by the infant's physical condition and by the circumstances of the delivery. First, we summarize our results in a tabular form (Table 2) comprising the quotations, comments, and themes and then we focus on the master themes as IPA's conclusions.

Master themes

Crisis & extended liminality

Very preterm babies were seen as existing between two worlds, not fully arrived in our shared reality yet. The father was hesitant and ambivalent about his role and, in some cases, was reluctant to build the bonding, as their future seemed unpredictable. Rapid alternations between mood states, hope and despair, and changing attitudes were characteristic of this early phase. In most cases, the birth was described in terms of a serious psychological trauma. Fathers mentioned physical symptoms such as trembling and crying, and used crisis metaphors (e.g. 'upside down'). Chaos is mirrored by sudden changes in temporal perspectives and in the disrupted sentence structure in the texts.

Contact with the baby

Seeing or touching the baby for the first time was an overwhelming experience. First, kangaroo care might be scary, and fathers seemed to be more aware of the risks than the benefits of the physical contact. They saw it as an important milestone in the development of father-child relationship and as a proof of the child's growing strength and predictable survival. In this case, physical contact also represented *hope*.

Paternal roles and responsibilities

Work – private life balance was completely upset. Both the child and the partner needed extra support, in ways that were often unusual, such as taking the mother's milk to PICU; or being around as much as possible so that the infant could feel the father's presence and feel encouraged to stay in this world. This emphasis on the significance of the bond is positive; but the responsibility of keeping the baby alive through these subtle communication channels might become a huge emotional burden, should the baby die.

PICU and the related health services

PICU equipment seemed frightening, up to the point of derealization experiences. (The word 'incubation' originally referred to a healing ritual in a sacred place outside everyday, easy-to-understand settings.) In the

Table 2. Quotations, comments, and themes.

Quotations (the respondent's pseudonym in parenthesis)	Comments	Themes
The birth: One of my worst moments in life (. . .) I was lost in time, space and in every ways (. . .) and I stopped working and started to cry and I was trembling (. . .) one is uncertain, having no knowledge (. . .) On Saturday, everything turned upside down (. . .) change was sudden (. . .) we could not experience the last phase (*of the pregnancy*) (. . .) they started an emergency Caesarean section (*Jason*). I did not even have the time to think it over. (*Charlie*) We were not prepared for this, what if . . . (*Aidan*) First, we were flustered and then we were standing in the middle of the room, embracing each other, and crying and then in a hurry again. (*George*) Neither the doctor nor we were prepared for this. (*Noah*) I felt angry and helpless that this happened, I like to plan things in advance. (*George*)	Feeling highly stressed, lost, and insecure. Chaos/out of order, unpredictable events, emergency, 'preterm parents'	first shock, onset of crisis, unpredictability helplessness
Seeing the baby, first contact: A tiny creature . . . how should I call it? . . . those paternal instincts, that love, I did not dare to, I did not know what was going to happen with that child, if he survives or not, and I . . . I did not dare to love, to feel anything, what is going to happen, you tried to protect yourself against this whole issue. (*Jason*). In fact, I could see my son only when they (*the ambulance men*) were waiting for the elevator (.) he was crying, in a way (. . .). Naturally, it was wonderful to have the child on me (*kangaroo care*), but of course a man has doubts, I had doubts. What is this all about? (*Robert*) I had not dared to hold them as they were so small, not until they were three months old. (*Siggy*) I have never seen such a tiny baby, neither in a photo nor in any other ways. (*Jack*)	The baby looks different and is crying differently. Struggling with the highly ambivalent emotional experience Defensive (trying to protect himself from a terrible but potential loss) Seeing the baby by chance	First contact Defense

(*Continued*)

Table 2. (Continued).

Quotations (the respondent's pseudonym in parenthesis)	Comments	Themes
Reasons: They were twins and she was not prepared for this. (*Will*) You know, it was even a bit too long, I mean her body, three children … (*Aidan*) … or, I, I don't know the exact diagnosis … maybe rupture of membranes, this is written in one of the documents (…) she lifted a heavy saucepan, she was a bit irresponsible. (*Jason*)	Searching for reasons, potentially blaming the mother/self-blame; attempts at interpreting medical diagnosis, uncertainty	searching for reasons, meaning making
The healthcare system: There was not any vacancies at Szeged, and then we were told to try Kecskemét, and if it does not work then Gyula (Hungarian cities) (…) The building was in ruins. (*Will*)	Lost in the healthcare system in an emergency, 'ruins'	Problems in the healthcare system
At PICU: The whole thing was a rollercoaster as was our own life. (Jason) There were a few days when her treatment was an open question … those days were really tense. (Charlie) I could see that they were in good hands. (*Will*) … and this is when I could learn that they are between life and death and are struggling for their lives. Whenever the phone rang it ripped in my heart as I did not know what news I was going to get. (*Zach*) I remember only the pleasures. (*Siggy*) I don't remember anyone caring about us, considering our mental state … we became fond of another child as we knew the parents and then he was not there anymore and I was, like I asked, I do not even remember if I asked about by the name, the baby's name, according to the baby's name or I don't know, uhm, and they answered that unfortunately he had deceased. (*Jason*) I did not get any help and I did not want any. (*Zach*) The only way this child could live at the moment … uhm, is that he is helped by the machines (…) It was a great moment, to see him without the artificial respirator. (*Robert*)	Change is permanent Trust and pleasures for those with a near term baby Mental care is not provided at PICU; other parents' loss – identification reflected by the chaotic sentence structure („could be mine"). For the PICU staff, such losses are part of their work, but for the parents, this is most frightening. Name as sign of personhood. The preterm baby is a person. Life-sustaining equipment; machines are a sign of the baby's condition that parents monitor	unpredictability & liminality (very preterm babies) experiencing loss without mental support equipment as a source of help and a sign

(*Continued*)

Table 2. (Continued).

Quotations (the respondent's pseudonym in parenthesis)	Comments	Themes
Communication at PICU: Me, me was not informed by anyone at all *(about the birth)*. She (*the doctor*) said that they were going to do everything they could and only these first few days are critical, and then some weeks are critical, and then we ended up with two months as critical. (*Jason*) As if this whole workplace was a great burden on them (PIC staff) but some of them were really nice. (*Charlie*) (*Explaining why they put a little sock on the baby's head*) . . . perhaps I am a bit imprecise as this is not my professional area. Perhaps their skin is not yet formed on their head and the baby would simply evaporate. (*Zach*) 600-gram babies also survive, she *(the health visitor at PICU)* said. There is no need to worry, there won't be any problems (. . .) I, as a layperson did not really understand these things as they were using technical terms, if only I knew it would be great . . . (*Noah*)	Lack of information, communication issues, mixed experiences with PICU staff	Communication at PICU
Paternal care: . . . and I should be there so that the child could feel that I am there, and this, this is important for him to survive. *(Charlie)* . . . so that we could give him colostrum . . . I always took it for him. (*Robert*) . . . and there was the little bed and everything but there was no child in it. (*Robert*) . . . a little mental support to Mummy, everything's fine, and then running to PICU. *(Zach)* Evidently, when they were at PICU I was the milkman and took the milk for the boys every morning. *(Siggy)* I was saying that I was willing to undertake overwork, but we should have a „paid" doctor (*Charlie*) *(Note: a „paid doctor" was a former 'grey' solution between state and private care and was due to doctors' very low salaries.)* They (*other parents*) just close this problem in a dark room in their brains and throw away the keys, but we are not like that, we are the ones who would try anything that might help. We would have agreed to everything if we had had the opportunity. (*Charlie*)	Immense responsibilities: help keep the baby alive; unusual tasks in caring; frustrations (waiting for the baby to come home and fill the empty space Assuming traditional paternal roles as a sign of care (overwork) responding to the problem by providing exceptional care exceptional long-term care is shown through comparisons; precondition for exceptional care is openness and giving up denial	altered and traditional forms of paternal care parental commitment to long-term care
Future chances: „ . . . can be healthy and normal (*referring to statistics*) (. . .) if he could live an autonomous life. (*Robert*)	estimating the chances; the child's future	worried about the child's future

domestic system, parents may not know for sure where the delivery will take place and the subsequent intensive care will be given – a source for further worries and loss of control experiences.

Communication

Communication was generally supportive but with major gaps: in the current study, one respondent was not informed about the emergency cesarean section in time; and parents were not informed that due to regular medical checks, the infant might be missing from the incubator, so they interpreted it as their baby's death. Technical terms, so natural for the PICU staff were often not understood by the fathers.

Coping strategies

These involved seeking information from the PICU staff, from the internet and from peers or family members having the same experience. Fathers searched for explanations, and they wanted to know the reasons for preterm birth. Help-seeking behavior was not present as they identified themselves as sources, and not recipients of support.

Discussion

Preterm birth is a major loss when „fundamental components of the assumptive world are challenged, including assumptions about the benevolence, predictability, and controllability of the world; one's safety is challenged, and one's identity and future are challenged" (Tedeschi & Calhoun, p. 5.) Traces of this seismic trauma were clearly seen in fathers' recollections. In our analysis, we highlighted the liminal features related to this crisis experience, the lack of psychological support and impairments in communication. The interviews have revealed that in these life-transforming moments, some of the sentences uttered by the PICU personnel echo in fathers' ears for years, but pieces of relevant information might be misunderstood or lost. Communication at PICU is mostly restricted to information related to the child's and the mother's physical condition. It is not always timely and is not tailored to fathers' understandings (medical jargon). Fathers are busy searching internet or may consult their peers for advice, but the information they have access to might not be valid, and empathy may be missing (also in Hollywood & Hollywood, 2011). Fathers' traumatic experiences and crisis state are not validated by the environment. Usually, they cannot share their experiences within their natural support networks (Lasiuk et al., 2013). Psychological support for fathers is missing. Fathers themselves often feel that the infant is the only one in need of help but evidence on parents' impaired mental health would challenge this notion. Further, as Robinson and Robinson (2022) point out, experiencing the trauma has an impact on the subsequent pregnancies.

The medical staff have their requirements on preterm parents' new roles that do not necessarily coincide with parents' own interpretations and capacities (Wigert et al., 2014). These requirements are posed on fathers in the middle of a deep crisis. In the Hungarian context, 'health issues' of a child and of the family are usually left to the mother. The long-term hospitalization of the child and the mother has a lasting impact on the life of the family (Karatzias et al., 2007), bringing new and unusual challenges into fathers' life. In this situation, there is an invisible change in primary roles in the first few days, as the father, who is much less prepared to deal with the medical aspects of delivery and care, must cope with this situation by himself. Recovery on family level may take a long time and lots of resources – many of which are missing.

Preterm birth may lead to a reduction in responsive parenting behaviors (Carson et al., 2015) while parents are often struggling to ensure high-level care for a sick baby and establish a work – private life balance (Thomson-Salo et al., 2017).

A potential limitation to the transferability of the results is that the respondents who were motivated to participate in the research were all married to or living with registered partnership with the mother. Data suggest an elevated risk for divorce in this population (Baldoni et al., 2021). Further, this was a retrospective study, and trauma narratives do change over time, though the sensory experiences that have not been translated into verbal representations remain stable (van der Kolk, 1998). We must note that abrupt changes in temporal perspectives and the somewhat chaotic sentence structure suggest that these stories have not been fully integrated into the personal stock of stories yet.

Implications

Currently, psychological support for the fathers (or for both parents) by trained counsellors is not available at PICUs in Hungary. Crisis intervention and referrals to counselling services are not routinely provided, and access to external mental health resources is also limited. Jotzo and Poets (2005) found that the introduction of structured psychological intervention for mothers, comprising early crisis intervention and continuing psychological support during the hospital stay and at critical times (e.g. due to the child's worsening medical condition) significantly reduced symptomatic responses to preterm birth. Fathers could benefit from similar services, and from more specific ones that focus on the acute tensions between their carer and earner roles.

For the fathers of preterm babies, the previous balance between private life and work is completely upset, and isolation from previous supportive networks frequently occurs. Continuing care could involve individual and family counselling (e.g. grief counselling) to promote posttraumatic growth after the loss of previous parental expectations. A 7/24 helpline could provide psychological first aid free from the time constraints of a daytime service, which can be a major benefit in this situation. This service network, adapted to fathers' needs, could facilitate better paternal functioning in the future and prevent longstanding mental health problems for the fathers.

Arnold et al. (2013) suggest preparatory tours at the neonatal intensive unit to minimize the initial shock for the parents. Communication on part of the PICU staff was mostly seen as supportive, but it had gaps and did not always match fathers' competencies – a potential area of specific trainings for the personnel.

As a form of continuing care for the carers, peer support is now available for the fathers in some Hungarian cities. Parents involved in the Early Mentoring Program are an invaluable source of help as experts of experience in this extremely burdening life situation. Peer support facilitates participation in individual and family counselling. Witnessing the healthy development of a previously preterm-born child can give the parents who are in the middle of the crisis hope. These programs, also encouraging help-seeking behavior and ensuring the continuity of care could be extended to cover every region (Zelena & Monostori, 2016).

Currently, neither the public nor the policy makers are aware of fathers' key role in the child's early psychological development. Employers and policy makers should be sensitized to the problem so that they give the fathers the necessary support, e. g. extra paid leave, flexibly available in the first year after preterm birth.

Further research, preferably involving cross-country comparisons, could add to our understandings the variety of fathers' experiences in other contexts.

Acknowledgments

We owe special thanks to the participants and the interviewers of this research.

Disclosure statement

No potential conflict of interest was reported by the author(s).

ORCID

Dóra Monostori http://orcid.org/0000-0001-6672-7083
Kinga Lampek http://orcid.org/0000-0003-4975-0411
Marta B. Erdos http://orcid.org/0000-0003-1618-9875

References

Anyasági és apasági szabadságok - a lista, amelyen Magyarország a világ élvonalában van. (Maternity and paternity leaves. A list where Hungary ranks among the first countries). (2023). *Portfolio*. https://www.portfolio.hu/gazdasag/20230311/anyasagi-es-apasagi-szabadsagok-a-lista-amelyen-magyarorszag-a-vilag-elvonalaban-van-602128

Arnold, L., Sawyer, A., Rabe, H., Abbott, J., Gyte, G. M., Duley, L., & Ayers, S. (2013). Parents' first moments with their very preterm babies: A qualitative study. *BMJ Open*, *3*(4), e002487. https://doi.org/10.1136/bmjopen-2012-002487

Baldoni, F., Ancora, G., & Latour, J. M. (2021). Being the father of a preterm-born child: Contemporary research and recommendations for NICU staff. *Frontiers in Pediatrics*, *9*, 724992. https://doi.org/10.3389/fped.2021.724992

Candelori, C., Trumello, C., Babore, A., Keren, M., & Romanelli, R. (2015). The experience of premature birth for fathers: The application of the Clinical Interview for Parents of High-Risk Infants (CLIP) to an Italian sample. *Frontiers in Psychology*, *6*, 1444. https://doi.org/10.3389/fpsyg.2015.01444

Carson C., Redshaw M., Gray R., & Quigley M. A. (2015). Risk of psychological distress in parents of preterm children in the first year: evidence from the UK Millennium Cohort Study. *BMJ Open*, *5*(12), e007942. https://doi.org/10.1136/bmjopen-2015-007942

Danis, I., Bóné, V., Hegedüs, R., Pilinszki, A., Szabó, T., & Dávid, B. (2020). Infancy in 21st century Hungary – a project introduction: Policy, theoretical and methodological framework and objectives of the first national representative parent survey on infant and early childhood mental health. *European Journal of Mental Health*, *15*(2), 111–144. https://doi.org/10.5708/ejmh.15.2020.2.3

Eatough, V., & Smith, J. A. (2013). Interpretative phenomenological analysis. In C. Willig & W. Stainton-Rogers (Eds.), *The SAGE Handbook of Qualitative Research in Psychology* (pp. 179–194). SAGE.

Ettenberger, M., Bieleninik, Ł., Stordal, A. S., & Ghetti, C. (2024). The effect of paternal anxiety on mother-infant bonding in neonatal intensive care. *BMC Pregnancy and Childbirth*, *24*(1), Article 55. https://doi.org/10.1186/s12884-023-06179-z

European Parliament. (2023). *Maternity and Paternity Leave in the EU*. https://www.europarl.europa.eu/RegData/etudes/ATAG/2023/739346/EPRS_ATA(2023)739346_EN.pdf

Genesoni, L., & Tallandini, M. A. (2009). Men's psychological transition to fatherhood: An analysis of the literature, 1989–2008. *Birth*, *36*(4), 305–318. https://doi.org/10.1111/j.1523-536X.2009.00358.x

Hollywood, M. A., & Hollywood, E. (2011). The lived experiences of fathers of a premature baby on a neonatal intensive care unit. *Journal of Neonatal Nursing*, *17*(1), 32–40. https://doi.org/10.1016/j.jnn.2010.07.015

Hungarian Central Statistical Office. (2022). *22.1.3.7. Csecsemőhalandóság. (Infant mortality)*. https://www.ksh.hu/stadat_files/nep/hu/nep0058.html

Ionio, C., Colombo, C., Brazzoduro, V., Mascheroni, E., Confalonieri, E., Castoldi, F., & Lista, G. (2016). Mothers and fathers in NICU: The impact of preterm birth on parental distress. *Europe's Journal of Psychology, 12*(4), 604–621. https://doi.org/10.5964/ejop.v12i4.1093

Jotzo, M., & Poets, C. F. (2005). Helping parents cope with the trauma of premature birth: An evaluation of a trauma-preventive psychological intervention. *Pediatrics, 115*(4), 915–919. https://doi.org/10.1542/peds.2004-0370

Karatzias, T., Chouliara, Z., Maxton, F., Freer, Y., & Power, K. (2007). Post-traumatic symptomatology in parents with premature infants: A systematic review of the literature. *Journal of Prenatal & Perinatal Psychology and Health, 21*(3), 249–260.

Lasiuk, G. C., Comeau, T., & Newburn-Cook, C. (2013). Unexpected: An interpretive description of parental traumas' associated with preterm birth. *BMC Pregnancy and Childbirth, 13*(Suppl S1), S13. https://doi.org/10.1186/1471-2393-13-S1-S13

Monostori, D. (2021). "Van élet a koraszülött intenzív ellátás után!" a koraszülő családok támogatási lehetősége. (There is life after preterm intensive care. Potential supports for the families with preterm babies). In M. B. Erdős & K. Talyigás (Eds.), *Kutatások a magyarországi szociális munka problématerületein (Studies in problem areas in social work in Hungary)* (pp. 56–63.) MTA Szociológiai Tudományos Bizottság Szociális Munka Albizottsága. https://ojs.lib.unideb.hu/public/journals/7/files/A_szocialis_munka_elmelete_es_gyakorlata_Tudomanyos_gondolkodas_es_kutatas_a_szocialis_munkaban_II_2.pdf-2021-11-18-01-22-15.pdf

Petersen, I. B., & Quinlivan, J. A. (2021). Fatherhood too soon. Anxiety, depression and quality of life in fathers of preterm and term babies: A longitudinal study. *Journal of Psychosomatic Obstetrics & Gynecology, 42*(2), 162–167. https://doi.org/10.1080/0167482X.2020.1808620

Rácz, J., Kassai, S., & Pintér, J. N. (2016). Az interpretatív fenomenológiai analízis (IPA) mint kvalitatív pszichológiai eszköz bemutatása. (Interpretative Phenomenological Analysis as a qualitative research method in psychology). *Magyar Pszichológiai Szemle, 71*(2), 313–336. https://doi.org/10.1556/0016.2016.71.2.4

Robinson, M., & Robinson, C. D. (2022). The silent cry: A psychiatric-mental health nurse's guide for fathers experiencing perinatal loss. *Journal of Psychiatric & Mental Health Nursing, 29*, 619–623. https://doi.org/10.1111/jpm.12849

Schaber, R., Kopp, M., Zähringer, A., Mack, J. T., Kress, V. E., & Garthus-Niegel, S. (2021). Paternal leave and father-infant bonding: Findings from the population-based cohort study DREAM. *Frontiers in Psychology, 12*. https://doi.org/10.3389/fpsyg.2021.668028

Stefana, A., Biban, P., Padovani, E. M., & Lavelli, M. (2022). Fathers' experiences of supporting their partners during their preterm infant's stay in the neonatal intensive care unit: A multi-method study. *Journal of Perinatology, 42*(6), 714–722. https://doi.org/10.1038/s41372-021-01195-3

Tedeschi, R. G., & Calhoun, L. G. (2004). Posttraumatic growth: Conceptual foundations and empirical evidence. *Psychological Inquiry, 15*(1), 1–18. https://www.jstor.org/stable/20447194

Thomson-Salo, F., Kuschel, C. A., Kamlin, O. F., & Cuzzilla, R. (2017). A fathers' group in NICU: Recognising and responding to paternal stress, utilising peer support. *Journal of Neonatal Nursing, 23*(6), 294–298. https://doi.org/10.1016/j.jnn.2017.04.001

van der Kolk, B. A. (1998). Trauma and memory. *Psychiatry and Clinical Neurosciences, 52*(S1), S52–S64. https://doi.org/10.1046/j.1440-1819.1998.0520s5S97.x

Wigert, H., Dellenmark-Blom, M., & Bry, K. (2014). Parents' experiences of communication with neonatal intensive-care unit staff: An interview study. *BMC Pediatrics, 14*(1). https://doi.org/10.1186/s12887-014-0304-5

World Health Organization. (2023). *Preterm Birth.* https://www.who.int/news-room/fact-sheets/detail/preterm-birth

Zelena, A., & Monostori, D. (2016). Kommunikáció a hozzátartozóval. A gyermekintenzív ellátás pszichoszociális és kommunikációs szemléleti változásainak spektruma. (Communication with family members. The spectrum of change in psychosocial and communication perspectives at the pediatric intensive unit). *Lege Artis Medicinae, 26*(9–10), 451–455.

Body as mediator: Case understanding in salutogenic-oriented general practitioner consultation

Ottomar Bahrs

ABSTRACT
An animate body offers itself in its material substrate as an object of causal-analytical thinking and, as such, requires an interpretative approach. In this regard, medicine and the health sciences are always hermeneutic, yet how is shared meaning constituted in the doctor-patient relationship if the patient does not verbalize the central questions of life? And what roles do caregivers' health concepts play? This paper uses sequence analysis (according to structural hermeneutics) to explore a video-documented conversation between a general practitioner and his patient, in which the overall shape of professional interactional patterns resulting from the rating procedure for solution-oriented interventions is evaluated. The case study illustrates how negotiating health goals goes beyond the patient's illness and touches upon their concerns and (life) goals. The paper suggests that shared decision-making must be preceded by mutual understanding, and that the health-promoting potential for a sense of coherence can be strengthened by interpreting symptom formation as a possible voice of the body if this expression is taken seriously.

1. Introduction

As a medical sociologist, I[1] have been concerned for the past 40 years with questions about how people deal with chronic illnesses. Initially, I was interested in those affected as well as their families. How, for instance, do they cope with their disease? What are the effects on their everyday life? How can meaning be attributed to what is considered as suffering? What changes over time? Is it possible to describe the typical course of the illness and the potential influencing factors?

In the examination of different illnesses (e.g. epilepsy, multiple sclerosis, diabetes, and heart attack), it became clear to me that 'mental health' is of central importance to those affected and that the way they deal with it sheds light on the more general question of living with chronic conditions (Hildenbrand, 1993, 1999). Health and illness are understood as an overall process. Hence, being healthy and ill are individually expressed in all their complexities. Thus, it seems reasonable to use a biographical approach to reconstruct the layering of meaning in the context of the respective systems (Hildebrand, 1999; Hildebrand & Welter-Enderlin, 2004) Sartre's existential questions of how it is possible to make oneself a condition of one's conditionality and thus become one who is is of central importance in this regard (Sartre, 1964).

Research and the accompanying primary care processes opened up another perspective for me. I learned that medical experts approach health problems objectifying and collect findings, whereas those affected begin from their state of being, but how can mutual understanding be achieved through encounters with such experts? Thus, this research focuses on negotiation processes between carer and patient, relational dynamics, and framing.

It addresses the relationship between person-centeredness and meaning-making by referring to anthropological medicine (von Weizsäcker, 1956) and salutogenesis (Antonovsky, 1987).

Weizsäcker observed that comparable organ damage can be accompanied by different courses of illness and concluded that those affected suffer their illness and develop it. Mental and physical processes are functional in shaping the ego – environmental relationship and can represent each other. Therefore, sick persons must be viewed as a whole, and symptoms must be understood in terms of expression.

Antonovsky attributed the ability to cope with a crisis to the degree of confidence that the situation is understandable and manageable from the perspective of the person affected, and that they have a meaningful task to fulfill. If meaning can be found, a sense of coherence is formed throughout life and affects the entire person.

As such, the case study (based on a video-documented conversation between a general practitioner and a patient suffering from chronic pain) will illustrate how negotiating health goals goes beyond the patient's illness. Instead, it implicitly touches upon the practitioner's concerns and the patient's (life) goals. Balint discussed how this can lead to a struggle between doctor and patient about values and (life) goals; both are involved in 'mutual missionary work' (Balint, 1957). Shared decision-making must be preceded by mutual understanding.

However, many individuals are unaware of their (implicit) life goals and search for meaning which can be represented through physical expressions.

Here, *the body* might come into play as a mediator, and could, in turn, be linked back to the concept of salutogenesis. This raises follow-up questions about how the 'sense FOR coherence' (Lindström & Koelen, 2016) can be strengthened and how person-centered medicine can consider the physician as a subject with biographically-based subjective theories of health and illness.

The case study is explored using exemplary sequence analyses according to the structural hermeneutics method. Additionally, the overall shape of professional interactional patterns is presented, resulting from an evaluation using a semi-interpretative rating procedures for solution-oriented interventions.

The paper first outlines my basic theoretical assumptions before presenting the case to be interpreted and its outline of evaluation methods. Finally, it summarizes how a practitioner's approach towards the patient can shape meaningful and goal-oriented conversations that have the potential to turn the quirk of illness into an opportunity.

2. Physical and living body[2]

As the French philosopher Jean-Paul Sartre posits, '*To live is to produce meaning.*' (Sartre, 1977–1979, p. 25). Accordingly, man is more than a thing among things. He has a double structure as an animate body. As a body, man offers himself in his material substrate as an object to causal-analytical thinking, as a meaning-producing subject. This causal way of being in the world requires an understanding approach. Thus, it can be argued that medicine and the health sciences are always hermeneutic (Rieger, 2023; von Weizsäcker, 1956).

This double structure becomes apparent in the interaction between the patient and doctor or, more generally, between the person seeking help and the person helping (Weizsäcker, 1956). Both instances explain the phenomenon against the background of their respective subjective concepts of reality (Coulter, 2014; Kreher et al., 2008; Witte, 2010), so that a double problem of understanding exists (Bahrs & Köhle, 1990). As such, it is integral that a shared (treatment) reality must be created based on joint participation in a meaning-dividing social structure.

In the following section, I will show, starting from a consultation in a general practitioner's office, how the body can function as a mediator to open up the world of meaning—even when it is barely mentioned.

3. Materials and methods

The starting point of my case study was a video-documented conversation recorded in 1997, with the actor's consent, as part of the Eurocommunication research project. Ethical approval was not required for most participating countries. We have used a successfully tested design in several other practice observation studies in Germany. The first was the BILANZ study funded by the Federal Ministry of Education and Research. The BILANZ study was reviewed by the University of Düsseldorf Ethics Committee and received a favorable vote in April 2012 (registration number: 3740).

3.1. Data collection

The EUROCOM study was conducted in parallel in six European countries between 1996 and 1999 with financial support from the EC under the BIOMED2 program. This study included 3695 patients and 190 general practitioners (898 patients and 43 GPs in Germany). The data were collected between 1997 and 1998. With patients' consent, 20 consecutive consultations with each physician were recorded using a permanently installed video camera. Documented conversations were coded according to the internationally validated Roter's Interaction Analysis System (RIAS) and comparatively analyzed (Bahrs, 2003; Van den Brink-Muinen et al., 1999). Individual case analyses in Germany have continued, one of which is presented here. This interview was selected because it documented a rare attempt to initiate support groups from a family doctor's office.

3.2. Evaluation methods

The conversations were transcribed for individual case analyses, and videos and transcripts were analyzed in several steps. The evaluation was conducted in two phases.

(1) The sequential interpretation of (selected) interview passages according to the structural hermeneutic method is fundamental (Oevermann, 1984, 2000; Oevermann et al., 1979). The aim was to determine the relevant patterns of interaction.
(2) Furthermore, we conducted a structured, semi-interpretative analysis of physicians' behavior as professionals according to the rating method of solution-oriented interventions (RLI; Schiepek et al., 1997). The aim was to identify conversation phases and turns relevant to change.

3.2.1. Structural hermeneutics

Structural hermeneutics was developed by Frankfurt sociologist Ulrich Oevermann and his group (Oevermann et al., 2021). They assumed that the social world is (also) an inter-subjectively produced world of meaning. It is organized in textual form, whereby agreement on the meaning of content is, in the last instance, ensured linguistically. However, utterances are ambiguous and can be used in different contexts: they are 'overdetermined'. Social interactions cannot simultaneously respond to all possibilities of meaning; they are interpretive and selective.

In the analysis, systematically unperceived options are of particular interest because they point to the rule according to which selection takes place and, thus, the formation of an interactional structure. The form, content, and order of the utterances were not random. The subjectively intended meaning and the objectively latent structure of meaning are categorically distinguished.

Social interaction protocols were analyzed within the group. Prior knowledge is systematically ignored in artificial naivety to capture possible ambiguities.

To approach the emerging rule of generation, utterances were analyzed step-by-step and then sequentially. Context is gradually included, and three forms of context can be distinguished.

- The *external context* refers to the framework; thus, the rule offers a priori to help structure the interaction.
- The *internal context* refers to the gradually generated structuring of actors' interactions.
- The *biographical context* refers to the interactants' former experiences. Throughout the analysis, a structure gradually becomes recognizable and can be generalized as a type regardless of how often it is realized.

3.2.2. Rating procedure for solution-oriented interventions

The RLI is a semi-standardized procedure for observing resource- and solution-oriented therapist behavior (Schiepek et al., 1997). It is considered a generic procedure that can be used independently of setting up a person, profession, or therapy school. The interrater reliability was high.

Doctors' utterances or interventions were rated on a five-point scale per minute. The assessment was based on a set of 23 items grouped into seven impact factors, which are:

(1) Problem analysis;
(2) Actualization of goals
(3) Concretization of solutions;
(4) Formation of relationships
(5) Resource orientation
(6) Alternative thinking and
(7) Reframing

The assigned value indicates the intensity and sophistication of the doctor's behavior regarding the respective aspects. A weighting of '0' means that the conduct was not observed, whereas a weighting of '4' means that the individual behavior occurred frequently and in a qualified manner.

In every type of conversation between help-seekers and helpers, aspects of influencing factors IV (shaping the relationship), I (problem analysis), and III (structuring the conversation and concretizing solutions) are indispensable. The more the possible behavioral repertoire is fully utilized, the more flexible the interaction, which suggests complex problem situations and precisely coordinated diagnostic-therapeutic processes.

4. Case study

4.1. Background information on the conversations analyzed

The consultation took place within the framework of a health checkup in a group practice in a rural area in northern Germany (Bahrs, 2011). The physician, Dr. Sachse,[3] was about 55 years old and ran a general practice focusing on primary psychosomatic care. The patient, Mrs. Buchholz, was a married housewife and mother of three children, aged approximately 40 years, who were not employed after finishing elementary school and vocational training. She had been a patient in the family doctor's practice for seven years, and in the previous year, there had been approximately 50 contacts with the doctor.

Frequent consultations preceded the present visit because of chronic back pain. Previously, Mrs. Buchholz underwent surgery on her intervertebral disc without success. Cardiological clarification of cardiac arrhythmia was initiated and briefly discussed at the beginning of the conversation. Dr Sachse planned to use conversation, which initially discussed the findings of a medical checkup, to persuade Mrs Buchholz to attend a cross-indication support group. However, he suspected a more profound problem behind her persistent pain and wanted to prevent it from becoming chronic (Brucks et al., 1998; Grol et al., 1985):

> You have your herniated disc, and you are in pain. I would like to know why the resistance is so enormous that I need to do something about the tension again, which always increases the whole thing. Tension arises once for you from the diversity of your activities, and why still? We have already talked a lot about this and looked at many things. However, I think many things need to become clearer to you than they have now become in our discussion. Further, I would like you to go into the group and listen more closely to yourself. (A42–A43) (For the complete (German) transcript see GeMeKo, 2005)

4.2. Doctors' behavior and course of conversation

Interaction and formal conversation analysis refer to each other during the research process. Regarding research logic, interaction analysis precedes conversation analysis. In research practice, the steps are intertwined in a spiral. Since interaction analysis is very elaborate and can only be presented suggestively, I first present the analysis results related to the conversation process for a better understanding.

To characterize the conversation, I have shown the process on the left (Table 1) and a visualization of the predominant forms of intervention on the right (Figure 1). Visualization is based on an evaluation using a semi-standardized rating inventory of solution-oriented interventions.

Table 1. Conversation phases.

Conversation phase	Time (Minutes)
Framing: Health check	1–3
Expanding the topic: from the organ to the person	3–6
Dealing with resistance	7–11
Order clarification	11–13 and 15
Ensuring the continuity of doctor-patient-relationship	12–13
Accompaniment in the group	4 and 14
Risks in the family	16–8
Framing: Balancing and reappointment	19–20

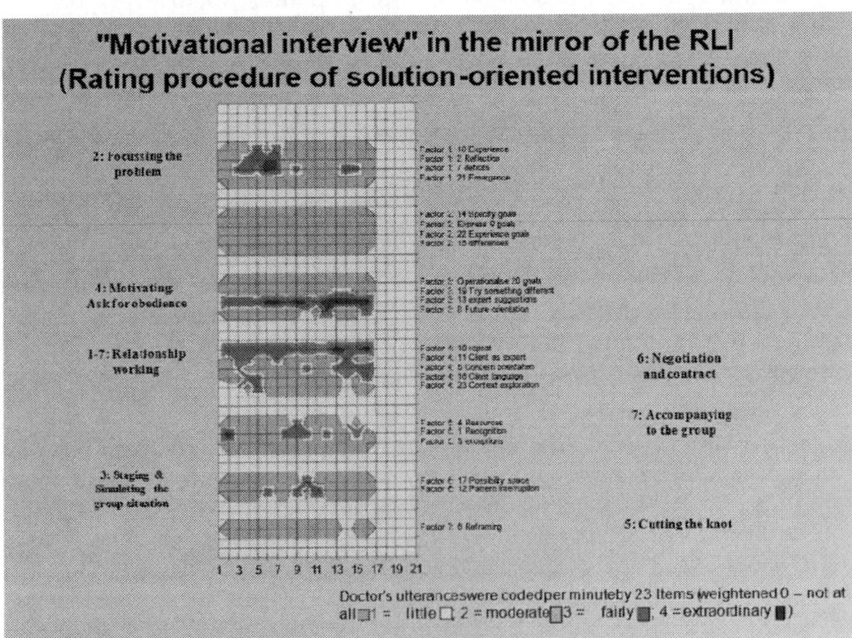

Figure 1. The motivational interview in the mirror of the rating procedure of solution-oriented interventions (RLI).

The shaping of the relationship (factor 4) is constitutive and is a component of every moment of the conversation. Furthermore, Dr Sachse structured the consultation (Factor 3) but picked essential hints from Mrs Buchholz. The motivational interview (Bahrs & Hesse, 1996) was framed by elements of the health examination at the beginning and end of the interview (Factor 1). Finally, Dr Sachse introduced the perspective of change (Factors 6 and 7) in a resource-oriented manner (Factor 5).

In this complex intervention, Dr. Sachse plays virtuously on the keyboard of interaction and uses almost all elements except for the explicit thematization of the patient's goals (Factor 2). A representative of a self-help counseling agency commented: '*Prescribed self-help cannot work.*'

4.3. Interaction analysis: Doctors' talks were conducted together

A glance at the conversation suggests that the physician strongly dominates the conversation; his share of conversations was 66.5%.

Nevertheless, Mrs Buchholz controlled the conversation. She supplies the doctor with the cue for an extended problem analysis with the lax wording '*my heart has a quirk*' (P22). '*Just the heart?*' Dr. Sachse comments (A25) and thus swings to her language level.

The core of this motivational interview was a resistance analysis. This focus is possible and necessary because, contrary to Dr. Sachse's repeated recommendation, Mrs. Buchholz did not visit the psychological-therapeutic self-help group because of the fear that she could not concretize further. She describes herself as defensive and reserved towards strangers, thus confirming the doctor's assessment that a psychotherapeutic intervention would currently be too much for her. "*However, one thing you can have right away is the group. Moreover, nothing can happen to you in the group. You say something, or you say nothing*' (A54). "*I say nothing*" (P51). Thus, Mrs Buchholz stages the expected relational situation in the group in the here and now of the doctor-patient relationship, repeating a previously shown pattern: '*I thought you were stupid at first, too.*" (P44) By pointing out that she can change her mind, she continues to refer to the potential for development that Dr. Sachse attributed to her.

Both actors experience themselves as powerless and find common ground for mutual recognition of distress. The doctor asks the patient to '*obey*' him as she would swallow a prescribed pill (A62). The seemingly weak argument '*just because the doctor wants me to*' (P57) thus becomes a motivation in the sense that '*I will try it out for the doctor's sake and my own sake*'. However, Mrs. Buchholz can only take this risk after Dr. Sachse assures her of the safe continuation of the doctor-patient relationship, even if she does not attend the group (P59, A64).

While Mrs Buchholz visibly struggles to decide – '*it is tough for me!*' (P64) – Dr. Sachse facilitates her going to the group by allowing her husband to drive her. In doing so, he returns to her earlier statement that she would immediately follow the group member (P33). From the perspective of being accompanied by a friend, Mrs. Buchholz is released from the staged group situation into the expected actual situation, thus initiating a detachment process to some extent. With targeted reappointment, the continuity of the relationship is emphasized simultaneously; Dr. Sachse will continue to be available as a *sparring partner* and *transitional object*, thus enabling emotional refueling (Helmich et al., 1991).

With the injection, the patient's apparent concern is addressed again in the concluding section. Notably, both actors brought their concerns to bear in the conversation.

In the course of the conversation, Mrs Buchholz hints at obstacles and resources and contributes to the formation of the hybrid between benevolent paternalism and shared decision-making into a consensual '*conditional obedience*' (Table 2).

4.3. Follow-up – the motivational interview as a developmental impulse

From a qualitative personal communication conducted four years later, I know that against a background of persistent pain and panic attacks,

Table 2. Conversation control by interactors.

Conversation phase	Patient intervention	Intervention of the doctor
Problem analysis	'The heart just has a quirk'. (P22)	'Just the heart?' (A25)
Request for obedience	'Do you want me to go there just because you want me to?!' (P57)	'I want you to try it'. (A61) 'Can I not command you, as I would write down a pill that you swallow?' (A62–A63)
Cut the knot	'Now I have a problem again! Now I go home with it – "Shit!" He sends me there!' (P65)	'Can cutting the knot and giving it a try be a way to deal with this resistance?' (A70)
Relationship work	'That is just the kind of guy I am. . . . I can also change my mind. At first I thought you were stupid too, now I do not think you are stupid anymore'. (P45/P46) 'What happens if I do not go there?' (P59)	'You need a little time'. (A51) 'I like the way you treat each other in the family'. (A53) 'You are a grown woman'. (A64) 'We have a contract, and next week, we will see each other again and chat about it'. (A106)
Staging the group situation	'I'm not saying anything.'(P51)	'You do what you can allow – you say something or say nothing'. (A54)
Accompaniment in the group	'If someone said: "Come on, I'll go with you".–then I would go with the person'. (P33)	'You are not a stupid cow either if you let your husband drive you there'. (A78)

The initial utterance is marked in yellow.

Mrs Buchholz attended a non-indication-specific psychological-therapeutic talk group for a year. But: *'I didn't say a word there.*" Nevertheless, she was able to take the next step and spent three months in a psychosomatic clinic. This experience has contributed to fundamental changes. Since then, she has attended another support group and has remained pain-free without medication. Without Dr Sachse's intervention and persistence, she would have stiffened her back. "*I was expecting more of a physical treatment, but that would not have been right.*'

She continues to see Dr. Sachse but much less frequently than before.

After the consultation, the patient was grateful, with one exception: she hoped for support in prevention and health promotion. She confirmed that Dr. Sachse had also considered these aspects, but she was highly dissatisfied with reframing the problem from a physical body to a biographically lived body.

In the follow-up interview four years later, she revised her evaluation: Only in the group, she learned you could discuss health and illness. From this point of view, she needed a 'kick in the butt'.

5. Body as mediator

Viktor von Weizsäcker suggested questioning symptom formation based on what is expressed. However, the body's language might betray what the patient speaks; thus, possible meanings require interpretation (Weizsäcker, 1950).

We are all born holistically into a preexisting social world of meaning that inscribes itself into the body, which plays out through our lives: 'The body as a social phenomenon can be examined sociologically in two ways: First, as a product, and second, as a producer of society'. (Gugutzer, 2022, p. 15). The body mediates multiple senses. Understanding is relationally mediated and occurs through dialogue. The counterpart must be benevolent and occasionally a critical companion to enable a shared experience.

In the present case, the person-centered approach (Mezzich et al., 2010) using active listening, strengthens the sense of coherence, as in the case of Mrs Buchholz (see Table 3), who was encouraged to open up to her 'felt sense' (Gendlin, 1993).

However, person-centeredness requires the physician to authentically engage in the interaction as a participant (Bahrs, 2022). According to Dr. Sachse,

> Psychotherapists teach us to use conversation as an instrument rather than a personal expression. (…) This psychotherapeutic attitude is not a GP

Table 3. Strengthening the sense of coherence through person-centered medicine.

Sense of Coherence (after Antonovsky, 1987)	Sense FOR Coherence (after Meier Magistretti, 2019)	Active listening
Sense of meaningfulness	Making coping tangible	Taking the patient seriously as a distinctive personality Convey the feeling that dealing with health and illness is worthwhile
Sense of comprehensibility	Provide security	Better access to the subjective meaning of symptoms and complaints
Feeling of manageability	Empower	Experience in controlling risks and problems and support from the doctor will help strengthen a possibly insufficient social network.

> attitude. After all, we experienced the histories of our patients with their own life stories. Therefore, we must be physicians in this regard. I reveal something myself to be credible. With my truthfulness, as I see it, I want to give the patient the chance to be truthful and honest with himself. (Interview, 1991)[4]

6. Summary and outlook

Understanding somatization can be helpful to patients if it is addressed as a valid form of self-expression. The success of this is dependent partly upon the practitioners' experience and theoretical knowledge. The practitioner who approaches the patient holistically is, as such, more likely to consciously enable greater patient authenticity whilst promoting the doctor-patient relationship.

The tension between mind and body is inherent in our culture and is repeatedly negotiated by each individual. This tension often arises during the care process, whereby the caregiver typically takes an 'objectifying' external view, while the patient's view is more (unconsciously) body-centered. However, this can vary depending on education and personal and professional experience.

The interaction analysis revealed that the physician played a prima vista-dominant role, but the patient also steered the conversation with the central utterances. The standard German term 'Das ärztliche Gespräch' (the doctor's conversation) should be replaced by 'the conversation between patient and doctor'.[5]

The fact that the dimension of a patient's goals does not become an explicit topic is not a unique feature of this conversation. It is still a rule that the practitioner designs the treatment plan and, in the best cases, considers the patient's priorities in the sense of shared decision-making, which may, eventually, enable a greater chance of the patient discovering their potential for meaning-making.

In the present case, Dr Sachse wanted to enable Mrs Buchholz to become more self-aware through her experiences in a self-help group. He assumed that Mrs. Buchholz could thus change her attitude towards herself and the world and develop her goals in the longer term (see Kofahl, 2021). At the time of the interview, Dr Sachse intuited that the patient's suffering was too acute to look this far ahead. Therefore, it is understandable that the dimension of explicit goal actualization was excluded from the conversation. This type of interaction results in a conversation characterized by the patient's conditional consent to follow the doctor's instructions instead, whereby the agreement is designed to be revoked.

However, the analyzed conversation inspired the development of an eventual review dialogue (Bahrs & Matthiessen, 2007; Bahrs & Henze, 2019; Bahrs et al., 2017). This new concept aims to enable patients and GPs to develop health goals jointly. Thus, the motivational interview presented is an excellent example of how solutions are designed in practice, which can anticipate and inspire further conceptual development.

7. Take home message

- The concept of 'body as mediator' links medical anthropology and salutogenesis, thus considering the unity of the health-illness process.
- Active listening promotes empowerment.
- Salutogenic orientation affects the entire organism and is not limited to mental health in the narrower sense. This is particularly important for individuals with diffuse complaints or chronic illnesses.
- Focus on the patient's long-term (usually latent) (life) goals, which may need to be made explicit.
- The doctor acts as a whole person to the entire person. Authenticity is crucial.
- It is not the extent but the quality of participation in a conversation that is decisive.
- Every interaction creates something new, and participative practical research is worthwhile.

Notes

1. The text also reflects my own history as a researcher, which is why I write in the first person except in the abstract. The introduction of the subject into medicine demanded by Weizsäcker should also be followed by the introduction of the subject into research – at least insofar as it reflects health-related interactions (Bahrs, 2022).

2. In German, we differentiate between *Körper* and *Leib*, that is 'having a body and being a body' (Plessner) in the phenomenological tradition. (See Plügge, 1967).
3. Names and biographical data are made anonymous.
4. Dr Sachse's experiences of illness in his family, his own crises and challenges in his medical work, alluded to here, cannot be presented here for reasons of space (Cf. (Bahrs, 2011)).
5. Increasing emphasis is being placed on developing communication skills in medical education. However, there is still talk of 'medical conversation' (see e.g. Simmenroth-Nayda et al., 2007), which does not capture bipersonality.

Acknowledgments

This EUROCOM study was coordinated by the NIVEL Institute (Utrecht) and funded by the EC (BMH4—CT96-1515).

I thank the EC, the EUROCOM study group colleagues, and the patients and GPs participating in the project; the study could only be conducted and presented successfully through their commitment and openness. This was particularly true for Mrs Buchholz and Dr Sachse (anonymized names), who were available for follow-up interviews years after the baseline study and agreed to further detailed analysis.

Furthermore, I would like to thank my long-time colleagues Susanne Heim, Karl-Heinz Henze, and Vera Kalitzkus for their numerous suggestions.

Disclosure statement

No potential conflict of interest was reported by the author(s).

Funding

This quantitative part of the EUROCOM study was funded by the EC [BMH4—CT96-1515]. The additional qualitative evaluations presented here were financed by own funding.

References

Antonovsky, A. (1987). *Unraveling the mystery of health: How people manage stress and stay well.* Jossey-Bass.

Bahrs, O. (2003). Mein Hausarzt hatZeit für mich – Wunsch und Wirklichkeit; Ergebnisse einer europäischen Gemeinschaftsstudie. *GGW*, *3*(1), 17–23.

Bahrs, O. (2011). Der Arzt als Partner – Biografie und ärztliches Handeln. *Balint*, *12* (3), 77–84. https://doi.org/10.1055/s-0030-1262519

Bahrs, O. (2022). Introducing the subject into primary care - person-centeredness in primary care needs participatory research. *Global Journal of Medical Research*, *22* (2), 65–75. https://doi.org/10.34257/GJMRBVOL22IS2PG65

Bahrs, O., Heim, S., Löwenstein, F., & Henze, K. H. (2017). Review dialogues as an opportunity to develop life course specific health goals. *International Journal of Person Centered Medicine, 7*(2), 98–106. https://doi.org/10.5750/ijpcm.v7i2.638

Bahrs, O., & Henze, K. H. (2019). From shame to pride – Initiation of processes of De-stigmatisation in review dialogues. In C. Mayer & E. Vanderheiden (Eds.), *Transforming shame in culture and context: Practical applications and exercises for growth* (pp. 363–378). Cham & Springer.

Bahrs, O., & Hesse, E. (1996). Das Motivationsgespräch - Chancen der Selbsthilfeförderung im Rahmen der ärztlichen Sprechstunde. In O. Bahrs, W. Fischer-Rosenthal, & J. Szecsenyi (Eds.), *Vom Ablichten zum im-Bilde-Sein: Video-Dokumentation von Arzt-Patienten-Gesprächen im ärztlichen Qualitätszirkel* (pp. 219–260). Königshausen & Neumann.

Bahrs, O., & Köhle, M. (1989). Das doppelte Verstehensproblem - Arzt-Patient-Interaktion in der Hausarztpraxis. In H. Neubig (Ed.), *The Balint group in clinic and practice* (Vol. 4, pp. 103–130). Springer.

Bahrs, O., & Matthiessen, P. F. (Eds.). (2007). *Gesundheitsfördernde Praxen - Die Chancen einer salutogenetischen Orientierung in der hausärztlichen Praxis*. Hans Huber.

Balint, M. (1957). *The doctor, the patient, and his illness*. Tavistock.

Bengt, L., & Maria, K. (2016). *The ETC healthy learning process*. ETC-PHHP.

Brucks, U., Wahl, W. B., & Schüffel, W. (1998). Die Bedingungen zur Veränderung erkennen – Salutogenese in der Praxis. In W. Schüffel, U. Brucks, & R. Johnen (Eds.), *Handbuch der Salutogenese – Konzepte und Praxis* (pp. 37–47). Ullstein Medical.

Coulter, A. (2014). *What patients want: Information, involvement, support* [Paper presentation]. The Health Coaching Conference, Lynford Hall.

Gendlin, E. T. (1993). Three assertions about the body. *The Folio, 12*(1), 21–33. https://www.focusing.org/gendlin/docs/gol_2064.html

Gesellschaft zur Förderung Medizinischer Kommunikation (Ed.). (2005). *GeMeKo Materialien "Was macht denn Ihre Macke?"* Gesellschaft zur Förderung Medizinischer Kommunikation.

Grol, R. P., & van Eijk, J. T. M. (1985). *Prävention somatischer Fixierung*. Springer.

Gugutzer, R. (2022). *Soziologie des Körpers* (6th ed.). Transkript.

Helmich, P., Hesse, E., Köhle, K., Mattern, H., Pauli, H., Uexküll, T. V., & Wesiack, W. (1991). *Psychosoziale Kompetenz in der ärztlichen Primärversorgung - Ein Lernbuch für Ärztinnen, Ärzte und Studierende*. Springer.

Hildenbrand, B. (1993). Eingefrorene Geschichten und auftauende Beschreibungen – begriffliche Überlegungen: Konstruktion von Chronizität. *System Family, 6*(3), 130–138.

Hildenbrand, B. (1999). *Fallrekonstruktive Familienforschung: Anleitungen für die Praxis*. Leske & Budrich. Qualitative Sozialforschung; Vol. 6.

Hildenbrand, B., & Welter-Enderlin, R. (2004). *Systemische Therapie als Begegnung*. Klett-Cotta.

Kofahl, C. (2021). Gemeinschaftliche Selbsthilfe und Gesundheitskompetenz – der Beitrag der Selbsthilfe zur Gesundheitsbildung des Einzelnen und der Bevölkerung. In K. Rathmann. (Ed.), *Gesundheitskompetenz* (pp. 1–12). Springer.

Kreher, S., Brockmann, S., Sielk, M., Wilm, S., & Wollny, A. (2008). *Hausärztliche Krankheitskonzepte: Analyse ärztlicher Vorstellungen zu Kopfschmerzen, akutem Husten, Ulcus crusis und Schizophrenie*. Hans Huber.

Meier Magistretti, C., Topalidou, A., & Meinecke, F. (2019). Sense FOR Coherence - der Sinn FÜR Kohaerenz: Annaeherungen an ein mögliches Konzept. In C. Meier Magistretti (Ed.), *Salutogenese kennen und verstehen* (pp. 119–135).

Mezzich, J., Snaedal, J., van Weel, C., & Heath, I. (2010). Toward person-centered medicine: From disease to patient to person. *The Mount Sinai Journal of Medicine, 77*(3), 304–306. https://doi.org/10.1002/msj.20187

Oevermann, U. (1984). Zur Sache. Die Bedeutung von Adornos methodologischem Selbstverständnis für die Begründung einer materialen soziologischen Strukturanalyse. In L. V. Friedeburg & J. Habermas (Eds.), *Adorno-Konferenz 1983* (pp. 234–289). Suhrkamp.

Oevermann, U. (2000). Die Methode der Fallrekonstruktion in der Grundlagenforschung sowie der klinischen und pädagogischen Praxis. In K. Kraimer (Ed.), *Die Fallrekonstruktion – Sinnverstehen in der sozialwissenschaftlichen Forschung* (pp. S. 58–156). Suhrkamp.

Oevermann, U., Allert, T., Konau, E., & Krambeck, J. (1979). Die Methodologie einer "objektiven Hermeneutik" und ihre allgemeine forschungslogische Bedeutung in den Sozialwissenschaften. In H. G. Soeffner (Ed.), *Interpretative Verfahren in den Sozial- und Textwissenschaften* (pp. S. 352–434). Metzler.

Oevermann, U., Allert, T., Konau, E., & Krambeck, J. (2021). Structures of meaning and objective hermeneutics. In V. Meja, D. Misgeld, & N. Steher (Eds.), *Modern German sociology* (pp. 436–447). Routledge.

Plügge, H. (1967). Der Mensch und sein Leib. In *Forschungen zur Pädagogik und Anthropologie* (p. 9). Niemeyer.

Rieger, H. M. (2023). *Gesundheit als Wandlungsfähigkeit - Viktor von Weizsäckers Beitrag zu einer kritischen Medizintheorie*. Springer.

Sartre, J. P. (1964). *Marxismus und Existentialismus*. Rowohlt.

Sartre, J. P. (1977–1979). *Der Idiot der Familie* (5 Bände). Rowohlt.

Schiepek, G., Honermann, H., Müssen, P., & Senkbeil, A. (1997). Ratinginventar Lösungsorientierter Interventionen (RLI) - Die Entwicklung eines Kodierinstruments für ressourcen orientierte Gesprächsführung in der Psychotherapie. *Zeitschrift für Klinische Psychologie, 26*(4), 269–277.

Simmenroth-Nayda, A., Chenot, J. F., Fischer, T., Scherer, M., Stanske, B., & Kochen, M. M. (2007). Mit Laienschauspielern das ärztliche Gespräch trainieren. *Deutsches Arzteblatt, 104*(13), 749–751.

Van den Brink-Muinen, A., Verhaak, P. F. M., Bensing, J. M., Bahrs, O., Deveugele, M., Gask, L., Mead, N., Leiva-Fernandez, F., Perez, A., Messerli V., Oppizzi L., Peltenburg, M. (1999). *The Eurocommunication-study - an international comparative study in six European countries on doctor-patient communication in general practice*. NIVEL.

Weizsäcker, V. (1950). *Diesseits und Jenseits der Medizin*. Koehler.

Weizsäcker, v. V. (1956). *Pathosophie*. Vandenhoeck & Ruprecht.

Witte, N. (2010). *Ärztliches Handeln im Praxisalltag: eine interaktions-und biographieanalytische Studie* (Vol. 8). Campus Verlag.

OPEN ACCESS

School organisational trauma during student suicide crisis

Clare Finegan

ABSTRACT

Recent qualitative research in Ireland illuminates the impact of student suicide on Irish school guidance counsellors and the school organisation. It exposes distinctive factors in the overall system contributing to their experience of organisational trauma when coping with suicide aftermath. A qualitative Interpretative Phenomenological Analysis study privileged the voices of this Irish cohort of first responders to student suicide. Much international literature highlights the often severe effects of suicide trauma on mental health professionals. Irish school guidance counsellors comprise some of this cohort who deal with suicide. As they are highly likely to encounter suicide due to the accelerating rate of youth suicide in Ireland, they are vulnerable to similar risks of adverse impact. This research helps fill a gap in the literature concerning the specific Irish school context. In this research, semi-structured interviews generated descriptions of what was indicative of vicarious and secondary trauma, moral injury, organisational trauma and lack of containment, systemic disconnect, ambiguity and organisational double-bind used as a defence strategy, which appears to have comprised crisis recovery for the entire system. This article draws on the research and argues for a review of the Irish school critical incident protocols and policy and the introduction of an external evaluation of their efficacy in containing trauma in Irish schools.

Introduction

The author's research study was conducted against the backdrop of accelerating rates of suicide worldwide, particularly in Ireland. At the time of research, Ireland was reported to have the fourth highest suicide rate among young Irish people in the European Union (UNICEF Innocenti, 2020). The National Office for Suicide Prevention (NOSP, 2021) annual report indicated a slight reduction in suicide numbers. The potential of a student suicide happening for the school guidance counsellor (GC) has increased as Ireland has one of the highest rates of mental illness in Europe, with 18.5% of the population recorded as having a mental health disorder, such as anxiety, bipolar, schizophrenia, depression, or alcohol or drug misuse (OECD / European Union, 2018). This Irish research study addressed a gap in the knowledge base regarding the impact of adolescent suicide on GCs in Ireland. There seemed to be a need for a more profound understanding of the challenges and dilemmas when dealing with school suicide. Irish GCs are responsible, together with management, for coping with suicide postvention, so their experiences offer significant insight and can contribute to the international perspective. Their efforts are supported by the National Educational Psychological Service (NEPS). NEPS is part of the Irish government's Department of Education and provides a range of important psychological services for Irish schools. At times of critical incidents such as suicide, their role is to advise and support school management, usually through the presence of one or two trained advisors who attend the school. Their role during postvention does not include clinical engagement with students.

Data collection and sample recruitment

A purposeful homogeneous sample was sought, consistent with the IPA orientation, which prefers to focus on a small sample to allow for depth of experience, interpretation and meaning to emerge (Smith et al., 2009). The participants needed were Irish school GCs who had experienced student suicide within the previous 5 years. The Institute of Guidance Counsellors (IGC) enabled the recruitment of the purposeful sample.

Participants

Details of suicides and years experience for participants are listed below in Table 1.

Table 1. Participant profile.

Pseudonym	Gender	Number of suicides experienced	Years in role of GC
Lenny	Male	1	5 or more
Tamlyn	Female	2	5 or more
Ted	Male	1	5 or more
Connie	Female	1	5 or more
Mandy	Female	1	5 or more
Tina	Female	1	5 or more
Nessa	Female	2	5 or more
Mona	Female	2	5 or more
Fran	Male	1	Less than 5
Sue	Female	1	5 or more
Ellen	Female	2	5 or more

Data collection and method

In this study, 11 participants were interviewed by the researcher, with typically 1-hour recorded, in-depth, semi-structured interviews. Before the interview commenced, informed consent to audio-record was once again sought. An interview schedule guided empathic researcher questioning and facilitated interviewees to take the lead. The open questions explored their understanding and lived experience of dealing with the aftermath of a school student suicide. Questions focused on interviewees' experiences from the moment they became aware of the suicide event through to the closure of the critical incident postvention. The researcher followed up with questions on how they made sense of the traumatic impact on themselves and the school system. What they perceived as challenges and barriers to individual and systemic traumatic healing were explored, and interviewees were invited to offer their thoughts on how and where improvements could be made to facilitate them professionally in their role in this context.

The researcher analysed the interview transcripts following the principles of IPA outlined by Smith et al. (2009). During the analysis phase, Smith et al. (2022) introduced new IPA terminology, a significant development in IPA. The new terminology was welcomed even at a late stage in this research as it offered better clarity and allowed for a more in-depth focus on the experience of the phenomenon. It was decided to keep the old terminology where it had been used and move to the new terminology at the analysis stage. This move is evident in the thesis, with some deliberate overlap to provide an understanding of the change.

(1) The researcher's interpretative engagement and analysis was carried out with each interview transcript in turn, as IPA is interested in 'idiographic' analysis, meaning engagement with the detail of individual lived experiences, before moving to the next interview. The process followed for each interview transcript reveals insights into

the participant's experience and the potential meaning attributed to it. Any patterns in thoughts, feelings expressed and meanings conveyed were noted and differentiated between conceptual, descriptive and linguistic observations. The exploratory comments were then reviewed and re-read in an iterative process to understand and reveal emerging themes. These were catalogued. When the transcript coding was complete, a clustering process was undertaken to condense and combine themes, reducing them to coherent emerging themes with underpinning examples of experiential participant comments. These clusters were then further refined to produce a final 'Themes Table' of participant Personal Experiential Themes (PETs) with subordinate themes and illustrative participant experiential statements, capturing the essential nature of the experience of the phenomenon. Finally, a pictorial representation was produced to illustrate the phenomenological superordinate themes (PETs) and their related subordinate themes. A narrative summary of the participants' rich and meaningful experiences of the phenomenon was then written, illustrated by the most compelling PETs in the transcript, representing the participant's 'voice' and researcher's 'positionality' to make sense of the phenomenon in unique ways (Smith et al., 2022).

(2) The researcher then commenced the same process for the subsequent interview transcript, and this procedure was repeated in turn for all 11 transcripts.

(3) After completing each analysis, a cross-case analysis led to emerging GETs. During the iterative 'Hermeneutic circling' process, the researcher referred to the PETs tables and the interview transcripts, repeatedly reviewing the experiential statements for each participant to reveal their most representative experiences. The cross-case analysis of all themes was divided into five stages, as pictured below.

Findings and discussion

Three significant Group Experiential themes (GETs) were identified: (1) Managing Emotions, (2) Feeling Disempowered – Organisational Context and (3) Relying on Personal Resources. See Table 2.

Group experiential theme (GET) 1 – Managing emotions

Participants echoed the struggle to manage their emotions while juggling many tasks and simultaneously attending to many distressed individuals. When Tamlyn remarked, 'Just show up with the fullness of your humanity . . . there's no word . . . I don't think there's a script for that', she was relating how

Table 2. Group experiential themes.

GET 1. Managing Emotions: *'You have to keep it together'.*	
Sub Theme 01	Appearing Resilient *'No . . . script for that.'*
Sub Theme 02	Fear of a Repeat *'On alert physically and mentally'.*
Sub Theme 03	Feeling pressure- the impact *of the Organisational Context* *'You have to put on your armour and just go . . .'*
GET 2. Feeling Disempowered - **Organisational context** 'A Tsunami of Students'	
Sub Theme 01	Needing Support *'Grasping at Straws'*
Sub Theme 02	Accountable but Powerless *'At the Mercy of Management'*
GET 3. Relying on Personal Resources *'Scars are on my Back'*	
Sub Theme 01	Still Feeling it: *'I don't think I'm over it all'.*
Sub Theme 02	Relying on self-compassion and self-care *'Doing the best you can do'*

no words could describe or prepare one for how one might feel, respond or operate when confronted with the reality of the student's death by suicide.

Each participant could still recall what they were doing when the news broke, suggesting an indelible impact. Some shared detailed memories of their behavioural, emotional and embodied visceral responses: 'Panic, anxiety, going into fifth gear, running' (Lenny) as well as 'flashbacks' using words like 'creepy . . . evil' to depict 'disturbing images . . . disturbed me, frightened me' (Ellen). Sue's mental health was also impacted: 'I had quite a bit of anxiety . . . trouble sleeping and waking up early . . . it would have been in my head . . . All I could think of was [him] . . .' (Sue). This rumination conveys her close bond with the student and the sense of personal loss she suffered at his death. Ellen and Tamlyn described their ongoing visceral responses every time they see a tree or ropes which remind them of the hanging body, 'When you look at a particular kind of tree and kind of think, "yuck" or ropes that kind of stuff just triggering it. That bad feeling that that sinking feeling' (Ellen, p. 10). The experience of profound loss, the shock and horror after witnessing the ultimate self-destructive act, could only have left them off-balance, retrieving, as best they could, their humanity. So intense was the loss, anger and anxiety that Ellen could not process it for many, many months. She recounts that years later, while on holiday, she had a spontaneous emotional response to a stranger's upset, finding release and restoring some equilibrium, '. . . that was the first time I cried, and I cried. And I cried, and I cried and cried' (Ellen, p. 11). This outpouring of grief where she felt safe, impressed how unsupported and unsafe she felt in the school. The lack of school containment proved a barrier to post-traumatic growth and ongoing resilience.

Feelings of regret, guilt and self-loathing co-existing with reproach at the student's destructive act and betrayal of her investment of time and heart-felt care had overwhelmed her. 'I was just so angry with what she had done and the chaos that she had actually unleashed' (Ellen, p. 11). Just as the child's self-loathing had become so unbearable, so too had Ellen's own feelings become unbearable, having been left to receive and contain these projected parts of the student. She expressed her feeling that the school staff were blaming her. 'blood on your hands in some peoples' eyes ... like she left scarred a number of us' (Ellen). While the student's feelings were projected into Ellen, it is possible that her felt response to the staff is better explained as projective identification, a defence of her own self-blame and self-loathing. A similar sense of projective identification could resonate with Ted, 'The sadness of a life lost ... totally unnecessary, totally futile and the pain and the permission that is released into our society to do something similar' (Ted). The regret and persecutory guilt left Ted with a sense of self-doubt and constant, hypervigilant dread he had not experienced before. 'It's the vigilance not to miss someone else ... It's more about not letting the ball drop ... God I hope I don't miss somebody else, you know. and there's another tragedy' (Ted). Mandy described it as having shaken her to the core, 'just a moment of madness ... there was no sign of him being upset or anything ... it's like a bolt out of the blue has rocked your world forever, and you never can undo that learning you know' (Mandy). This absolute shock resonated with Nessa, 'Oh God it was horrible, and it came from nowhere' (Nessa). Connie still remembers the sound of the immediate impact, 'You could hear it actually, as the news broke, just the wall of grief. It definitely ... took its ... I'm brought right back to it' (Connie).

Ted's countertransference of feelings of helplessness shows itself, 'the helplessness, of them and us. And the not knowing what to say', so he suggested that they 'rattle off a few prayers to get them speaking ... You don't have to think when you're praying; it does something to your unconscious'. The 'rhyming off things' served to pacify, but for some students, he believed it allowed them to process '... that kind of stuff that's going on inside you comes more and more to the fore' (Ted).

The participants' responses to empathic working with those affected by the trauma of suicide were indicative of Vicarious Traumatization (VT) and Secondary Traumatic Stress (STS).

GET 2. Feeling disempowered – Organisational context

A Tsunami of Students

This GET refers to the pressure participants describe when operating as 'normal' in a 'not normal' situation and unprepared, '.... I was learning what to do for these kids while I was supposed to be doing something for them ... it would have rattled me for a more elongated amount of time if we hadn't had the following death [a second suicide]' (Tamlyn). Ellen describes the powerlessness experienced in her nightmares, 'I was having nightmares because I was very anxious about the students. I couldn't get to them as I was flat out' (Ellen). Ted recalled the anger he felt at the lack of consultation regarding student suicide ideation: 'If someone had told me . . . I was angry . . . I believe that if I had of been told, he [the boy] wouldn't have died' (Ted). Anger surfaced at what he perceived as systemic failings to connect with what was needed to keep the boy safe. Again, revealed here is projective identification into the deceased boy and his parents, the school management and the mental health support agency 'CAMHS' to whom he had communicated his concerns and the lack of feedback, 'If only . . .' (Ted).

The term 'Moral Injury' describes an individual's trauma response to a life experience that violates their moral values, beliefs and standards. Ted, Mandy, Tamlyn and others had expectations of those who had the power and were in the position to make a difference. 'I find when I think of that I take a sharp intake of breath' (Ted). He was left to contain unimaginable regret, rage and persecutory guilt. So too was Mandy as she says, 'If someone had come to me . . . we could have prevented it' (Mandy). Tamlyn's similar projective identification is highlighted '. . . how a parent could get a phone call from their child's school . . . and then . . . don't do anything with that . . . it makes me angry and guilty at the same time in equal measure cause I don't really know whats going on' (Tamlyn).

The impact was overwhelming as they stated how unprepared they felt for the reality of dealing with a suicide aftermath. The pressure of expectation to feign professionalism while denying feelings of powerlessness and inadequacy affected their self-worth, professional integrity and agency.

Participants interpreted the lack of containment of the trauma as a disconnect between what they saw as needed at ground level (therapeutic containment) to support the vulnerable and what school management and the NEPS decided was needed. Participants' accounts evidenced toxic organisational dynamics, a contempt for lack of consultancy, a lack of inclusion in decision-making, and a lack of acknowledgement and empathy for the scale and reality of the pastoral support needed, 'a tick box exercise' and 'a puppet show', leaving them to 'pick up the pieces'. . . 'They [management] are the people setting out the parameters in which you can work'; '. . . made me realise how vulnerable we are in this role . . . you're at the mercy of your manager' and 'lives could be saved if we had time and if we had resources' (Mandy). Tina expressed her contempt at the charade of support from management, '. . . once there is a guidance counsellor in the school that, that's grand as we've got that box ticked, you know' (Tina). All participants expressed feedback about the lack of support from the external support agency 'NEPS'. Nessa gave a clear insight into the feelings shared by many others: 'suited and booted . . . and beyond useless . . . (Nessa). '. . . the follow up afterwards, there was never any, you know, disaster . . . They provided us with absolutely nothing. They were shocking . . ., but Lord save us a child had died' (Nessa). Sue describes 'a tsunami' of students needing support and her experience, 'All very difficult . . . it all came to my door . . . [the service] came, they came and went. . . . I would have liked more support . . . there they were [students] all lined up . . .' (Sue). She used a powerful metaphor to describe her response to the lack of support, 'It's like someone pouring overflow in a cup, and you're taking all their emotions on and where do you go with it? . . . The effects of it are far-reaching' (Sue). The burden of powerlessness is tangible here: '. . . the only support I felt was from my colleague who was having the same, the same situation' (Ellen). 'When the **** hits the fan, there's no loyalty. . . . It shattered my trust in my manager' (Ellen). She projects with a derogatory comment about being silenced: 'You don't want to lose the student on your watch, and what I learned from this experience is that you have no control . . . You're muzzled' (Ellen).

It was apparent that the school management exacerbated her anxiety and could not deal with the widespread traumatic emotional impact, evident in the manifestation of the dehumanisation of the participants and the lack of autonomy or support given.

GET 3 – 'Relying on personal resources'

Scars are on my Back

This final superordinate theme encapsulates participants' thoughts and feelings about personal and professional coping while feeling unsupported and scarred from their experiences. While many, with the benefit of hindsight, felt armed with new knowledge, skills, insight and understanding, all participants reported the need for empathic support from their leaders to understand the effects on the GC, and trauma-specific training to be able to contain the trauma. With the hindsight of having felt dehumanised, boundaries were necessary to self-protect, while self-compassion and self-care were also deemed a necessity for longer-term resilience. Ellen expressed how she felt scarred, '. . . she [the deceased] left scarred, a number of us . . . its scarred me profoundly . . . because I've lived those experiences now and the scars are on my back . . .', '. . . it changed how I work in that I would now add a layer of minding myself' (Ellen). This voices the need for a supportive organisational culture which could contain the experience of 'death and dying'.

Tamlyn acknowledged that she had done her best for her students, 'I'm doing everything I possibly can within my remit', inferring the need for self-affirmation including protective boundaries. Lenny expressed a similar need to let go of remaining persecutory guilt, 'Let yourself off the hook, nothing to be guilty of because you did your best with two things, the information you had and the skills that you had . . . you might acquire a skill later on that you could have used, but if you hadn't got it first time round, let yourself off the hook' (Lenny).

Fran took consolation from his self-affirmation of having helped the bereaved students as best he could, 'To be able to give that space where a child can acknowledge the death' (Fran).

Some care was necessary in interpreting the many emotional experiences related. For example, one participant remarked on how isolated her manager seemed, possibly projecting into him her own difficulties at being unable to bear the effects of suicide. It could also be interpreted that he indeed was acting out his own difficulties.

Discussion – Organisational trauma

A brief critique of IPA

The main research question for this study focused on the Irish school guidance counsellor's experiences of the aftermath of student suicide in Ireland. The researcher believed the IPA approach would best serve her needs to explore and understand the participants' experiences. However, she felt a need to enhance the transparency of the analysis process by introducing a variance of the IPA-suggested protocol for clustering PETS. While the randomised selection and grouping of PETS written on pieces of paper is effective, it lacks transparency and seems insufficient to gain the reader's trust. It was decided to make this random selection process demonstrable by clustering on a spreadsheet and using multi-stage random selection, avoiding the risk of privileging one theme when presented in list format (Smith & Nizza, 2022). This provided visual evidence of the process for the reader's benefit (Appendix).

Organisational trauma

In this study, a systemic lens was required to view and make some further meaning of the personal internal psychological world and external professional world to which the participants belong. The interrelationships between managerial, psychological, relational, training, and supervision support and the participants' sense of psychological resilience, competency, efficacy and agency defined their overall experiences. They existed in relation to others in their school organisation or ecological system (Bronfenbrenner, 2005). The individual psyche and the collective psyche needed to be understood. A system's ongoing interrelationships are influenced by the interaction between the individual and the environment (Bronfenbrenner, 2005). Some participants experienced several student suicides.

Like these individuals, organisations can have their own historical or prior trauma, as Fraiberg et al. (2003) posits. The impact of painful memories of previous traumas, unprocessed and unaddressed, for some, was triggered and relived. Bloom (2013) defines the term 'trauma-organised' as an individual or an organisation that unconsciously organises itself around the impact of chronic and toxic stress, undermining its adaptive ability. According to Bloom, a lack of learning and reflection on the past can facilitate 'organisational learning disabilities', resulting in a traumatised organisation (Bloom, 2013).

Only one participant in the study related her concern about the possible impact on the school principal. The fact that he seemed isolated and alone in his grief at the loss of the student impacted her. She was also concerned for the teachers who had witnessed the scene of the suicide and who she believed, as was her experience, would most likely not get the therapeutic support needed to contain the trauma. This shows how trauma could affect every level of the hierarchy and potentially collapse the system (Hopper, 2003). His work points towards the potential for lack of leadership direction when the leader in a traumatised organisation falls at risk of psychological and emotional impact, rendering it challenging to bring into effect the very qualities needed in a time of crisis. Ineffective leadership resonates with the feelings of mistrust, detachment and contempt expressed by the participants in this study regarding school management. Symptoms of depersonalisation, chronic stress, detachment and negative emotions in school leaders can be a barrier to managing their 'professional burden' (Szempruch, 2018). It can negatively influence their capacity to create organisational conditions for trust, openness, collective responsibility and empathic collaboration. It is worth adding that trauma can develop in school staff without their conscious 'realisation' (Parker & Henfield, 2012, p. 137).

Dutton et al. (2002) state that 'trauma leads to pain, confusion and disruption of daily routines which has a huge impact on the level of anxiety of the organisation' (p. 55). They maintain that leaders (management) need to 'demonstrate compassion, thereby unleashing a compassionate response throughout the whole organisation' (Dutton et al., 2002, p. 55). Steinkamp and de Vries (2014) posit that compassion must go beyond empathy and provide 'context for meaning' and 'context for action'. He suggests that leaders use communication to establish an environment for free expression and open discussion of the event to facilitate employees and management to go into grief mode. In this study, a few of the participants remarked on the lack of an opportunity to go into grief mode and resistance to their outward expression of grief, something which they felt was a barrier to their recovery. The leadership direction was reported as unhelpful, defensive and overcontrolling. Many felt a strong sense of moral injury because of the injustice to vulnerable students and staff, who they feared would not get the care needed.

While the guidelines published by National Educational Psychological Service (2016) refer to **'the few'** when highlighting students who may need further attention, which points to a systemic disconnect. The guidelines and school policies failed to recognise the potential for student suicide to impact **very many** students, as was the reality for all participants. The **'tsunami'** of students, including siblings, friends and other vulnerable students needing support highlights these guidelines as being disconnected from the scale of the crisis and the support required. It is worth quoting Parsons, 'In the case of suicide, proceeding as "normal" is not only abnormal but potentially quite damaging for the survivors' (Parsons, 1996). Counsellors need to assist the school community in pushing through such denial and implement a proactive, preventive, postvention response aimed at helping all survivors work through their grief" (Parsons, 1996, p. 78).

Participants spoke about dealing with role ambiguity, role conflict and 'double-bind'; drawing on the concept of double-bind (Bateson et al., 1956). They reported imposed contradictory demands. They described feeling pressured to go into operation mode to comply with the prescriptive protocols to move the students back to functioning as normal, despite the 'not normal' context and not feeling 'normal'.

Power-dependent relationships perpetuated the double bind some participants experienced. Bateson et al. (1956, p. 3) defined the double-bind as an 'unresolvable sequence of experiences' a predicament which leaves the subject pulled in opposite directions, 'a situation in which no matter what a person does he can't win' (Bateson et al., 1956, p. 1).

While it was implicit that the participants and students should resume normality, it forced a denial of their authentic reactions and true feelings. Management's instructions were ambiguously communicated and implicitly expected to be fulfilled. It strongly suggests the purposeful use of ambiguity by school management as a strategy, relying on participants' vocational diligence to attempt to do more than was realistic. The school could then appear to move forward while participants were 'left to pick up the pieces long after . . .' (Tina). Speaking about management's denial, Nessa comments '. . . he felt he was covered . . .' (Nessa).

A classic case of a double-bind is the quantity-quality dilemma, where employees can either try to accomplish an excessively high amount of work or fulfil expectations regarding the attention paid to detail but, realistically, will not be able to achieve both (Bateson et al., 1956). Contemporary research increasingly acknowledges double-binds as a workplace reality (Tracy, 2004; Visser, 2010 as cited by Hornung et al., 2016) in 'Dealing with Organizational Double-Binds'. Hornung asserts that role conflict and ambiguity are associated with undesirable personal and organisational outcomes, such as lowered performance, satisfaction, commitment, increased turnover intentions, psychophysical strain and impaired mental health (Hornung et al., 2016). It was apparent that Dutton & Frost's strategy was not adopted, as no opportunity was created by school Leaders to openly discuss the suicide event to 'demonstrate compassion, thereby unleashing a compassionate response throughout the whole organisation' (Dutton et al., 2002, p. 55). This phenomenon of using denial as a coping defence mechanism is not peculiar to a school organisational context. The strategic use of denial, resulting unintentionally in exacerbating primitive anxieties and moral injury, is featured in Menzies (1960) study of a nursing service. She speculated that a hospital organisation is set up to protect nurses from their primitive anxieties because to do otherwise would undo the regimented workings of the hospital system. She believed that it allowed for a 'rational madness' because the belief was that a certain amount of chaos could not be controlled without upsetting the entire system, which functioned regardless of how well it functioned, despite the impact on the anxiety levels of carers and nurses.

In this study, the lack of autonomy and dehumanisation experienced by the participants parallels the nurses' experiences in Menzies's study. In her selected essays 'Containing anxiety in institutions' (Menzies Lyth, 1988), she describes how anxiety is compounded by a 'task-list' system that inhibits 'full person to person' relationships developing between nurse and patient. The implicit aim is depersonalisation: '... nurses often talk about patients not by name, but by bed numbers or by their diseases or a diseased organ: "the liver in bed 10" or "the pneumonia in bed 15". Nurses themselves deprecate this practice, but it persists'. She continues, '... Socially permitted differences between nurses tend to be restricted to a few major categories, outwardly differentiated by minor differences in insignia on the same basic uniform ...' (p. 52). 'They can be very upset by what happens to patients, by deaths, doctors' or nurses' mistakes, pain and emotional stress ... The emotional disturbance is denied as far as possible and dealt with by brisk, though kindly, remonstrances of the "pull yourself together" variety. ... strong feelings are discouraged ... This learned attitude of denial of stress offers some protection against its conscious experience ... Further ... against spread of the distress among nurses ...' (p. 104). Menzies continues to explain how, in an effort to lessen stress, '... nurses are implicitly or explicitly forbidden to make decisions about certain things' (p. 105). Menzies's vivid accounts demonstrate demoralising and dehumanising experiences similar to those described by the participants in the school research study.

It was not a lack of awareness that allowed psychological distress to go unacknowledged and unsupported in the participants' schools. Rather, as with the nurses' management, it served the School management as an active denial and defence strategy '... a puppet show' (Mandy, p. 19). Managements' inability to engage empathically or facilitate therapeutic support resulted in tension being allowed to threaten participants' equilibrium and sense of moral professionalism. Moral injury results from 'feelings of guilt and shame that arise after one has transgressed one's ethical norms' (Alford, 2016, as cited in Cullen, 2020, p. 3).

Participants' sense of duty of care to their charges was compromised, as happened to Menzie's nurses. A lack of individuated, competent, critical-thinking and empathic leadership failed the school organisation. As described in Hopper (2018), 'Groups of people can also be traumatised in a variety of ways ... such as management failures or other events that break the boundaries of containment and cause group members to feel profoundly unsafe'

(p. 93). This, in turn, compromises the overall system's mental and moral well-being and ability to recover from traumatic impact. 'As a defence against anxieties . . . the group shifts toward . . . relationships . . . based on merger of the sort one might experience at a political rally or sports event, rather than authentic relatedness base on integrated interaction and communication that typifies an effective workgroup' (Hopper, 2018, pp. 95–96).

Implications and recommendations

The study calls for an updated school suicide and critical incident postvention model, which includes a formalised on-site suicide de-briefing and triage service to assist the GC. This intervention can be broadened to include the provision of additional clinical care and support for the many students affected. An interim support service could be made available that can receive and manage high-risk students for some time after a suicide and provide one-to-one trauma-focused supervision for the GC.

There is much focus on the negative impact of organisational trauma and systemic disconnect on all participants in the study. Given the wealth of literature on the subject of organisational trauma, it is unfortunate that it appears to remain largely untapped for the benefit of schools in Ireland. The school is a perfect example of an ecosystem, with relationships and dynamics that extend beyond the school oganisation, into the community, the layers of governance and up to the policymakers and back. It indicates not just need for enhanced trauma-informed training for school principals, but the necessity to enact theory-informed organisational trauma training for all involved in the school system's management and governance. The object is to encourage supportive, open, transparent empathic leadership and an understanding of organisational culture. Clinical supervision is also critical for the GCs and management in monitoring and supporting this process. In the specific case of the GCs, defining clear leadership roles could address the reported lack of autonomy and agency.

There is considerable scope and a need for further study into the individual experiences and the complexity of the organisational trauma and systemic disconnect revealed. An openness to researching the school organisation as a particular site of trauma may bring a more detailed understanding.

The critical incident support service guidelines and intervention policy were experienced as a mismatch to the issues encountered and a contributory factor in creating a systemic double-bind, bringing contradictory messages to the GC during this time of acute stress. The NEPS guidelines, while comprehensive and valuable, still failed to address the issues encountered. There is a clear need for review and update of the detail in the guidelines and intervention protocols. The review could also benefit by referencing international theoretically informed overarching frameworks that could expose the resources and clinical expertise needed to support trauma-impacted school communities.

There is no external evidence available to date on how the 'NEPS' trauma-informed approach has been effective in addressing the trauma impact on the school community, such as improved behavioural, clinical management or staff burnout outcomes. Openness to an evidence-based, rigorous internal and external evaluation of the NEPS suicide postvention interventions is recommended.

Conclusion

The research study which informs this article is the first Irish qualitative IPA research study to explore Irish secondary school guidance counsellors lived experiences of coping with a school suicide. Adding to the literature on school organisational trauma, it provides insightful perspectives on the management of trauma in Irish schools. The study unearths and exposes contributory factors that exacerbate the adverse impact on the GC, including systemic double-bind, strategic ambiguity, denial and avoidance of responsibility, leading to the potential for moral injury and compassion fatigue. In the Irish context, it has important clinical and policy implications. It makes a case for external review and assessment of the efficacy of Irish school critical incident policies and intervention protocols, with a clear focus on the clinical care of students, staff and management.

Disclosure statement

No potential conflict of interest was reported by the author(s).

References

Bateson, G., Jackson, D. D., Haley, J., & Weakland, J. (1956). Toward a theory of schizophrenia. *Behavioral Science, 1*(4), 251–264. https://doi.org/10.1002/bs.3830010402

Bloom, S. L. (2013). *Creating sanctuary: Toward the evolution of sane societies.* Routledge.

Bronfenbrenner, U. (2005). *Making human beings human: Bioecological perspectives on human development.* Sage.

Cullen, J. G. (2020). Moral recovery and ethical leadership. *Journal of Business Ethics,* 1–13.

Dutton, J. E., Frost, P. J., Worline, M. C., Lilius, J. M., & Kanov, J. M. (2002). Leading in times of trauma. *Harvard Business Review, 80*(1), 54–61.

Fraiberg, S., Adelson, E., & Shapiro, V. (2003). Ghosts in the nursery. A psychoanalytic approach to the problems of impaired infant-mother relationships. In J. Raphael-Leff(Ed.), *Parent-infant psychodynamics: Wild things, mirrors and ghosts* (pp.87–117). Routledge. https://doi.org/10.4324/9780429478154

Hopper, E. (2003). *The social unconscious: Selected papers (International Library of Group Analysis, 22).* J. Kingsley Publishers.

Hopper, E. (2018). *Trauma and organizations.* Routledge.

Hornung, S., Lampert, B., & Glaser, J. (2016). Dealing with organizational double binds: Three-way interactive effects of role stressors and coping on worker exhaustion. *Psychological Reports, 118*(2), 487–509. https://doi.org/10.1177/0033294116637732

Menzies, I. E. (1960). A case-study in the functioning of social systems as a defence against anxiety: A report on a study of the nursing service of a general hospital. *Human Relations, 13*(2), 95–121. https://doi.org/10.1177/001872676001300201

Menzies Lyth, I. (1988). *Containing anxiety in institutions*. Free Association Books.

National Educational Psychological Service. (2016). *Responding to critical incidents, NEPS guidelines and resource*. Department of Education and Skills.

NOSP. (2021). *National office for suicide prevention - Annual report 2020*. Health Service Executive.

OECD / European Union. (2018). *Health at a glance: Europe 2018: State of health in the EU cycle*. https://doi.org/10.1787/health_glance_eur-2018-en

Parker, M., & Henfield, M. S. (2012). Exploring school counselors' perceptions of vicarious trauma: A qualitative study. *The Professional Counselor, 2*(2), 134–142. https://doi.org/10.15241/mpp.2.2.134

Parsons, R. D. (1996). Student suicide: The counselor's postvention role. *Elementary School Guidance & Counseling, 31*(1), 77–80.

Smith, J. A., Flowers, P., & Larkin, M. (2009). *Interpretative phenomenological analysis - Theory, method and research*. Sage.

Smith, J. A., Flowers, P., & Larkin, M. (2022). *Interpretative phenomenological analysis - Theory, method and research*. Sage.

Smith, J. A., & Nizza, I. E. (2022). *Essentials of interpretative phenomenological analysis*. American Psychological Association.

Steinkamp, M., & de Vries, M. K. (2014). *Behind the masks of silence: How leaders can overcome organizational trauma* [Unpublished master's thesis]. INSEAD, Fontainebleau.

Szempruch, J. (2018). Feeling of professional burnout in teachers of secondary schools. *New Educational Review, 54*(4), 219–230. https://doi.org/10.15804/tner.2018.54.4.18

Tracy, S. J. (2004). Dialectic, contradiction, or double bind? Analyzing and theorizing employee reactions to organizational tension. *Journal of Applied Communication Research, 32*(2), 119–146. https://doi.org/10.1080/0090988042000210025

UNICEF Innocenti. (2020). *Worlds of influence: Understanding what shapes child well-being in rich countries. Florence* (Innocenti Report Card 16). UNICEF Office of Research.

Visser, M. (2010). Constructing organisational learning and knowledge socially: An interactional perspective. *International Journal of Knowledge and Learning, 6*(4), 285–294. https://doi.org/10.1504/IJKL.2010.038650

Appendix

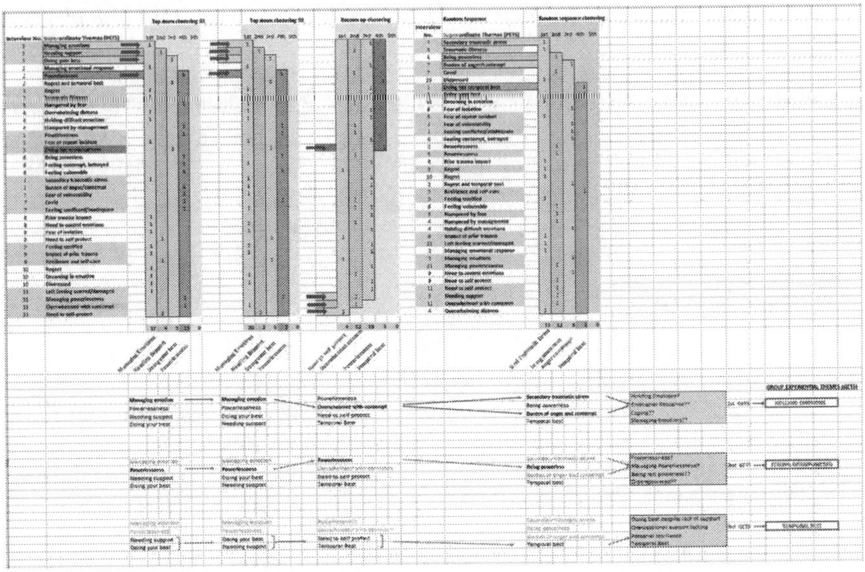

Analysis sheet 01 showing multiple varied cycles of initial clustering of PETs, yielding 3 dominant GETs.

OPEN ACCESS

Living with and living by tattoos: Discursive analysis of a bodily practice

Csilla Csekő, Anna Csekő Szél and Péter Bodor

ABSTRACT
In this case study, we present a discursive analysis of tattoos related to significant autobiographical events, examining their pictorial, interpretative, embodied and discursive characteristics in a remembering process. Tattoos are pictorial motifs of a culturally defined system, while tattooed persons as active agents endow them with personal meanings connected to their motives. This study presents the connection between motif choosing and individual motives, as well as the embodied positions of tattoos with their discursive consequences. Our paper underscores that not only new or reinterpreted meanings are created in this practice, but persons also construct their own positions, their own situated selves and identity in a positioning process. Through these discursive identity positions, that are assigned both in everyday conversations and in wider social-cultural discourses, persons construct more positive self-images, thus creating a device for coping with crisis situations.

Introduction

This article presents a case study about how a 26-year-old woman applies her tattoos to cope with her grief through creating meanings, and how she participates in different discourses. Tattooing is a culturally defined practice, an active pictorial body modification found in various ages and cultures (Caplan, 2000). In traditional cultures, tattoos and tattooing usually connect to rites of passages (Rush, 2005) and their normativity is more transparent than in our late-modern cultures. Tattooing and tattoo-wearing became popular in Western culture amongst the youth in the late 1990s, and although these individual tattoos can be preferred for aesthetic reasons, fashion, or self-expression, they also frequently memorialize significant life events or crises. Therefore, the psychological investigation of this cultural practice and its application can be relevant and effective for both academic research, as well as psychotherapy and counseling. Exploring its interpretative and communicative aspects can contribute to a better understanding of the phenomenon and the consideration of its therapeutic applicability.

We investigate the psychological aspects of tattooing in a discursive psychological framework. Discursive psychology is a social constructivist approach to social psychology, which offers a social epistemological direction to understand different psychological topics, such as memory, categorization, attitude, self or selves, and identity in social actions (Potter & Wetherell, 1987). The main questions of discursive psychology are who a person is in relation to others and how they act in these relations, given that these socially interpreted actions take place in a culturally constructed, common and shared value system, according to local moral rules (Harré & Gillett, 1994). Discursive psychology conceptualizes language and the discursive process as dynamically changing social action and employs novel methodological points of view. Two different directions of discursive psychology can be distinguished (Korobov, 2010). One is the rhetorical, methodological approach of Edwards and Potter (1992), which is based on the study of conversational interactions and the techniques of conversational analysis (Billig, 2009; Korobov, 2010). The other one is the discursive psychology of Harré and Gillett (1994), a hermeneutical perspective, studying meanings, intentions, purposes, and rules in a cultural context. In this conception, persons are defined as actors in a discursive process, using symbols or symbolic instruments like language, pictures, and symbolic cultural acts to fulfil their intentions (Harré & Gillett, 1994). In this study we perceive tattooed persons as agents who use tattoos as pictures for a definite purpose, and to create or construct meanings in order to realize these intentions. Therefore, we follow this hermeneutical method to explore these motives and meanings. Discourse is often interpreted on two distinct levels: a macro discourse connected to social discourses, and a micro discourse that is the vehicle of everyday conversations (Burr, 2015). We perceive these levels as interreacting (Csekő & Bodor, 2021), since discourse involves not only interactions, but interconnected cultural conventions and informal rules as well (Harré & Gillett, 1994). Therefore, while tattooing may have a more individual usage in Western culture, it still belongs to a socio-culturally defined local moral order, both in the process of creating meanings and in discursive settings.

Furthermore, since tattoos are pictorial manifestations recorded on the body for a memorial purpose, one of the main focal points of our inquiry is the remembering of respective autobiographical events, related images, and the body with its discursive implications. In our article we interpret remembering as a socially constituted activity (Middleton & Edwards, 1990), a relational and procedural accomplishment in and within discourses (Harré & Gillett, 1994). Hence, in this case study, we explore tattoos as pictures in a remembering process with their cultural and constructed meanings and their discursive presence. Picture theory has distinct traditions in picture analysis, and we follow a philosophical and art historical approach, which perceives the image as non-language-based, but interweaving entity with a manifest illocutionary force and representation (Mitchell, 1994). Most recently, scholars have interpreted the image as an actor with visual agency (Bredekamp, 2017). We interpret tattoos as pictures with illocutionary force and visual agency, not only because their wearers define them that way while selecting from a visual (online) repertoire, but also because autobiographical stories and motives are developed from pictures. These pictures appear on a specific canvas, the human body. We define bodies in the theoretical framework of discursive body and embodied self-conception (Csekő & Bodor, 2021; Wiggins & Cromdal, 2020), and analyze how identity and selves are construed over discourses (Wiggins, 2014). When considering tattoos, the body can be regarded as a surface, a subject of a rhetorical picture and body description, yet in diverse discourses, it is an active discursive constituent, possessing an illocutionary force, with its own positions and positioning possibilities.

In addition to the fact that the image and the body both retain a constant and contextual position and illocutionary force, speakers can also assume or be assigned different positions in interactions. We use the positioning theory to illuminate and analyze these positions. Positioning theory was conceptualized by Davies and Harré (1990) through the reflection on and critique of Goffman's role theory. According to these authors, in Goffman's dramaturgical model, social roles are relatively static relational subject positions defined by scripts and frames (Davies & Harré, 1990). On the contrary, in positioning theory, positions are personal identity utterances that constantly change during discourse and in different discursive situations (Davies & Harré, 1990). Harré and Langenhove (1999) model the discursive positioning process in the positioning triangle. This includes three discursive components: position, speech and other acts, as well as a storyline (Harré & Langenhove, 1999). These components dynamically change during interactions, and a change in one automatically alters the others (Harré & Moghaddam, 2003). All three elements of positioning retain both personal and social factors (Harré & Moghaddam, 2015). Speech acts, image acts, embodied acts and their illocutionary force belong to a linguistic and social system, just as the storylines are narratively constructed and contextual. Positions refer to who, what, and how can say and act in a discourse and they also manifest under local moral order (Harré & Moghaddam, 2015). These positions can be explicit or implicit self-positions, explicit or implicit positioning of others, explicit or implicit positioning by others, or a specific move within discourse. Any given utterance can be taken as a special kind of speech act, an implicit or an explicit 'identive' (Bodor, 2012). Since discourses are both constructed and constructive, a contradiction of positions and agency are important questions concerning the self-construction process in them. Participants have possibilities to choose self-identical and coherent positions, and to act as an agent by changing storylines or topics in a definite interaction (Davies & Harré, 1990).

To examine positions as identity utterances, we associate position theory and Harré's complex selves theory. This concept includes four aspects of selves: the embodied self, autobiographical (narrative) selves, social selves and cultural selves (Harré & Moghaddam, 2015). The embodied self is defined as a unique, singular, continuous self-aspect, based on bodily identification. Narrative selves are multiple, variable, inconstant and contextual, formed by narrative construction. Social selves are described as multiple, discursive, contextual, and constructed, while cultural selves are multiple and connect to social representations as well as cultural values and rules (Harré & Moghaddam, 2015). Over discourses, these selves-aspects are constructed, manifesting in positions that are continuously changing identity utterances contextually in a definite discourse.

We hence explore the characteristics and details of a tattoo connected to grief as a significant autobiographical event. More specifically, we focus on the discursive practice of embodied recording, transforming cultural symbols and creating meanings, and we analyze various discourses in which selves are being constructed through the positions of tattoos and their wearers.

Materials and methods

The collection of interviews we rely on in the present case study consists of 11 interviews with women and men aged between 24–37, together referring to ca. 50 tattoos. All interviewees connect their tattoos to autobiographically significant life events, which include loss, grief and abuse.

In our qualitative research, we used explorative, in-depth, active interviews with loose interview-outlines (Holstein & Gubrium, 1997). The unstructured interviews followed the progress of everyday conversations about tattoos and related life stories. Interviews were coded by two independent coders with Interpretative Discourse Analysis (IDA), comprised by three different analyses. Although the designation/denomination IDA is used by Wash for an interpretative public policy and critical discourse analysis (Wash, 2020), we use IDA as a means for the interpretation of thematic, discursive, and positioning aspects. As a first step, using content analysis, we identified topics that interviewees talk about ('what subjects talk about') and developed topic categories from which we created three main categories. The first category contains the autobiographical event connected to the making of the tattoo, the personal motivations for making it, the process of choosing the motif and its meanings related to the cultural context. The second category pertains to the positions of tattoos on the body and its discursive consequences, such as the control of its visibility, including its coverability and disclosability. The third category applies to different discourses, such as inner discourse (self-dialogue), private conversations or possibly different public communication situations in which the tattoo appears with its embodied position and/or its personal or cultural meanings. Our second step of analysis and interpretation examined communication situations focusing on their cultural and personal context, constructed meanings and interpretations. This part of the analysis investigated how interviewees use language and cultural connotations ('how subjects talk') for making meanings in different contexts. Thirdly, we applied position analysis concerning the various discourses to separate and determine identity utterances (Davies & Harré, 1990). This analysis shows explicit and implicit self-positions, explicit and implicit positioning of others, and finally, explicit and implicit positioning by others in definite discursive settings (Bodor, 2012).

In this paper, we chose a single mourning tattoo to present in detail for several reasons. Firstly, mourning tattoos are strongly represented in our sample, and because grief and the grief process are common therapeutic topics, they warrant emphasis. Additionally, due to the fact that our interviewee chose tattooing specifically for the purpose of processing her grief, we employed her case to gain insight into her mourning process through her intentions, goals, interpretations, chosen tattoo location and various discourses.

Analysis of a mourning tattoo

Description of the participant and her tattoos

Our interviewee is a 26-year-old woman, whose pseudonym in this context is Kate. She has three tattoos, all of which she got in her early adulthood, between the ages of 18 and 22. She formulates her main motive to have tattoos this way:

> . . .and for some reason, I felt that the basic idea that arose in me, was so significant, that I wanted to remember this . . . and I wanted not to forget it so hard, so deep that I felt I want it to be imprinted on my body, so it will always be there with me and I will always remember it.

Thus, all her tattoos implicate important events, carefully thought-out and significant main ideas with long-term meanings and messages to remember.

Her first tattoo is a dayfly (Figure 1), from when she was 18, 'a little dragonfly-like thing. . .an animal, which lives just a very short time'. In her interpretation, it means that everything is changing, fleeting, and the most difficult things are as temporary as all good things. She wanted to remember this wisdom: everything that can be experienced in the present is in flux and she relates this idea to her difficult adolescence.

Her second tattoo is an owl (Figure 2), capturing a painful autobiographical event when she was 19: her older brother's death and her grief process with several motives that we present in detail below.

She got her third tattoo when she was 22, and it is a mountain range (Figure 3) with three or four peaks and valleys symbolizing her intense struggle for even the simplest resources and skills on the one hand, and her persistence, strength and endurance on the other hand.

The first and the third tattoos have a common context and connotation regarding her burdensome life story and childhood experience of being poorly provided for by her parents. But, as the meaning of dayfly connects to the past and brings closure to her childhood, the mountain range symbolizes her own endurance and refers to the present and the future. These motives and meanings show the dynamics of stability and change, remembering and oblivescence, as well as the combined application of the more stable, imprinted picture and the changing verbal narratives of the event.

The coverability of the three tattoos also shows a dynamic progression from the first until the third. The dayfly tattoo is positioned on her abdomen in a fully concealable place, since it possesses a personal and intimate meaning and because Kate is not ready to talk about her tattoo. The second one, the owl, is on a more public but easily coverable part of her body (upper

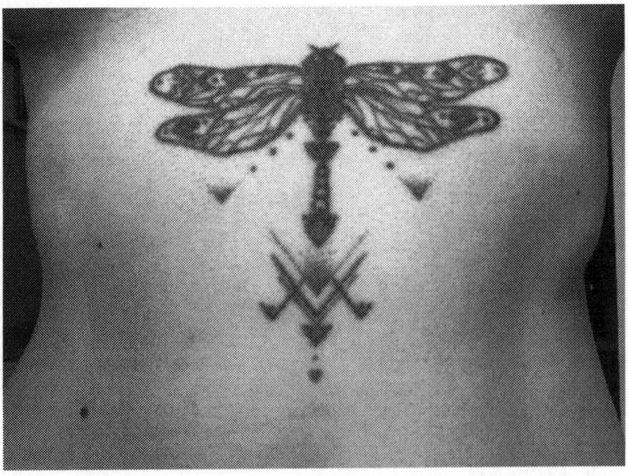

Figure 1. The dayfly.

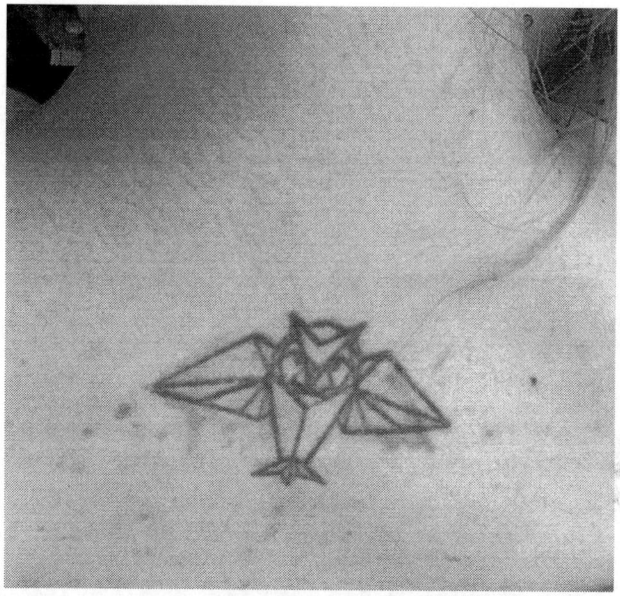

Figure 2. The owl.

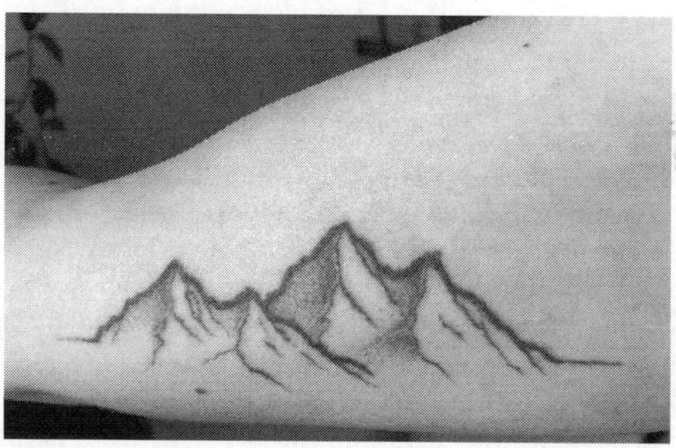

Figure 3. The mountain range.

back), but the topic and motives remain personal, not to be shared with anyone. In the case of the mountain range, not only does the meaning become less 'internal', but also Kate learns to participate in different discourses. As she says:

> But it may also have happened in the meantime, that with the time passing by, I began to find it less threatening, or not threatening, but burdensome, the questioning or teasing of others about why you had to get this tattooed on yourself, and why was it not enough just to get it sorted out in your head

> etcetera., but I felt like O.K., I am ready for these conversations, even if it comes from strangers on the bus, in a bar, or anywhere.

As she says, her 'being ready for conversations' is the reason for choosing a more public part of her body to position the tattoo (medial side of upper arm).

Autobiographical events, motives, picture choice and meaning construction

As mentioned earlier, the abstract, watercolor owl was created in time between the two life-experience tattoos and also relates to a difficult autobiographical event, her older brother's death and her grief process. This unexpected death and the complexity of their relationship led to compounded grief, a crisis to cope with. The owl tattoo was made four months after the loss of her brother.

The motif and meaning were chosen together, since, as she says: '. . .the pattern was occasioned by this because the owl is an animal said to carry the dead to the afterlife. Therefore, this motif also signifies farewell and saying goodbye'. This meaning of the owl as a guiding animal has roots in European tradition connected to Pre-Christian beliefs of spirit animals (Pócs, 2019) and ancient Greek tradition on soul guides (Burkert, 1987). Although this cultural background is not widely known, the meaning is, resulting in several grief tattoos depicting specific species of birds (e.g. owls or swallows), as well as related images of wings, feathers, aerial animals, and imaginary winged animals, such as unicorns. Accordingly, Kate applies a culturally shared motif system with multiple meanings to cope with this crisis. Her motives for having the owl tattoo were as complex as her grief process; furthermore, they both evolved during her mourning journey and varied in different discourses. Indeed, one of her most important motives is to imprint her brother's death as an immensely significant autobiographical event on her body. As she says: '. . .because I experienced it as very significant, and I felt [. . .] that would be like . . . have its imprint. I felt that I was ready for it right there and right then'. In this case, the wearer is an agent who, herself alone, chooses the significant event and makes it eternal; thus we have an activity of the person, an action that expresses agency by the act of embodied remembering – indicating that the body and soul are inseparable.

Our interviewee's second most crucial reason for using this tattoo is that both tattooing and wearing this tattoo are memorial acts to draw up an inventory of their relationship, itemizing actions that could and could not happen in their relationship.

> I think it is distinctive from the beginning in every single grief process, that some things become unsolved, and one needs to do an inventory of it, and one

> has to say goodbye, one has to make peace with the fact that this is going to be like this.

The most consequential part of this list connects to the fact that their adult relationship had just begun when this fatality happened. Accordingly, the lack of a deep emotional connection and the never-fulfilling desire for it causes the complexity of this grieving process.

> But yeah... this was a really complex thing from that perspective, and, like, quite weird. Not necessarily sad, [...] more like ... that weirdness [...] that you were important to me, but we will not have the opportunity anymore.

This 'weirdness', this 'complexity' of grieving somebody whom she does not know, relates intimately to her complicated grieving process, and this aspect integrates the inter- and intrapersonal aspects of processing her loss.

The third significant motive is associated with intrapersonal aspects, namely an intended commemoration: '...I wanted to know you, [my brother]; you were important to me, but we will not have the opportunity anymore'. The commemoration is about the significant other as a person, their personality, attributes and values from the perspective of the mourner. In this case, Kate's knowledge of her older brother's personality and values is lacking; therefore, she is partially grieving an imagined person whose cardinal attribute is his significance as a brother.

The fourth main idea for getting this owl tattoo is to ensure her brother's well-being: 'I hope you find what you're looking for, or not that you find it, but that I hope that you are going to be well. That you're well'. This concept also connects to the brother as a person and to an integral part of the cultural tradition where the meanings of this tattoo are created. Although the mourner does not consider herself religious, the image of a place where her brother feels good is an important part of her grieving and seems necessary for feeling reassured.

On the whole, this owl tattoo and its meanings voiced in the respective discourse segments attest to a complex grieving process. The process not only includes the mourning of the brother as a person, but in a sense, also getting over this significant and emotionally complex relationship, as well as accepting the loss of an unrealized brother-sister relationship. Although this tattoo as a picture and its meaning(s) are rooted in a traditional cultural field, they relate to the mourner's personal motives, and together they form the first important discursive determinant, which defines the discourses in which this tattoo takes part. These different discourses can be defined by the topic, the shared cultural knowledge and meanings, along with the intention of the mourner to divide diverse personal motives, connotations and their complexities.

Position of the picture on the body and its discursive consequences

The second important discursive aspect that influences discourses is the position of the picture on the body. This embodied position also has an impact on its illocutionary force and discursive consequences. In most cases, the place of the tattoo is consciously choosen by the tattooed person and reflects their intention and purpose of their tattoos.

The owl tattoo is located on Kate's back, between her two scapulas, close to the neck, and she formulates very clearly her intentions: '... to be honest, it was the first step, which was important for me, to be the one who controls who can see [the tattoo], who knows about it'. 'And really, the fact that [the tattoo] is being mentioned in a conversation is fully under my control ... ' 'And on the other hand, I did not feel the need for everyone should see it' [...] 'I felt rather like, those to whom I'll tell it myself, share it, will know'.

As we mentioned earlier, controlling the visibility of tattoos and orientating the different discourses through this is a priority for this mourner in all her tattoos. Her aim with having the owl tattoo is to create an inner place, a self-discourse to elaborate on her loss and form different discourses with her close friends and family members. For that very reason, she does not want a more public place on her body to wear her tattoo.

> New things can still emerge, but this is now just an internal process in me. Not a back-and-forth discourse. Or that if something pops into my mind, there will be no answer to that, and that there is nothing wrong with it.

Accordingly, she chooses a place on her body that is a boundary between private and public. Although, according to several interpretations, the human skin itself is a boundary between private and public (Valsiner, 2020), different parts of the body also possess varying amounts of publicness depending on their spatiality, movement, actions and coverability. These qualities ensue from the physical existence of the body, but this is not separable from its cultural entity as clothing, hairstyle, and rules connected to bodily actions, and collectively eventuate a situated visibility.

In this case, the situated visibility arises jointly from the boundary position of the tattoo and its coverability.

> This is also a motif that can be covered quite well, as I have relatively long hair [...], so I can cover it when I want and not cover it when I don't. And it can also be covered in high percent with my clothes ...

This is a conscious decision, so the intentions and purposes of the tattooed person conduct the choosing of bodily position and lead to the situated visibility, controlling gazes and discursive possibilities. The embodied position of the tattoo determines whether the motif goes into a discourse, what kind of discourse it takes part in and how it participates.

Discourses with implicit and explicit self-positions

As we have demonstrated earlier, cultural and personal meanings of the tattoo and its position on the body regulate whether a tattoo takes part in a discourse and in what way. The third main aspect is the positioning of participants. In this section, we introduce some of these positions related to two topics: the fact of tattooing, and the motif and its meaning(s) connecting to the motives of the tattooed person. We can differentiate diverse discourses in the interviewee's narrative, namely, inner discourse or self-dialogue, and variants of private and public discourses. Henceforth, we instantiate all three forms of discourse.

Public discourse

Public discourse occurs on the social media platform of the tattoo studio, where the tattoo was made. These interfaces are used by tattoo artists to post and present their works as artistic creations, and for followers to react to them. This discourse is defined by the rules of social media and data protection regulation, and it is only about the motif as an artwork on the body without the life story or personal motives. The implicit and explicit self-positions and the implicit and explicit positioning by others coincide with each other. The self-position, which is an implicit self-position when the tattoo is posted by the artist on social media, becomes explicit when the interviewee elaborates it in an interview: 'I am wearing this tattoo and [followers] like this motif'. The implicit position assigned by followers that becomes partly explicit in an interview is: 'You are a tattooed person and we like the post/motif'. These concurring positions connect to her social identity as a tattooed person and form, affirm, and validate this identity. Although this positioning is connected solely to the motif, the fact of getting a tattoo, the motivations are also confirmed implicitly through this validation.

Inner discourse or self-dialogue

The second discourse is the inner discourse or self-dialogue of this woman connected to the autobiographical event and her grief process, which includes all her motives, as well as explicit and implicit self-positions. Her main position is explicit: 'I am a grieving sister' because 'My brother died'. This main self-position follows from not only the autobiographical event and familiar relation, but also her personal attitude to these. Her further motives and positions are all part of this main position and specify her mourning process. The first and most important self-position is: 'I am the one who imprints'. This self-position includes the personal decision the fact of recording and which autobiographical event is recorded, making this event eternal on the body, as well as the process of constructing her embodied self and identity. Therefore, this imprinting covers the fact, the object and the manner of remembrance. This embodied remembrance by a tattoo as a picture as an embodied 'lieu de memoire' (Nora, 1984–1992) leads to the next step in the grief process, to the memorial act in which the self-position is 'I am who is remembering'. The memorial act consists of both the inventory of this relationship and the commemoration of the significant other as a person, along with the hope for his well-being in a good place.

The motives and this self-dialogue demonstrate mostly that the autobiographical event chosen by the tattooed person is the starting point, and the meaning-making process happens through the picture. The picture has an original illocutionary force, and the embodied picture includes the illocutionary force of both the picture and the embodied positions. This embodied pictorial remembering, with its meanings connected to the motives of the wearer and the embodied positions of the tattoo, results in diverse discourses and discursive remembrance. The autobiographical, the social and the cultural selves are equally part of the discourse, but are defined mostly by the embodied self and its discursive consequences.

Private dialogue

The third form of discourse is instantiated as a private dialogue that can happen with family members and other intimate relationships such as friends or partners, but in this study, we only focus on the examples of private dialogues with family members.

This private dialogue with older family members has two distinct parts with sharp changes of positions between them. The first part of the dialogue is about the fact of tattooing connected to her first tattoo, mentioned by Kate:

> There came some remark from a distant family member anyway, which said 'well-well, I understand that there is an important message behind it, but why did you absolutely have to get this tattooed on yourself then, why couldn't you just keep it in your head.

These 'distant family members' not only conceptualize Kate in an evidently Cartesian ontology, separating soul and body, while she unifies these instances phenomenologically both in her experience and in her discursive rendering, but also assign discursive positions.

The implicit position of the wearer formed by older family members is 'I am a young woman in our family' and this position in a familial, social and cultural context is that young women do not have the right to tattooing, but older male family members have the right to express their disagreement concerning being tattooed. Therefore, the rights and duties are as defined by local cultural order as positions are shaped by it. Most of our interviewees change their socially and culturally defined position to an embodied direction, referring to their embodied self-position, and evocating the right to modify their body, asserting 'my body, my choice' in similar discourses, or using complex self-positions reflecting the inseparability of bodily and psychological experiences.

Kate chooses another discursive solution in this situation connected to her second tattoo, the owl, remaining in the cultural context and employing her cultural position while she changes the topic from the fact of tattooing to its meaning.

> At this tattoo of mine, these questions were not even raised, since no one, somehow no one felt like saying, well, 'but why couldn't you just say farewell to him inside yourself' (laughs) or something like that ... because it's a much more taboo topic.

So, this private dialogue with the same family members about the tragic life event through this meaning concerns a cultural taboo, resulting in a difficult to manage discourse in which Kate actively changes position. Her explicit position is: 'I am wearing a tattoo because of my brother's death' and her implicit position is: 'I am grieving, so I have the right to grieve in that way I want'. She sees the advantages of her active positioning by meaning of the tattoo and the cultural values and rules of grief, so she uses the main meaning without its complexities in other discourses also.

> Because I knew that there would not be so much teasing in connection with that, but people would say 'Oh, I'm sorry (for your loss)'. And then I would say 'ok, no problem, I mean no problem, I can talk about it', but somehow there were not such kind of clarifying questions in that case.

Death and grief as a topic and a discourse can be regulated, culturally bounded or even taboo. At the same time, the fatality can provide an opportunity not only to comply with these rules but also to escape from them by finding new solutions for grieving.

Discussion

Our aim was to present that tattoo-wearing can be interpreted as an embodied remembering, imprinting a respective significant autobiographical event on the body via a picture. This remembering practice is also a crisis-elaborating process, which can have several therapeutic implications.

The therapeutic implications of our study are related to the latest literature on tattoo research (Alter-Muri, 2020, Buckle & Dwyer, 2021; McCarty, 2019; McCarty & Christian, 2023; McCarty et al., 2023; Naude & Naudé, 2024) in several respects. Especially in areas emphasized by the social constructivist approach to therapy (McNamee & Gergen, 1992) and the collaborative dialogical practice (Anderson, 1997; Anderson & Gehart, 2007, 2022), such as the therapeutic relationship and the discursive nature of the construction of narratives, interpretations and selves. The acceptance of tattoo-wearing by a therapist validates life experiences and coping strategies of the client and leads to a trustful collaborative therapeutic relationship (McCarty, 2019). By engaging in dialogue about tattoos as pictures and as recorded symbols of significant life events, a therapist can gain valuable knowledge about life experiences, motivations, and purposes of their clients (McCarty & Christian, 2023). Tattoo series can help draw up a life path with significant events and their meanings (Buckle & Dwyer, 2021). Tattoo-narratives and storylines reveal the elements of the meaning-making process and allow insight into the cultural, relational, and personal values and beliefs of client (McCarty & Christian, 2023; McCarty et al., 2023). This supports the understanding of these values and beliefs, and results in a more sophisticated collaborative meaning-making process. Narrative and discursive strategies of clients in meaning-making reveal their self-conception (Naude & Naudé, 2024), their complex identity, and its temporal and contextual evolution (Buss & Hodges, 2017). These dynamic changes of storylines and discursive strategies often lead to more complex and positive interpretations and indicate personality development, as well as spur agency (Alter-Muri, 2020; Buckle & Dwyer, 2021).

The most important contribution of discursive psychology to counselling is that it highlights the performative nature of language and image, as opposed to its representational approach (Lester et al., 2018). Furthermore, analyzing different forms of discourses shows that self-aspects and positions are complex, dynamic, and constructed in social interactions (Lester et al., 2018). Tattooed bodies are both visual surfaces and communicative interfaces (Kosut, 2000), hence the bodily position of tattoos carries information about clients' relations to their body, their relations to the events imprinted, their communicative intentions, and purposes to conceal or to reveal them. Coverability and disclosure can connect to the intimacy or publicness of an event, and can provide information about their elaborated status and reveal how the attitude of tattooed persons changes dynamically over additional tattoos. Visible and invisible tattoos give rise to diverse discursive situations, identity positions and storylines. These positions are shaped in a social, cultural and interpersonal context, and are informative regarding the client's experienced agency, as well as their communication possibilities and strategies in these settings.

In sum, tattooing can be a self-supporting way of remembering and coping with crises, and engaging in conversation about tattoos with clients can be included in the therapeutic process. Further research would be necessary to clarify how life history tattoos appear in the therapeutic space, what kind of meaning construction processes they can initiate or mediate. Furthermore, a point of inquiry may be what kind of discourses result from everyday and therapeutic situations, and what positioning processes and agencies are connected to them. Additional research could examine what meaning constructions and positioning situations are created by tattoos specifically related to identities, and how these can be utilized in therapy and counseling.

Disclosure statement

No potential conflict of interest was reported by the author(s).

Funding

The research was reviewed and approved by the Hungarian United Ethical Review Committee for Research in Psychology (EPKEB) on the following reference number: [2023-98].

Data availability statement

In order to protect personal data, the interviews that support the findings of this study will not be released to third parties.

References

Alter-Muri, S. (2020). The body as Canvas: Motivations, meanings, and therapeutic implications of tattoos. *Art Therapy*, *37*(3), 139–146. https://doi.org/10.1080/07421656.2019.1679545

Anderson, H. (1997). *Conversation, language, and possibilities: A postmodern approach to therapy*. Basic Books.

Anderson, H., & Gehart, D. R. (2007). *Collaborative therapy: Relationships and conversations that make a difference*. Routledge/Taylor & Francis Group.

Anderson, H., & Gehart, D. R. (2022). *Collaborative-dialogic practice: RelationshIps and conversations that make a difference across contexts and cultures* (1st ed.). Routledge. https://doi.org/10.4324/9781003156260

Billig, M. (2009). Discursive psychology, rhetoric and the issue of agency. *Semen*, *27*. https://doi.org/10.4000/semen.8930

Bodor, P. (2012). IdentitY in discourse: The case of ascribing "Schizophrenia" to Europe and Hungary. In M. Heller & B. Kriza (Eds.), *IdentIties, ideologies and representations in post-transition Hungary* (pp. 117–153). ELTE Eötvös Kiadó.

Bredekamp, H. (2017). *Image acts: A systematic approach to visual agency*. De Gruyter. https://doi.org/10.1515/9783110548570

Buckle, J. L., & Dwyer, S. C. (2021). Embodied meaning making: Memorial tattoos as a visual expression of grief. *Death Studies*, *47*(1), 1–9. https://doi.org/10.1080/07481187.2021.1983889

Burkert, W. (1987). The dead, heroes, and chthonic gods. In W. Burkert (Ed.), *Greek religion* (pp. 190–215). Basil Blackwell.

Burr, V. (2015). *Social constructionism*. Routledge.

Buss, L., & Hodges, K. C. (2017). Marked: Tattoo as an expression of psyche. *Psychological Perspectives*, *60*(1), 4–38. https://doi.org/10.1080/00332925.2017.1282251

Caplan, J. (2000). *Written on the body: The tattoo in European and American history*. Princeton University Press.

Csekő, C., & Bodor, P. (2021). Embodiment a pszichológiában: a diszkurzív pszichológia olvasata [Embodiment in psychology: The discursive psychological interpretation]. *Replika*, *121–122*, 73–81. https://doi.org/10.32564/121-122.6

Davies, B., & Harré, R. (1990). Positioning: The discursive production of selves. *Journal for the Theory of Social Behaviour*, *20*(1), 43–63. https://doi.org/10.1111/j.1468-5914.1990.tb00174.x

Edwards, D., & Potter, J. (1992). *Discursive psychology*. Sage.

Harré, R., & Gillett, G. (1994). *The discursive mind*. Sage.

Harré, R., & Langenhove, L. V. (1999). *Positioning theory: Moral contexts of intentional action*. Blackwell.

Harré, R., & Moghaddam, F. (2003). Introduction: The self and others in traditional psychology and in positioning theory. In R. Harré & F. Moghaddam (Eds.), *The self and others: Positioning individuals and groups in personal, political, and cultural contexts* (pp. 1–11). Praeger Publishers/Greenwood Publishing Group.

Harré, R., & Moghaddam, F. (2015). Positioning theory and social representations. In G. Sammut, E. Andreouli, G. Gaskell, & J. Valsiner (Eds.), *The Cambridge handbook of social representations* (pp. 224–233). Cambridge University Press. https://doi.org/10.1017/CBO9781107323650.019

Holstein, J. A., & Gubrium, J. F. (1997). Active interviewing. In D. Silverman (Ed.), *Qualitative research: Theory, method and practice* (pp. 113–129). Sage Publications.

Korobov, N. (2010). A discursive psychological approach to positioning. *Qualitative Research in Psychology*, *7*(3), 263–277. https://doi.org/10.1080/14780880902822321

Kosut, M. (2000). Tattoo narratives: The intersection of the body, self-identity and society. *Visual Sociology*, *15*(1), 79–100. https://doi.org/10.1080/14725860008583817

Lester, J. N., Wong, Y. J., O'Reilly, M., & Kiyimba, N. (2018). Discursive psychology: Implications for counseling psychology. *The Counseling Psychologist*, *46*(5), 576–607. https://doi.org/10.1177/0011000018780462

McCarty, D. L. (2019). Tattoo narratives and counseling. *Theses and Dissertations, 3344*. https://scholarworks.uark.edu/etd/3344

McCarty, D. L., & Christian, D. D. (2023). Assessing the Adlerian lifestyle through tattoos narratives. *Journal of Constructivist Psychology*, *36*(2), 248–267. https://doi.org/10.1080/10720537.2022.2164532

McCarty, D. L., Christian, D. D., & Henderson, R. R. (2023). The usefulness of tattoo narratives for expressing life-story constructs. *Journal of Constructivist Psychology*, 1–23. https://doi.org/10.1080/10720537.2023.2294327

McNamee, S., & Gergen, K. J. (1992). *Therapy as social construction*. Sage Publications.

Middleton, D., & Edwards, D. (1990). *Collective remembering*. Sage Publications.

Mitchell, W. J. T. (1994). *Picture theory. Essays on verbal and visual representation*. University of Chicago Press.

Naude, F., & Naudé, L. (2024). (Tat)who Am I? Tattoos as an expression of narrative identity. *Identity*, *24*(2), 79–94. https://doi.org/10.1080/15283488.2024.2310845

Nora, P. (1984-1992). *Les lieux de mémoire. I-III*. Gallimard.

Pócs, É. (2019). Preface. In E. Pócs (Ed.), *Body, soul, spirits and supernatural communication*. Cambridge Scholars Press (pp. x–xvi).

Potter, J., & Wetherell, M. (1987). *Discourse and social psychology: Beyond attitudes and behaviour*. Sage Publications.

Rush, J. A. (2005). Scarification and tattooing: A cultural history of pain. In J. A. Rush (Ed.), *Spiritual tattoo: A cultural history of tattooing, piercing, scarification, branding, and implants*(pp. 1–76). Frog Ltd.

Valsiner, J. (2020). Embodiment in action: The making of the body. In J. Valsiner (Ed.), *Sensuality in human living* (pp. 23–34). Springer Briefs in Psychology. Springer. https://doi.org/10.1007/978-3-030-41743-7_2

Wash, I. (2020). Interpreting public policy dilemmas: Discourse analytical insights. *Humanities and Social Sciences Communications*, *7*(1), Article 129. https://doi.org/10.1057/s41599-020-00621-9

Wiggins, S. (2014). On the accountability of changing bodies: Using discursive psychology to examine embodied identities in different research settings. *Qualitative Psychology*, *1*(2), 144–162. https://doi.org/10.1037/qup0000012

Wiggins, S., & Cromdal, K. O. (2020). *Discursive psychology and embodiment*. Palgrave Macmillan. https://doi.org/10.1007/978-3-030-53709-8

OPEN ACCESS

Towards a psychotherapy publishing ethics concordat

Gary Winship, Ann Scott and James Edgar

ABSTRACT

The changing landscape of data management and privacy have far-reaching implications for psychotherapy research regarding confidentiality, informed consent, and data de-identification in scientific publications. This paper reports on discussions among international psychotherapy journal editors regarding ethical guidelines governing publishing qualitative case study research. A range of psychotherapy journals have been examined and it notable that there is a variegated approach to consent and data-identification, and there are contested ethical standpoints when it comes to publishing research. These contestations are presented and six key areas for debate are set out, i) explicit informed consent, ii) prospective and retrospective consent, iii) data de-identification and bricolage, iv) withdrawing consent, v) education and training, and vi) inconsentable circumstances. These are set out as base for further discussion towards the development of a Psychotherapy Publishing Ethics Concordat (PEC).

Case study as research

Psychotherapy practitioners make discoveries that provide vital knowledge beneficial to clients and colleagues alike, and it is a professional obligation for psychotherapists to share knowledge of good practice, and crucially, when psychotherapy has not been effective, or where there has been an has adverse outcome. A core method of research in psychotherapy is the social science convention of a case study approach where in-depth material, drawing from the client's case history, is presented with a longitudinal account of the process of the clinical work. The detail of the case is examined to understand both the causal pathways of distress, and a means to identify which aspects of psychotherapy have affected a positive or negative outcome. Taken on their own, these fine grain qualitative single case study accounts might offer only preliminary insights into theory and practice, but as Rustin (1996) points out, over time when amalgamated with other case studies from fellow

Supplemental data for this article can be accessed online at https://doi.org/10.1080/13642537.2024.2384864

practitioners, these accounts incrementally knit together a critical mass of generalisable evidence that can influence practice and education in the field.

Until recently, most psychotherapy and psychoanalytic journals have allowed authors to choose from a range of approaches to protect patient and client privacy in order to ensure confidentiality and anonymity, confidentiality, but there are changes in attitude towards data protection and consent that have seen most publishers setting out more rigorous requirements for consent when publishing case study material. For example, in 2021 the publisher Wiley asked the *British Journal of Psychotherapy* (BJP) editorial board to review its position regarding publishing ethics and confidentiality. The guidance for authors at that time was explained in 'Notes on Confidentiality',

> Authors will be aware that there is a conflict between the privacy of patients on one hand, and the need when writing up cases for publication to provide lucid and transparent clinical material, on the other. No perfect solution to this dilemma exists, although there are a number of methods which authors tend to use: disguising material, consent from patients (preferably written), composite material from a number of comparable cases, or the report of colleagues' or supervisee's clinical cases, are various methods in use for protecting confidentiality . . . follow requirements that your professional organization has in relation to obtaining consent from the patient, and identify these in the covering email with your submission. Your manuscript should make explicit that all identifying details have been disguised. (BJP, Author Guidelines)

Wiley asked that the BJP editorial board to review these guidelines with a view to adopting informed consent as the standard approach to publishing case material, and this petition for informed consent was reflected in negotiations by other publishers and psychotherapy journals at large. The request for a standard position of informed consent has been embraced by some journals such as the *Journal of Analytic Psychology*, but most other journals have convened more protracted debates considering the possible hinderances and limitations of informed consent. Loewenthal (2022) argues that we are seeing a demise of the case study approach, and that this is a fundamental threat to the psychotherapy profession which will alter the traditional process of psychotherapy research and will have a deleterious impact on student and trainee experience where in-depth case discussion is less central to the pedagogic process

The new stringencies for publishing psychotherapy case studies have been driven by the increased accessibility of journals (Holloway, 2022) and the changes in the law regarding data management under the auspices of General Data Protection Regulation (GDPR) which came into effect with the 2018 UK Data Protection Act introducing a Europe-wide law replacing the UK Data Protection Act 1998.

Increased concern about how personal data is managed has been reflected in the research community insofar as online publishing has widened the audience far beyond print subscribers. Psychotherapy journals are available through thousands of institutional libraries across the globe, and accessible to individual readers on-line, communication via social media is rapid, and we are challenged to consider the use of clinical material beyond publications, including broadcasts, podcasts, conferences, and the pedagogical use of case accounts for trainees. Psychotherapy journal editors, publishers, and authors are all now grappling with the concerns about the privacy and security of individuals' data and identity protection. The therapist has a fiduciary duty of care to the client, but equally, there is a professional obligation to share new knowledge with colleagues in the interest of alleviating the suffering of many.

Whether consent or disguise has been adopted, it has been standard practice in publishing psychotherapy research to ensure that any personal details of the client are anonymised, with all identifying specific details removed, such as, name, age, address or references to specific places and any identifying physical markers such as tattoos or other identifying bodily characteristics (Gabbard, 2000). And it is worth noting that this approach has so far been largely effective in protecting patient and client identity, enabling the body of psychotherapy knowledge to grow. There have been very few incidents whereby patients have recognised themselves. In the BJP, across 40 years since its inception, there has only been one case where a client has asked for their case account to be redacted. And there has not been a case in the *International Journal of Psychoanalysis* (IJP), as far as can be recalled, where an analysand has complained about being described in case account (Grier, personal communication).

Data management law – a changing landscape?

The GDPR guidelines in fact carry only 24 mentions of the word 'research' across the entire act, pertaining to only a minor part of 7 of the 173 Recitals. In terms of the ethical management of data, we might surmise that the evolution of GDPR is clearly not the result of an ethical failure of researchers managing data sets, but rather a response to the failure of large corporations to protect details and identities of millions of customers, the loss of bank details, identity theft, scamming, phishing and so on. For example, the data breach at Yahoo (2013, 3 billion accounts exposed), Aadhaar (2018, 1.1 billion Indian identity and biometric information exposed), LinkedIn (2021,

700 million users), Sina Weibo (2020, China, 538 million accounts) and Facebook (2019, 533 million), to name a few of the best known.

The management of personal data in social science research, we might argue, has been unhelpfully impacted by the consequences of data breach scandals in fields that lie outside of the social and health scientific research community insofar as researcher now must include several pages of print about data protection which potential research subjects are expected to read.

That is not to say that there are not serious shortcomings in health research, for instance, Randomised Clinical Trials (RCTs) from 49 Cochrane Review Groups from May 2020 to April 2021, were found to be poorly constructed or 'bad' trials, accounting for up an estimated £8 billion in misspent research funding (Pirosca et al., 2022). But notably, none of these trials were considered bad science because of poor ethics, instead bias, methodological flaws and weak analysis, were the problem.

It is timely to consider the ethical implications for psychotherapy research and other qualitative research that seeks to generate small scale levels of case study data, and to consider how GDPR might shape the ethical steps in psychotherapy research. GDPR has cast a long shadow, and we might wonder if qualitative researchers have done enough to de-couple the stringencies of GDPR from the sort of data management which is the province of health and social science research. GDPR helpfully offers protection to individuals from large companies that hold the personal data of millions of customers but may have unhelpfully changed the research landscape by increasing anxiety and concerns about litigation, engendering a more defensive research culture in health and social sciences that in long term may impinge on progress, and might even threaten the future of the profession of psychotherapy (Loewenthal, 2022).

Publishing psychotherapy case studies –towards a psychotherapy concordat

This next section sets out six key areas for debate. The intention is not to necessarily to set out resolutions here but rather identify areas or principles where we may agree to disagree. The six areas are, i) explicit informed consent, ii) prospective and retrospective consent, iii) data de-identification and bricolage, iv) withdrawing consent, v) education and training, and vi) inconsentable circumstances.

Explicit informed consent

At the heart of current debates is the question of informed consent and then the implications for publishing thereafter. GDPR Recital 159 (5) sets out the following guidance, 'To meet the specificities of processing personal data for scientific research purposes, specific conditions should apply in particular as regards the publication or otherwise disclosure of personal data in the context of scientific research purposes'. The 'specific conditions' that apply in psychotherapy research publications have been well established, and as discussed earlier, as a research active community of practitioners, patient and client data has been published with great care. The Committee for Publication Ethics (COPE), which is a body governing publishing standards representing over 13,000 journals, strongly recommends that informed consent is sought prior to publication. This guidance has been adopted by a number of health research and psychotherapy publishers and a number of journals have adopted informed consent as a default position, *Journal of Analytical Psychology, The Journal of Family Therapy, International Journal of Applied Psychoanalytic Studies, Counselling and Psychotherapy Review, Counselling and Psychotherapy Research, Psychology and Psychotherapy: Theory, Research, Practice.*

Not all psychotherapy journals and organisations have adopted a uniform position in regard to informed consent. See, for instance, a statement from the British Psychoanalytic Council (BPC) on publication ethics,

> For some, the inequality between therapist and patient and the influence of transference in the analytic situation make it questionable whether patient consent to use of clinical material can ever be regarded fairly as informed consent, that is to say, consent freely or autonomously given. Therefore, it is argued, the problematic nature of consent means that, even with consent, disguise is always necessary. However, even then, disguise cannot be relied upon as a cure since it is often ineffective or effective only at the expense of clinical truth. Even with consent and effective disguise, further ethical considerations arise regarding the therapist's ethical duty not to do harm and the intrusion of the request for consent into the analysis; the impact on the patient of such request depending upon its meaning for them in their internal world and with their particular personal history; and the further impact on them of later learning what their therapist has said or written about them and their analysis.

Francis Grier, the Editor of the *International Journal of Psychoanalysis*, has concerns about the pressure to move towards informed consent and has agreed with the publisher Taylor Francis that informed consent is not adopted as a default position for the journal, 'At IJP, we have never asked for informed patient consent, and we are not going to do so now. If an author asks for patient consent, we would not seek to stop them . . . but our concern in such cases would be even more to check that real anonymisation has occurred'. (Grier, personal communication).

Prospective and retrospective consent

The process of consent is not normally established ahead of therapy, but in the circumstances where research is formalised, either by an institution such as a university, or as part of a funded research programme, then it is a requirement for the patient or client to consent to this process before the commencement of therapy. This approach to case study research will ordinarily be required to proceed through seeking a favourable ethical opinion from an ethics committee or ethics body. A record of such consent should be kept by the author and noted in the paper.

GDPR Recital 33 (3) states, 'Data subjects should have the opportunity to give their consent only to certain areas of research or parts of research projects to the extent allowed by the intended purpose'. The area of psychotherapy research here would be that of seeking consent from the patient or client to disseminate certain details about the therapy. Consent forms are often used, specifying that the client agrees to material being published, and that their identity will be disguised. It is worth saying, however, that not all patients or clients will wish to be anonymous, and there are instances where therapist and client may be joint authors, perhaps the best-known example of this is Barnes and Berke (1971) *Two Accounts of a Journey Through Madness*. In the instance of a co-constructed publication, or where the client has asked to be identified, the benefits and potential disbenefits of identification will need to be discussed with the client.

Many practitioners will only consider writing up a case study after therapy has been completed. Seeking consent during therapy might well disrupt the therapeutic alliance, or create unease for the client, or disrupt the transference relationship in a way that would jeopardise the treatment (Davids, 2022). Arguably, seeking consent after therapy is completed is best practice because the therapy itself should not be sullied by an intent to do research on the therapist's part, and seeking consent from the client to undertake research may unnecessarily be distracting for them too. Seeking retrospective consent after therapy has finished might be optimal and should be subject to discussion in supervision. But there are occasions where seeking retrospective consent might be contra-indicated, impractical and potentially unethical (Winship, 2007). For example, to make unsolicited contact, especially if it some years after therapy has finished, could be unhelpful to the client and contact through email or letter might be a breach of confidentiality. And if it is many years after treatment, the contact details for the client may have changed.

De-identified data and bricolage

The term anonymisation is used interchangeably with the term de-identified data (Tucker et al., 2016). In all instances, even where consent has been agreed, it is onerous on the author to ensure that the identity of the patient or client is not recognisable. In the process of writing up a case study or multiple case studies, data should be pseudonymised, that is, all records adopt a pseudonym from the outset ensuring that the name of the patient is not identified anywhere in written records. It is noteworthy that according to GDPR Recital 26, that, 'The principles of data protection . . . [do] not apply to anonymous information, namely information which does not relate to an identified or identifiable natural person or to personal data rendered anonymous in such a manner that the data subject is not or no longer identifiable. This Regulation does not therefore concern the processing of such anonymous information, including for statistical or research purposes'.

Where clinical material has been sufficiently de-identified to the extent that that no-one including the client are recognisable, then explicit consent is not required by the GDPR. The use of de-identified data or disguise entails finding the right balance between reducing the risk of identification and at the same time maintaining the accuracy of the case data to ensure the fidelity of the findings. High levels of data de-identification, such as altering gender or birth order detail, may result in data that cannot accurately answer the research question(s), or may result in misleading or inaccurate interpretation of the findings (Tucker et al., 2016).

The International Psychoanalytical Association (IPA) has a set out guidance for members who are considering publishing case material in books and journal articles (International Psychoanalytical Association, 2018), referring to the 'ethical asymmetry' in seeking consent from an analysand. Ethical asymmetry here refers to the inherent power imbalance in the therapist-client relationship which means that consent cannot be de-coupled from transference. Instead, the IPA sets out a case for ensuring that there is a 'community of concern' that protects the patient. This takes the shape of a culture of confidentiality in which protection of the patient's privacy is a paramount concern at every point in the development and dissemination of clinical material, from discussion with supervisors, tutors or senior colleagues, through to the scrutiny of peer reviewers and journal editors.

Although one hundred percent anonymisation is optimal, in most cases it is not possible, and a residual risk of re-identification must be factored in. There may be instances where the client will not identifiable by a third party but the client may still recognise themselves. This is a general challenge for all fields of research, and the caveat for presenting data that might be identifiable, is the question whether the identification will be harmful or be used for the purpose of an attack by another person or agency. There will be some case accounts where more exacting details are required, for example, working with a client who suffered the loss of a limb, and as such it may be deemed that anonymisation is not possible, and seeking consent may be the optimal ethical choice.

Another approach to ensuring that data is de-identified can involve the use of composite case material, that is, overlaying details from different case accounts to disguise one individual. We might think of this approach to composite case study as bricolage. A composite approach to case study is a newly constructed case that is based on two or more actual experiences of working with a client. With a composite case study, the risk of presenting material that is too thinly disguised, thereby increasing the risk of identification, is precluded. Equally, a composite approach removes the possibility that an overly thick disguise will sacrifice so many key details that the fidelity of the case material is lost.

Guidelines for generating composite case material are limited, but from those that do exist (Duffy, 2010) there appears to be an approach that resembles bricolage (Levi-Strauss, 1962). The bricolage involves the imaginative development of a single case account that builds from a clinical dilemma or experience and draws together material selected from actual case material which is then supplemented with the subjective experience of the therapist. One of the disadvantages of a composite approach would be that the fidelity of the material is compromised and lacks authenticity. One of the key advantages of having consent as recommended practice is that it ensures that case material is drawn from lived experience, ensuring that authors and researchers are not misleadingly fabricating data.

Withdrawing consent

There is a question of whether informed consent can be taken in perpetuity. Duffy (2010) argues,

> Clients may comply at one point in time because they feel honoured and special to have been asked and then years later may reread the account for which they originally provided consent to have published and feel trivialized, angered, or retraumatized by the rereading. (Duffy, 2010, p. 143)

It is worth ensuring that the client is aware that by providing consent, it is difficult, if not impossible to withdraw it in the future. That is, while on-line versions of papers can be edited, paper copies in circulation cannot. For these reasons it may well be ethically diligent to take a position that consent is lasting and cannot be withdrawn.

What might happen if a patient or client consented to publication, but later withdrew their agreement after the article was published? The Committee for Publication Ethics (COPE) states that, 'once the information has been published, revocation of the consent is no longer possible' (Barbour, 2016, p. 3). Some publishers, such as Wiley, do argue that it is possible to consider retracting an article, or part of an article, after publication, if a client subsequently withdraws consent. This would prioritise patient privacy over published records and would be consistent with Article 17 of GDPR where there is a right to erasure (right to be forgotten). The same principle would apply where a paper had been published without informed consent, and a patient recognised themselves in a paper, and requested that the paper or section of the paper be redacted.

Education and training

The use of illustrative case study data material is essential for all psychotherapy trainings, and tutors need to draw on case material in order to effectively educate students and build their capacity for research-based practice (Greenwood & Loewenthal, 2005). The pedagogical culture of all psychotherapy trainings should adopt and extend the type of 'community of concern' approach recommended by the IPA. As such, all case study data should be de-identified in accordance with ethical guidance on confidentiality, and this should be modelled in the presentations of tutors and lecturers, and then followed through in the micro-indicators for assessment, ensuring that students are demonstrating a capacity for de-identifying case material data. This demonstrable knowledge should follow through into qualifying papers, and thereafter in publications and conference dissemination activities.

And it might be onerous on training organisations, as well as therapeutic associations, to ask all clients, before the commencement of therapy, to grant permission for the subsequent publishing of any anonymised case study content. It is onerous on trainings and psychotherapy organisations to hold the burden of responsibility to ensure that there is an ethical footing for publishing research. Developing and delivering an ethical framework for research and publishing research requires a concordat that is generated across stakeholders, from organisations, trainings, practitioner authors and then journal and journal editors.

Inconsentable circumstances

Anagnostaki (2022) describes the process of submitting a paper to a journal, and how the journal then requested that she get written consent from the family described in the case study, and how this was a challenge because the family centre had closed down. Other inconsentable circumstances might include the death of the patient or client, or where treatment has finished many years previously so retrospective consent would be difficult because the client's contact details might have changed. The author and supervisor might agree that publishing an account of therapy where the outcome has been poor, would be of great benefit to colleagues. Where the client has died, a suicide for instance, there might be great value in a practitioner sharing their knowledge and experience, but it would be unethical to contact grieving relatives. The author, the supervisor or expert peer, might conclude that seeking consent would inappropriate, but that there are justifiable grounds for setting out the case with the ethical caveats for de-identified data and case disguise.

Conclusion

The publisher Taylor & Francis (2023), with input from an advisory group chaired by Stephen Seligman, has now stipulated that all clinical material must be published in reliably anonymised form. They set out that authors are required to give specific and detailed undertaking of how the case material is anonymised, and that authors, reviewers, and editors keep a record of their decision-making. Taylor and Francis argue that these steps will mean that editors and publishers can be confident that clinical material will contain no information that will allow a third party to identify the patient or client and minimise the risk clients will recognise themselves. With these measures, Taylor and Francis assert that the client will find no grounds for complaint about breach of confidentiality or reputational damage.

The guidance from Taylor & Francis is robust, though it does not have the nuance and detail that we have set out in this paper. And it does not resolve discrepancies between the journals when it comes to consent, for instance, the *International Journal of Psychoanalysis* maintains not having consent as a default, while the *Journal of Analytical Psychology* does have consent as a default. In this paper we have discussed circumstantial caveats and have proposed a middle ground in the consent debate and provided detail about the approach to data disguise. With the considerations we have discussed, we concur that the requirements set out by Taylor and Francis for anonymisation should be universally adopted, and these clarify what is expected of authors also helpfully shaping what reviewers should be looking out for. Author guidelines can be updated to carry information about the process of anonymisation including the stipulation that they set out in the paper the decisions they have taken. In this way the journal will have a record of the recommendations and decisions taken by the reviewers and editors, thereby ensuring that process of the review itself should be sufficiently transparent and robust.

The psychotherapy research community must engage with debates about consent that cut across the broad scientific research community. Psychotherapy research seeks to generate and harness a vibrant body of practitioner research knowledge that has methodological fidelity and authority as evidence which can inform policy and commissioning. At the same time, psychotherapy must ensure that it is not conflated with medical research, and so not governed by research ethics where approaches and treatments are invasive or pharmacological.

The changes in the ethical landscape might open up new opportunities for evolving case study research and writing. Holloway (2022) considers the value of co-authored accounts of therapy ahead of a consenting process,

> If therapy is currently ongoing, could therapist and patient writing cooperatively and co-constructively together about the process of therapy become an aspect of the therapy itself, and an extension of the therapeutic process?. (p143)

The idea of client-therapist co-authored accounts is not new (Barnes & Berke, 1971). It would be enfranchising and potentially enriching to our knowledge of psychotherapy to see an up-lift in co-authored papers. We might expect, and perhaps even welcome, autoethnographic accounts of the lived experience of psychotherapy from patients themselves. There would still need to be careful consideration of whether a patient wishes to be identified in an autoethnography or co-constructed paper, taking into account the longer-term consequences of revealed identity.

Although one might equally be cautious about sharing writing with clients, as Donachy (2022) notes,

> Anecdotally, I think there is a fear that by showing our patients what we have written about them, especially when this involves details of traumatic and/or abusive life experiences, we will cause harm, which is, of course, the antithesis of our objective. (p390)

In Donachy's (2022) paper she goes on to recount her experience of sharing her case account with her client towards the end of therapy ahead of a plan to publish the case study, and indeed, Donachy tells us that the client, who had otherwise progressed well, was taken back to a place of self-doubt and that the client 'became upset and her negative view of herself came alive' (p392). Nonetheless, the client consented to Donachy publishing the paper.

There is possibility that stipulating informed consent as a default position, that we might unwittingly increase the likelihood of complaint. Patients and clients might say, 'I consented when I was in a vulnerable position as client'. Preparing case material should happen in discussion with a clinical supervisor or experienced qualified peer (another practitioner with more than five years post qualification and experience in publishing psychotherapy case studies), and then finally editors and reviewers will consider the ethical positioning of a potential publication. Taken together, this sets out the type of 'community of concern' that the IPA calls for.

Authors are encouraged to go beyond a simple statement of obtaining research ethics approval, instead highlight potential issues (for example, with vulnerable clients) and how these were addressed. This is important both for transparency and sharing learning with colleagues. In all circumstances authors are advised to keep a record of their discussions regarding the decision to publish, detailing the opinions of supervisors, or experienced colleagues. It is onerous on authors to have evidence of their process in determining their decision to publish. Psychotherapy journal editors and reviewers can offer an feedback and ethical opinion to authors, but ultimately the responsibility for ensuring the ethical protection of the client in a published paper lies with the author.

The Declaration of Helsinki on the Ethical Principles involving Human Participants states that authors should address and confirm in a cover letter, either that the research was granted approval by an authorised ethical body stating the name of the organisation, or where a study was conducted without such a body, authors should state the ethics jurisdictions of this context and describe in detail how they complied with, for instance, an ethics code of practice of a professional association. Authors should confirm whether participants provided informed consent and specify whether this was written or verbal assent, and with research involving children under 16 years, following written consent by a parent or legal guardian. Authors should confirm in writing that they have obtained written informed consent but the written consent itself should be held by the authors themselves. The process of consenting is discussed in supervision and considerations given to identifying the best time for seeking consent (usually this would be recommended towards the end of therapy). A record of such consent should be kept by the author lead and made clear in the paper. If a study presents service level activity data, authors should confirm that they have received approval from a relevant research governance body, for example, the National Health Service.

Acknowledgments

The following colleagues have been consulted and have informed the debate developed in this paper, The International Council of Editors of Psychoanalytic Journals, The British Journal of Psychotherapy Editorial Board, Francis Grier (Editor, *International Journal of Psychoanalysis*), Arthur Niesser (Editor, *Journal of Analytical Psychology*), Universities Psychotherapy & Counselling Association (UPCA).

Disclosure statement

No potential conflict of interest was reported by the author(s).

ORCID

Gary Winship http://orcid.org/0000-0001-6336-3317

References

Anagnostaki, L. (2022). The process of gaining consent, retrospectively, when the institution has closed down. *Journal of Child Psychotherapy*, *48*(3), 398–405. https://doi.org/10.1080/0075417X.2022.2125044

Barbour, V. (2016). *COPE council. Journals' best practices for ensuring consent for publishing medical case reports*. COPE. http://bit.ly/2h8WvrS

Barnes, M., & Berke, J. (1971). *Two accounts of a journey through madness*. Ballatine Books.

Davids, J. (2022). Publishing: An act of intrusion and/or collaboration? *Journal of Child Psychotherapy*, *48*(3), 378–388. https://doi.org/10.1080/0075417X.2022.2137836

Donachy, G. S. (2022). Seeking consent: Some thoughts about sharing a draft with a patient. *Journal of Child Psychotherapy*, *48*(3), 389–397. https://doi.org/10.1080/0075417X.2022.2139401

Duffy, M. (2010). Writing about clients: Developing composite case material and its rationale. *Counseling and Values*, *54*(2), 135–153. https://doi.org/10.1002/j.2161-007X.2010.tb00011.x

Gabbard, G. O. (2000). Disguise or consent: Problems and recommendations concerning the publication and presentation of clinical material. *International Journal of Psychoanalysis*, *81*(6), 1071–1086. https://doi.org/10.1516/0020757001600426

Greenwood, D., & Loewenthal, D. (2005). The use of case study in psychotherapeutic research & education. *Psychoanalytic Psychotherapy*, *19*(1), 35–47. https://doi.org/10.1080/02668730512331341564

Holloway, R. (2022). Consent for publication and the future of psychoanalysis. *Journal of Child Psychotherapy*, *48*(3), 406–415. https://doi.org/10.1080/0075417X.2022.2138943

International Psychoanalytical Association. (2018). Report of the IPA confidentiality committee. https://www.ipa.world/IPA_DOCS/Report%20of%20the%20IPA%20Confidentiality%20Committee%20(English).pdf. Accessed 30/05/23.

Levi-Strauss, C. (1962). *The savage mind*. Paris.

Loewenthal, D. (2022). Is psychotherapy fundamentally threatened, with the demise of published case studies, to become neither an art and/nor a science? *European Journal of Psychotherapy & Counselling*, *24*(3), 263–268. https://doi.org/10.1080/13642537.2022.2115646

Pirosca, S., Shiely, F., Clarke, M., & Clarke, M. (2022). Tolerating bad health research: The continuing scandal. *Trials*, *23*(1), 458. https://doi.org/10.1186/s13063-022-06415-5

Rustin, M. (1996). The generation of psychoanalytic knowledge: Sociological and clinical perspectives. *British Journal of Psychotherapy*, *13*(4), 527–541. https://doi.org/10.1111/j.1752-0118.1997.tb00338.x

Tucker, K., Branson, J., Dilleen, M., Hollis, S., Loughlin, P., Nixon, M. J., & Williams, Z. (2016). Protecting patient privacy when sharing patient-level data from clinical trials. *BMC Medical Research Methodology*, *16*(1), 77. https://doi.org/10.1186/s12874-016-0169-4

Winship, G. (2007). The ethics of reflective research in single case study inquiry. *Perspectives in Psychiatric Care*, *43*(4), 174–182. https://doi.org/10.1111/j.1744-6163.2007.00132.x

Wished I'd been there: Reflections on the special issue's articles as refracted through my appreciations for qualitative researchers' innovativeness

Tom Strong

ABSTRACT

Since the early 1990s, the innovativeness and critical responsiveness of qualitative researchers in studying psychotherapy and mental health has been astonishing to witness. A social constructionist or postmodern (e.g. with narrative, solution-focused, and collaborative approaches) therapist who went on to conduct, teach, and supervise qualitative research, I bring an appreciative view of this recent history to comment on the articles of this Special Issue. This history shows qualitative researchers developing and refining their methods to pose new questions and ways of answering them in line with therapist curiosities about meaning making. Qualitative research also became a tool for surfacing social justice concerns, or for answering or addressing questions in novel contexts. The innovativeness of qualitative researchers often derives from how new ideas, concerns, and sense-making practices are honed by methodical rigors that extend beyond the one-off understandings or hunches therapists develop through working with clients. Though use of any method has limitations on what can be claimed from its use, what matters most is that good qualitative research offers useful understandings. From this appreciation of qualitative research's recent history and its potential usefulness to therapists and mental health workers, I selectively comment on the following articles.

Taking up the EJPC's editor's invitation to review this special issue's articles and comment on them reminded me of how dynamic and innovative qualitative research has been in its recent history. A veteran of conferences like this one yielding these articles, I read them as a recently retired white male Canadian professor having a process-oriented, meaning-making focus on therapy. These articles showcase different qualitative research topics, methods, counselling-related contexts, epistemological-ontological considerations, outcomes related to varied processes, ethical and procedural issues, and researcher reflections on their work. They also raise concerns about how qualitative research is conducted and used in this era of evidence-based practice. Qualitative research of psychotherapy and mental health concerns is relatively new, as are many approaches to qualitative research, though case studies have informed understandings of therapy since the days of Freud. Each research approach poses questions and answers them in different ways, informed by distinct ideas on what data is to be collected, how that data should be analyzed, and how knowledge claims from such analyses are made. In this manner, qualitative research of therapy and mental health often invites readers and knowledge users to understand therapy and mental health phenomena in new ways. Some qualitative research can substantiate what therapists hear anecdotally from clients or what they might hear from prospective clients in unfamiliar contexts of practice, but what matters in reading qualitative research is whether they learn something useful for their practice. The articles do not cohere under a common theme but showcase recent issues, methods, and outcomes of qualitative research addressing contemporary psychotherapy and mental health concerns.

Context

For readers unfamiliar with qualitative research conferences on mental health, at these events researchers present study results, while highlighting methodological and theoretical aspects of conducting and reporting on their research. The findings here will interest many readers, depending on their methods and contexts of practice. However, the research methods and ideas informing them also show innovative ways to make sense of client concerns and the processes of therapy. Such conferences bring together researchers of diverse cultures (i.e. ethnicities, research methodologies, theoretical orientations, professional identities) reflecting different curiosities, research customs, and contexts of practice. While therapists may consider their approaches to practice pluralistic (e.g. Cooper & McLeod, 2009), qualitative research has been diversifying at an exciting and near-dizzying pace. The questions of qualitative researchers have also been changing, often requiring new 'theory-methods' combinations (Clarke, 2005) to answer them. A scan of the tables of contents for Denzin and Lincoln's six editions (1994, 2000, 2005, 2011, 2016; Denzin et al., 2023) of the Sage Handbook of Qualitative Research shows how qualitative methods and issues relating to using them have been rapidly changing. Early qualitative methods primarily comprised phenomenology, ethnography, focus groups, grounded theory, and case studies. Qualitative research has had modern and postmodern phases, extending into what some now refer to as a posthuman era (Taylor & Hughes, 2016), to address how to understand how humans are influenced by their technologically mediated realities. Today, handbooks encompass various approaches for each early method – while similar handbooks showcase newer methods like narrative analysis, discourse analysis, and action research. Therapy had its first qualitative research book in McLeod (2000) and the American Psychological Association reluctantly accepted qualitative methods just over a decade ago (Levitt, 2013). That reluctance will be familiar to many readers here and for years was seen by quantitative researchers as dividing 'serious researchers' from those of us doing qualitative research.

This reluctance was also my backdrop as a qualitative researcher of the then new postmodern or discursive therapies. The reluctance derived from a belief that the hypothesis-testing methods of the natural sciences were required for answering important social science questions. In this positivist way, social scientists tried to prove or disprove hypotheses consistent with the theories or assumptions they already had regarding the variables to be measured and questions to be answered. For today's qualitative researchers, to be accused of positivism is to be insulted. Answers to their qualitative questions are typically arrived at in an exploratory, inductive, bottom-up manner, through interviews, observations, and interpretive methods. Quantitative researchers used theory-informed measures and procedures which controlled how and what respondents could say about a topic of interest, and then statistically analyzed responses to these measures. Grounded theory, an early qualitative method (Glaser & Strauss, 1967), was developed in part to learn what study participants might say that was not already framed and worded for them by research questionnaires and scales. Qualitative research is interpretive and messier than quantitative research but increasingly accepted by therapists who find useful information and insights into client concerns and their conversational work with clients.

Qualitative methods: Eras and issues in bringing meaningful order to messy complexities

Unlike the well-controlled studies of quantitative researchers, qualitative researchers seem at home in the 'messy' (Law, 2004) complexities of mental health and psychotherapy. Their varied methods innovatively diversify in response to theoretical and other debates, enabling new ways of posing and answering questions. Whether established or innovative, qualitative methods may help bring sense-making order to messy complexities, though their analytic findings often come with a partializing and reductive cost (Valsiner, 2023). Such outcomes (e.g. themes, discourses, narratives, etc.) inform via interpretive part answers, but practicing therapy involves responding to the holistic confluence of client concerns, circumstances, and immediacies of therapy interaction. Thus, therapists reading and using qualitative research face knowledge translation challenges: are the qualitative results useful to practice? Translating such knowledge also brings up Ryle's (1945) famous distinction between knowing that some phenomenon of research interest generally is what it is, and knowing how any knowledge should be used therapeutically. Knowing that a concern can be understood in particular ways can orient therapists to what might be salient to discuss though knowing how to facilitate that discussion is another matter. The researchers contributing to this special issue used varied qualitative methods to understand the thats and hows of messy human concerns in more rigorous ways than therapists might anecdotally reflect on them.

Part of the reason qualitative research diversified its methods in such a dramatic manner was because of questions raised by practitioners, but also in response to other researcher preoccupations. Linguistic insights, changing ontological assumptions, social justice concerns, and technological advances prompted new lines of inquiry difficult to conceptualize or answer using 'traditional' qualitative methods. This doesn't mean that newer methods of qualitative research make the older methods obsolete by any means. Early qualitative researchers (e.g. feminist scholars) invited participants to answer questions from their own experience, in their own voices or language (Lincoln & Guba, 1985). Therapists, like most qualitative researchers today, continue to rely on conversational data of this kind. As use of qualitative methods expanded further questions arose. The answers led to refinements in research methods, new standards in reporting qualitative research (Levitt et al., 2018), and fulsome debates at conferences like the one from which the articles following were derived. Critique can be an ally of innovation, though a few therapist-critics (e.g. Loewenthal, this issue) are concerned that some developments in qualitative methods have strayed from factors relevant to practicing therapy.

A postmodern and social constructionist era in the 1980s and 1990s greatly influenced how therapy and qualitative research developed. First person accounts of experience seemed inadequate once language and how it was used became a focal concern (e.g. Bruner, 1986; Lakoff & Johnson, 1980; Potter & Wetherell, 1987). Words, narratives, discourses, and ways of talking came to matter to many therapists and researchers – sometimes in similar ways, but often very differently. Diversity, power, and complexity became central concerns of qualitative researchers. Postmoderns and social constructionists also brought an appreciation for researcher reflexivity and collaboration that translated into new forms of feminist and action research. Questions came to be seen as tools for constructing preferred realities or deconstructing taken-for-granted understandings. Where quantitative researchers went to great lengths to control researcher bias, action researchers (e.g. Reason & Bradbury, 2001) saw their research relationships as fostering constructive and deconstructive curiosities.

Another development seeming to stray even further from therapy has been informing some recent approaches to qualitative research: posthumanist (e.g. Braidotti, 2013) or socio-materialist considerations (Barad, 2007; Latour, 2013). Subjectivity, for posthumanists and socio-materialists, is complicated by the ways humans are interwoven with their environments and technologies. What we experience, do, foresee, and overlook relates to how we are situated. Our horizons of knowing and possibility shift with our entanglements in different configurations of social, material, and technological reality (Barad, 2007). This is not news for eco-systemic family therapists influenced by Gregory Bateson (1972), but research methods have been slow to catch up with his insights. Relatedly, and borrowing from the process-ontological thinking of Deleuze (2005), our situated subjectivities can be seen as engaged with the emergent challenges and opportunities through which we become who we are. Subjective experience, by this view, is a moving target and efforts to describe its essence obscure how people are situated in emergent engagements with their socio-material circumstances (Stenner & Nichterlein, in press). We are somewhat different people depending on the horizons of our actual and virtual circumstances. Developing qualitative methods that make sense of these situated and complex ways of being and becoming has been a new kind of research frontier (e.g. Clarke et al., 2017). Such emergent methods may yield results that can sensitize therapists to salient contextual and process-oriented features of client experiences while avoiding understandings normally seen as character or personality oriented.

Finally, it is important to acknowledge that qualitative research of therapy and mental health in this era of evidence-based mental health is still often seen as preliminary to eventual randomized clinical trials where qualitative knowledge can be more robustly proven using hypothesis-testing measures. Evidence-based practice in mental health presumes a hierarchy (pyramid) of evidence with systematic reviews of meta-analyses of randomized, clinical trials (i.e. quantitative) (e.g. Berlin & Golub, 2014), though that need not sideline qualitative researchers from having useful things to say about mental health practice (Lester & O'Reilly, 2015). One trend within qualitative research of mental health has been a meta-synthesis approach to inform clinical policy and practice (e.g. Horton, 2020). Meta-syntheses involve aggregating then identifying patterns in the findings of different qualitative studies focused on similar research questions, often encompassing studies using different qualitative research methods. Having been involved in these kinds of studies recently (e.g. Tseliou et al., 2021), I was reminded of a core distinction between quantitative and most approaches to qualitative research – for single studies or across studies – namely, the centrality of interpretive work to qualitative analyses. Where the findings derived from quantitative measures enable objective statistical analyses, qualitative studies rely on trustworthy interpretive judgments regarding meaningful patterns or significant details in different kinds of data, arrived at through transparent and inter-subjective processes. Whether identifying experiential themes, narratives, cultural discourses, or interactional practices – these qualitative ways of sense-making typically attain their rigor by adhering to interpretive protocols corroborated through the judgments of other researchers. By extension, readers of qualitative studies afford another level of interpretive quality control by reading the research processes and judging for themselves if the researchers' interpretive findings are plausible, trustworthy, and useful to their ways of practice.

For readers trained in the last couple of decades, understanding or conducting qualitative research was often part of their training, though typically they learned only a few common methods (e.g. grounded theory, phenomenology, case studies). While some qualitative researchers developed or revised methods incorporating challenging social constructionist or socio-materialist insights, others made their methods (and the findings of those methods) more accessible. This latter direction is most evident in the cases of Thematic Analysis (TA, Braun & Clarke, 2023) and Interpretative Phenomenological Analysis (IPA, Smith & Nizza, 2022). Use of these methods has become increasingly common in mental health and psychotherapy research and feature in some of this special issue's articles. Theoretical purists may claim that important nuances are sacrificed in the flexible interpretive claims-making by researchers using TA (in finding common themes in qualitative data) and IPA (for interpreting lived experience within and across participants). Though findings from such studies may not seem conclusive, they can sensitize readers (Blumer, 1954) to potentially relevant or salient features of a circumstance, process, or client concern. While the aims of qualitative researchers and therapists may differ, both share an interest in bringing rigor to making sense of human concerns, the processes and practices of therapy included. My hope, by responding to the articles which follow, is that therapist-readers join me in finding helpful things to reflect on, and useful understandings of client and therapist circumstances and concerns.

My resonances with the special issue articles

The first article, 'Psychotherapeutic Research and Practice: Do we need to talk about "Efficacy"?' (Talens et al., 2024), is conceptual and addresses issues associated with how qualitative researchers relate to the assumptions informing evidence-based practice (EBP). An import from medical research, EBP came with a host of medicalizing assumptions (Strong, 2017) about the nature and intended outcomes of psychotherapy practices, and about practice-salient research and knowledge. Does therapeutic efficacy derive from precision use of evidence-based and standardized intervention protocols? Therapy funders tend to think so and regard standardized use of EBP interventions as ensuring practice is done safely and efficaciously. For this article's authors, however, an EBP logic is encroaching on therapy's dialogic relationships, extending to activities like training, supervision, and professionalization. Use of an EBP approach standardizes therapists' conversations with clients, holding both to what is supposed to develop within their conversations – to be efficacious and evidence-based. As the author(s) highlight, therapists adopting a hermeneutic, relationally oriented, approach are dialogically open to indeterminate developments (e.g. unexpected answers and needs for elaboration). This article zeroes in on the tension many therapists face navigating expectations between a quantitative, positivist EBP approach to therapy and a more discovery-oriented, qualitative (i.e. hermeneutic) approach.

The next article 'Travelling in time' (Smith, 2024) tackles a phenomenological challenge: how to make sense of changing experiences when using IPA. This is an example of when a research approach's theory-methods package is found lacking and in need of an innovation that doesn't invalidate the approach's foundational assumptions or practices. Here, the anomaly is how to address the immediate (i.e. lived) experience of talking with a researcher or therapist in ways that link a phenomenon (e.g. experience of a therapeutic intervention) to past or future experiences. While this temporal continuity focus is normal for narrative researchers, as the author discusses, the phenomenological focus here is on linking transformational self-experiences over past and projected future times. The article illustrates how IPA researchers, like many other qualitative researchers, adapt their methods to attain otherwise elusive understandings. Such innovations spark animated debates at qualitative research conferences, but in this case, in my view, they also help better align research and therapy.

While some psychological researchers and therapists focus on presumed universal features or essences of what it means to be human, others (e.g. social constructionists and socio-materialists) focus on differences that come with being humanly situated. The authors of 'Uncertainty and existential thinking' (Ullmann, 2024) adopt this latter focus, exploring the historical situatedness of existentialist thinking, and what that situatedness means for human subjectivity. Problematizing Yalom's existentialist 'givens' of uncertainty (external: death, freedom/internal: isolation and meaninglessness), the authors explore how these 'givens' are reflected in the thinking ('being' for Nail, 2018) evident across different historical eras. This historicizing of the 'givens' draws on other authors' accounts of thinking and subjectivity across time (this was not an interview study) and concludes with a similar presentation of postmodern subjectivity and its existentialist concerns. Readers of Foucault, Norbert Elias, or Charles Taylor will feel at home here, but those agreeing with Yalom, which universal existentialist themes are evident in life's uncertainties, may feel challenged here by the view that existential responses to uncertainty can vary with time.

One area of innovation in qualitative research has been on what constitutes analyzable data while another pertains to combining normally distinct qualitative methods. The authors of 'Using medical records in qualitative research. Advantages and limitations' (Bryniarska, 2024) turned to unconventional data to better understand how adolescent patients, parents, and professionals cooperated during anorexia nervosa treatment in a hospital setting. Combining the analytic procedures of Consensual Qualitative Research (CQR) in a Comparative Case Study (CCS) approach, the study brought therapists together to compare parents' emotional attitudes toward hospital treatment of their adolescent child as documented by an interprofessional treatment team. CQR is an interpretive process for arriving at consensual interpretations of qualitative data – in this case, of the non-standardized note-taking of the treatment staff. The CCS methodology was selected to enable the authors to contrast treatment team comments regarding a cooperating and a non-cooperating family (chosen after reviewing data for 37 patients) over hospital treatment that included a critical incident. This use of contrasting case studies from within a broader study (the CQR analyses of 37 patient families) is a way to more closely probe a clinical phenomenon for therapy-relevant understandings. Case studies have also been foundational to psychotherapy's early and continuing development.

An expanded, Bakhtinian (e.g. Bakhtin, 1981), view of dialogue within therapy informs the 'dialogic self' approach of Hubert Hermans (e.g. Konopka et al., 2019). It is an approach focused on people's dialogic engagements with others in their external world, but also with the inner dialogues they have within themselves. Facilitating a reflexive ability to use one's inner voice for self-compassion is the aim of the practice-focused inquiry: 'Developing reflexivity and self-compassion in group psychotherapy: A dialogical and narrative approach' (Viou & Eugenie, 2024). The researchers in this study tracked participants over 20 group therapy sessions – for shifts in their self-reflexive disclosures, from self-blaming to self-compassion. A combination of qualitative methods were used to classify and trace development in the kinds of self-disclosures (participant narratives) voiced in the group. Consistent with dialogic self-theory, participants' increasing abilities to spontaneously vocalize self-compassion in the group denote therapeutic progress. I am a fan of such research of therapy that produces practice-based evidence, and typically it relies on client feedback on therapist practice (e.g. Green & Latchford, 2012). Seldom does qualitative evidence from within actual therapy sessions get used to monitor client and therapist progress in ways consistent with models of therapy used by practitioners (see also Strong et al., 2008). This theoretically sophisticated article nicely exemplifies how therapist and researcher lenses can combine to answer practice relevant questions in useful ways.

The primary data of most qualitative researchers (and therapists) remains the words people use. However, meanings for any word's use are indexed to specific contexts, a limitation of one of qualitative research's most common methods: content analysis (Krippendorff, 2004). The authors of 'Exploring the grief journey of bereaved spouses: insights into the impact of sedation within palliative care' (Sani et al., 2024) use lexical software technology (ALCESTE) to quantify and contextualize the co-occurring words of bereaved spouses following palliative care. Thus, therapist readers are brought into layered contexts of grief (supporting a dying spouse with cancer, medical treatment of the dying spouse, and sedation as part of palliative care) in ways that help make sense of subjective nuances in meaning. The results illustrate the potential for some of the interpretive work of qualitative researchers to be done with content analytic software, helping researchers to become more focused on meanings associated with what the authors refer to as 'units of context'. As larger qualitative data sets and advances in artificial intelligence develop, I am curious to see what lexically oriented technologies like ALCESTE enable for future contextualized analyses of qualitative data.

Another medical context is the focus of inquiry by the authors of '"Lost in space and time": Fathers' experiences of preterm birth"' (Bognarne et al., (2024). Like the aims of the previous study, better understanding the emotional experiences of supportive family members in medically challenging circumstances can help to inform policies, education, and professional sensitivities when responding to their needs. The authors used IPA to probe these experiences for seemingly peripheral participants when there are preterm births. The themes derived from analyses of interviews with fathers experiencing preterm births helpfully highlight how hospital staff can prepare and respond to this subset of expecting fathers. IPA studies like this are increasingly common because they offer a useful way to gain insights into counselling-relevant phenomenon.

Trying to understand how therapists and clients make sense of and respond to each other in the emergent immediacies of their conversing has been a focus of many psychotherapy process researchers. The author of 'The body as mediator: Case understanding in salutogenic-oriented General Practitioner consultation' (Bahrs, 2024) adapt an innovative hermeneutic approach to closely examine the interactions between a patient and doctor where somatization has been a concern. The theoretically sophisticated case study reported is from a larger study and adopts a sequential view of a medical consultation. Focal to the analyses are actual responses of patient and doctor rated at each step in their interactional sequence, including the patient's embodied responses elicited as a felt sense by the doctor. This study reminded me of the great lengths therapy process researchers go to explicate meaning making as it occurs in the emergent immediacies of therapy interactions. The results of such studies offer new insights yet still incomplete understandings of subjective and inter-subjective therapy experiences that can sensitize therapists to how clients respond to them as they pursue therapeutic goals (Sidis et al., 2023).

Part of a therapist's role can involve responding to group experiences of trauma. Recent history suggests that developing group interventions to address trauma can problematically lag evidence supporting using the interventions, as was the case for Critical Incident Stress Debriefing. While quantitative researchers debate whether such interventions are helpful or harmful, their focus is largely on how well controlled (i.e. standardized) the intervention and research of its use has been (e.g. Stileman & Jones, 2023). The lived experience of participants of such interventions is seldom elicited and understood using methods like IPA, which is the focus of 'School organisational trauma during student suicide crisis' (Finegan, 2024). This study of 11 Irish guidance counsellors' experiences following student suicide that makes sense of what occurs and can be done in a school context. The results illustrate how qualitative findings from relatively few participants can helpfully inform professional practices and organizational policies.

People's experiences are seldom only communicated in words. We convey our meaning with tones of voice, choices of clothing or hairstyle, and in the case of 'Living with and Living by Tattoos – Discursive Analysis of a Bodily Practice' (Csekő et al., 2024) – through tattoos. A growing area of qualitative research has focused on data elicitation using visual methods (e.g. Pain,

2012). The authors of the case study here adopt a discursive psychology approach (e.g. Lester et al., 2018), which links the personal meanings the participant said about her tattoos to identifiable positions in cultural discourses. Positioning theory (Harré & Moghaddam, 2015) is indirectly related to the Bakhtinian voicings discussed earlier in my review of these articles and regards people as users (conscious and unconscious) of the words and visual tropes of cultural discourses. This participant's tattoos conveyed personal meanings, whether visible only to herself and intimate others (or not), and the kind of dialogues and reminders they might elicit from herself and others. In therapy, clients present many visual cues as to what matters to them, cues perhaps worthy of such discursive exploration.

The final article of this series reflects upon qualitative data ethics related to privacy. Personal data as it has been collected and used on online platforms (e.g. Meta) has been likened to a form of indentured servitude (Zuboff, 2019). In 'Towards a psychotherapy publishing ethics concordat' (Winship et al., 2024) the authors outline how recent trends in aggregating qualitative studies for meta-synthetic analyses, presents unforeseen ethical issues when clients consent to having their anonymized therapy participation documented for one study, but later find identifying details of themselves reported in meta-synthesis publications and presentations. This circumstance is especially likely to occur when case study data is aggregated and details used, like quotes or other recognizable features of one's participation in therapy. Ethics, like qualitative research of therapy, is in constant evolution. In Canada, national research ethics have been substantively revised to accommodate developments in qualitative research, and research with First Nations participants (Government of Canada, 2022). Here, the focus is on how journals publishing psychotherapy research can keep up with the meta-syntheses articles, given the privacy issues and lack of specific consent given by participants. The article surveys such journals and consults journal editors on the issues, enabling a more focused discussion ahead on the issues.

Discussion

I want to think Del Loewenthal for asking me to read and comment on these articles for this special issue. They pleasantly reminded me of the many conversations I had with students and colleagues regarding what would make their or our qualitative research practical, fundable, useful, defensible, and ultimately publishable. These special issue articles give a glimpse into the diverse presentations on offer at qualitative research conferences that broadly focus on therapy and mental health today. Those attending such conferences would typically consult their programmes to select presentations in a more focused way, say for IPA presentations or psychotherapy process research sessions only. I chose to read and respond to the articles here as someone who came late to qualitative research (at the turn of the millennium) but then dove right into its innovations, debates, and conferences. Nerdy as it might read, in my final years as an academic I came to think of the developments within qualitative research as more interesting than those occurring in approaches to therapy. My comments came from where each reading transported me, given my own immersion in recent developments in qualitative research of therapy and mental health.

I want to wrap up by commenting on Del Loewenthal's article. For me, it served as a reminder that qualitative research, like therapy dialogues, is a fickle activity that yields humble and invariably partial findings (see also, Valsiner, 2023). Del proposes equating aspects of phenomenological research and psychotherapy practice, particularly with respect to probing tacit knowledge. His concern is about how many therapists and qualitative researchers stray from describing subjective experience to focus on causal explanations of human concerns and therapeutic outcomes. We share a view that language can at best 'approximate' what clients and therapists attempt to use it to describe and that such attempts are specific to emergent developments in the conversation each has with the other. What matters, by this view, is finding language together (in therapy and research) that arrives humbly, inconclusively, yet still usefully, at what Wittgenstein (1953) described as 'perspicuous representations'.

Disclosure statement

No potential conflict of interest was reported by the author(s).

References

Bahrs, O. (2024). The body as mediator: Case understanding in salutogenic-oriented General Practitioner consultation. *European Journal of Psychotherapy & Counselling*, this issue.

Bakhtin, M. (1981). *The dialogical imagination* (M. Holquist, Ed.; C. Emerson & M. Holquist, Trans.). University of Texas Press.

Barad, K. (2007). *Meeting the universe halfway: Quantum physics and the entanglement of matter and meaning.* Duke University Press.

Bateson, G. (1972). *Steps to an ecology of mind.* Chandler.

Berlin, J. A., & Golub, R. M. (2014). Meta-analysis as evidence: Building a better pyramid. *JAMA*, *312*(6), 603–606. https://doi.org/10.1001/jama.2014.8167

Blumer, H. (1954). What is wrong with social theory. *American Sociological Review*, *19*(1), 3–10. https://doi.org/10.2307/2088165

Bognarne, E., Márta, G., Monostori, D., & Lampek, K. (2024). "Lost in space and time": Fathers' experiences of preterm birth. *European Journal of Psychotherapy & Counselling*, this issue.

Braidotti, R. (2013). *The posthuman*. Polity Press.

Braun, V., & Clarke, V. (2023). Is thematic analysis used well in health psychology? A critical review of published research, with recommendations for quality practice and reporting. *Health Psychology Review, 17*(4), 695–718. https://doi.org/10.1080/17437199.2022.2161594

Bruner, J. S. (1986). *Actual minds, possible worlds*. Harvard University Press.

Bryniarska, A. (2024). Using medical records in qualitative research. Advantages and limitations. *European Journal of Psychotherapy & Counselling*, this issue.

Clarke, A. E. (2005). *Situational analysis: Grounded theory after the postmodern turn*. Sage.

Clarke, A. E., Friese, C., & Washburn, R. S. (2017). *Situational analysis: Grounded theory after the interpretive turn* (2nd ed.). Sage.

Cooper, M., & McLeod, J. (2009). *Pluralistic counselling and psychotherapy*. Sage.

Csekő, C., Szél Csekő, A., & Bodor, P. (2024). Living with and living by tattoos – discursive analysis of a bodily practice. *European Journal of Psychotherapy & Counselling*, this issue.

Deleuze, G. (2005). *Pure immanence: Essays on a life*. Zone.

Denzin, N. K., & Lincoln, Y. S. (Eds.). (1994). *The sage handbook of qualitative research*. Sage.

Denzin, N. K., & Lincoln, Y. S. (Eds.). (2000). *The Sage handbook of qualitative research* (2nd ed.). Sage.

Denzin, N. K., & Lincoln, Y. S. (Eds.). (2005). *The Sage handbook of qualitative research* (3rd ed.). Sage.

Denzin, N. K., & Lincoln, Y. S. (Eds.). (2011). *The Sage handbook of qualitative research* (4th ed.). Sage.

Denzin, N. K., & Lincoln, Y. S. (Eds.). (2016). *The Sage handbook of qualitative research* (5th ed.). Sage.

Denzin, N. K., Lincoln, Y. S., Giardina, M. D., & Canella, G. S. (Eds.). (2023). *The Sage handbook of qualitative research* (6th ed.). Sage.

Finegan, C. (2024). School organisational trauma during student suicide crisis. *European Journal of Psychotherapy & Counselling*, this issue.

Glaser, B. G., & Strauss, A. L. (1967). *The discovery of grounded theory: Strategies for qualitative research*. Aldine Transaction.

Government of Canada. (2022). *Tri-council policy statement: Ethical conduct for research involving humans – TCPS 2 (2022)*. https://ethics.gc.ca/eng/policy-politique_tcps2-eptc2_2022.html

Green, D., & Latchford, G. (2012). *Maximising the benefits of psychotherapy: A practice-based evidence approach*. Wiley-Blackwell.

Harré, R., & Moghaddam, F. (2015). Positioning theory and social representations. In G. Sammut, E. Andreouli, G. Gaskell, & J. Valsiner (Eds.), *The Cambridge handbook of social representations* (pp. 224–233). Cambridge University Press. https://doi.org/10.1017/CBO9781107323650.019

Horton, L. (2020). Making qualitative data more visible in policy: A critical appraisal of meta-synthesis. *Qualitative Research, 20*(5), 534–548. https://doi.org/10.1177/1468794119881953

Konopka, A., Hermans, H., & Goncalves, M. (Eds.). (2019). *Handbook of dialogical self theory and psychotherapy: Bridging psychotherapeutic and cultural traditions*. Routledge.

Krippendorff, K. (2004). *Content analysis: An introduction to its methodology* (2nd ed.). Sage.

Lakoff, G., & Johnson, M. (1980). *Metaphors we live by*. University of Chicago.

Latour, B. (2013). *An inquiry into modes of existence: An anthropology of the moderns*. Harvard.

Law, J. (2004). *After method: Mess in social science research*. Routledge.

Lester, J. N., & O'Reilly, M. (2015). Is evidence-based practice a threat to the progress of the qualitative community? Arguments from the bottom of the pyramid *Qualitative Inquiry*, *21*(7), 628–632. https://doi.org/10.1177/1077800414563808

Lester, J. N., Wong, Y. J., O'Reilly, M., & Kiyimba, N. (2018). Discursive psychology: Implications for counseling psychology. *The Counseling Psychologist*, *46*(5), 576–607. https://doi.org/10.1177/001100001878046

Levitt, H. M. (Ed.) (2013). *Qualitative psychology* (Vol. 1). American Psychological Association.

Levitt, H. M., Bamberg, M., Creswell, J. W., Frost, D. M., Josselson, R., & Suárez-Orozco, C. (2018). Journal article reporting standards for qualitative primary, qualitative meta-analytic, and mixed methods research in psychology: The APA Publications and Communications Board task force report. *The American Psychologist*, *73*(1), 26–46. https://doi.org/10.1037/amp0000151

Lincoln, Y. S., & Guba, E. (1985). *Naturalistic inquiry*. Sage.

Loewenthal, D. E. (this issue).

McLeod, J. (2000). *Qualitative research in counselling and psychotherapy*. Sage.

Nail, T. (2018). *Being and motion*. Oxford University Press.

Pain, H. (2012). A literature review to evaluate the choice and use of visual methods. *International Journal of Qualitative Methods*, *11*(4), 303–319. https://doi.org/10.1177/160940691201100401

Potter, J., & Wetherell, M. (1987). *Discourse and social psychology: Beyond attitudes and behaviour*. Sage.

Reason, P., & Bradbury, H. (Eds.). (2001). *Handbook of action research: Participative inquiry and practice*. Sage.

Ryle, G. (1945). Knowing how and knowing that: The presidential address. In *Proceedings of the Aristotelian Society* (Vol. *46*. pp. 1–16).

Sani, L., Chemrouk, Y., Le Berre, R.,Ducos, M., Peyrat-Apicella, D., & Bacqué, M-F. (2024). Exploring the grief journey of bereaved spouses: Insights into the impact of sedation within palliative care. *European Journal of Psychotherapy & Counselling*, this issue.

Sidis, A. E., Bøe, T. D., Karlsson, B. E., Lidbom, P. A., Moore, A. R., Pickard, J., & Deane, F. P. (2023). In defence of loose ends: Psychotherapy process research in the real world. *New Ideas in Psychology*, *69*, 1–7. https://doi.org/10.1016/j.newideapsych.2023.101011

Smith, J.A. (2024). Travelling in time: Using interpretative phenomenological analysis (IPA) to examine temporal aspects of the personal experience of issues in mental health and well-being. *European Journal of Psychotherapy & Counselling*, this issue.

Smith, J. A., & Nizza, I. E. (2022). *Essentials of interpretative phenomenological analysis*. American Psychological Association. https://doi.org/10.1037/0000259-000

Stenner, P., & Nichterlein, M. (in press). Postmodernity in process: A new past for a future postmodern therapy. In O. Smoliak, E. Tseliou, T. Strong, S. Bava, & P. Muntigl (Eds.), *The Routledge international handbook of postmodern therapies*. Routledge.

Stileman, H. M., & Jones, C. A. (2023). Revisiting the debriefing debate: Does psychological debriefing reduce PTSD symptomology following work-related trauma? A meta-analysis. *Frontiers in Psychology*, *14*, 1248924. https://doi.org/10.3389/fpsyg.2023.1248924

Strong, T. (2017). *Medicalizing counseling: Issues and tensions*. Palgrave Macmillan.

Strong, T., Busch, R. S., & Couture, S. (2008). Conversational evidence in therapeutic dialogue. *Journal of Marital & Family Therapy*, *34*(3), 288–305. https://doi.org/10.1111/j.1752-0606.2008.00079.x

Talens, P. (2024). Psychotherapeutic research and practice: Do we need to talk about 'efficacy'? *European Journal of Psychotherapy & Counselling*, this issue.

Taylor, C., & Hughes, C. (2016). *Posthuman research practices in education*. Palgrave Macmillan.

Tseliou, E., Burck, C., Forbat, L., Strong, T., & O'Reilly, M. (2021). How is systemic and constructionist therapy change process narrated in retrospective accounts of therapy? A systematic meta-synthesis review. *Family Process*, *60*(1), 64–83. https://doi.org/10.1111/famp.12562

Ullmann, T. (2024). Uncertainty and existential thinking. *European Journal of Psychotherapy & Counselling*, this issue.

Valsiner, J. (Ed.). (2023). *Farewell to variables*. Information Age Publishing.

Viou, M. & Georgaca, E. (2024). Developing reflexivity and self-compassion in group psychotherapy: A dialogical and narrative approach. *European Journal of Psychotherapy & Counselling*, this issue.

Winship, G., Scott, A., & Edgar, J. (2024). Towards a psychotherapy publishing ethics concordat. *European Journal of Psychotherapy & Counselling*, this issue.

Wittgenstein, L. (1953). *Philosophical investigations* (E. Anscombe, Trans. & Ed.). Blackwell.

Zuboff, S. (2019). *The age of surveillance capitalism*. PublicAffairs.

Reading with love: Developing therapeutic imagination through purposeful engagement with qualitative research

John McLeod

ABSTRACT

This Special Issue of the *European Journal of Psychotherapy and Counselling* on Qualitative Research and Mental Health comprises a collection of papers that show how qualitative inquiry can be used to explore aspects of social experience that are relevant to counselling, psychotherapy and mental health, alongside other pieces that addresses methodological issues associated with this type of research. The present paper discusses these articles in relation to the question of how counsellors and psychotherapists can make use of routinely reading published research reports to support and enhance their work with clients. In particular, reading strategies are described that promote the development of therapeutic imagination.

Introduction

Psychotherapeutic work involves the capacity to draw on different ways of knowing (McLeod, 2016). The most fundamental way of knowing, for psychotherapeutic practice, is *moral* – an appreciation of the importance of care, hospitality and solidarity, and sensitivity to hurt and moral injury. Next comes *cultural* knowledge – the way the world looks from the world-view of a particular community, tradition, or heritage. Then *personal* knowing – what has been learned from reflecting on life experience. *Practical* or procedural knowing consists of being able to do things, such as begin or end a therapy session, or attend to several levels of action and communication (bodily, verbal, internal) at the same time. *Theoretical* knowing accesses stories, concepts, theoretical models and explanatory conversational strategies to identify patterns and cause-effect sequences, make sense of experience and anticipate future consequences. Finally, there is *scientific* knowing, generated by a global network of researchers committed to creating and disseminating knowledge products or packages (mainly written articles and reports) that are driven by four key principles: ongoing collegial critical dialogue around what counts as knowledge, commitment to transparency around how information was collected and analysed, responsibility to show how new knowledge claims sit alongside what is already known, and use of some kind of standardised reporting format.

There are undoubtedly other frameworks for thinking about ways of knowing (Bergner, 2006; Mika et al., 2020). However, whatever framework is adopted, the key point is that being able to separate out different ways of knowing makes it possible to view real-life practical dilemmas from a range of perspectives, with the effect of opening up new possibilities for action and understanding. One example of how this can be applied to counselling and psychotherapy practice is around the question of sharing personal biographical information about oneself, with a client. At a practical level, most therapists have been trained to avoid doing this, and have been schooled in a theoretical rationale that rationalises a distanced stance in interaction with clients. At the same time, personal knowledge inevitably enters a therapist's awareness during therapy sessions with a client, and possibly also a cultural voice reminding one that sharing personal stories is a valuable everyday strategy for developing a relationship with another person. To resolve this somewhat contradictory set of perspectives around how to handle therapist self-disclosure, over the course of my own career I have found it enormously helpful to read research studies – mainly qualitative investigations of client and therapist experience – that explored various aspects of this topic. A particularly valuable dimension of this area of scientific knowledge has been how it evolved over a thirty-year period, from a starting point of somewhat tentatively establishing that therapist self-disclosure could in some instances be helpful, through to the development of practice guidelines, and then eventually to a recognition of therapist self-disclosure as an act of solidarity (Goates et al., 2023).

Adopting a multiple ways of knowing framework makes it possible to see how and why research evidence can contribute to the practice of counselling and psychotherapy. Most of the time, a therapist is able to respond in the moment to a client, on the basis of deeply over-learned or 'metabolised' (Betan & Binder, 2010) personal, practical and theoretical ways of knowing. In some instances, however, these familiar perspectives fail to arrive at a secure means of moving forward. These moments represent potential *points of contact* between practice and research (McLeod, 2016). It is not feasible for all aspects of therapy to be research-informed – what happens between a client and therapist is too complex and emergent for that to be a realistic option. Instead, research knowledge offers a uniquely de-centred perspective that can be called on when necessary. A crucial element of research knowledge, during such episodes, is that it is not grounded in a position of certainty that specifies one right course of action. Rather, psychotherapy research studies are always framed as a dialogue in which alternative ways of understanding a phenomenon or ways of responding to a situation are weighed up. This is particularly the case in mature areas of research, such as therapist self-disclosure, which have evolved over time to produce a highly differentiated set of insights.

A capacity to *read* actual research studies is an essential dimension of being able to use scientific knowledge to inform practice (McLeod, 2015a, 2015b). Within therapist training, the experience of designing, conducting and participating in research is clearly valuable in terms of preparing the minority of practitioners who might go on to become researchers at a later stage in their careers. The experience of doing research also allows trainees to learn how to evaluate published studies on the basis of an appreciation of the real-life challenges and compromises associated with conducting an investigation. At the same time, reading research studies is vital preparation for doing research, because it allows a novice researcher to acquire an image of what a good study looks like, and the methodological options that are available (McLeod, 2022). Summaries of research studies in professional magazines, newspaper articles, textbook chapters, and systematic reviews, can be a good way to learn about what research is, or has been, carried out on a topic. However, such sources generally offer only headline news from a study, and seldom mention how the authors of a study reflected on the limitations of what they did, or made links between their approach and that adopted by other studies available in the literature. In addition, in respect of qualitative, autoethnographic and case studies, such summary accounts inevitably omit contextual detail or the emotionally evocative voices of participants.

There are many ways that skills and habits around reading research studies can be supported within training programmes, such as workshops on the structure and critical analysis of research papers, highlighting key studies as essential reading in respect of all topics in the curriculum, identifying appropriate use of research evidence within all assignments as a marking criterion, and trainers talking about studies that have had an impact on their own practice. It can be energising and informative for trainees to have opportunities to meet in groups to discuss specific research studies that are meaningful to them. In my career as a counsellor educator, I have generally advised students to commit themselves to reading at least one research paper each week, expect it to be a painful and frustrating experience at the start but – similar to acquiring any skill – an activity that will become easier and more rewarding over time.

Articles in this Special Issue

The articles in this Special Issue on Qualitative Research and Mental Health include both studies that use qualitative methods to explore areas of experience that are relevant to counselling, psychotherapy and mental health care and articles that examine the use of different methodologies and philosophical perspectives in qualitative inquiry. While quantitative therapy research has generally been viewed as providing evidence to inform policy-making, qualitative research has been characterised as being more relevant for actual practice, though its capacity to enrich practitioner awareness and understanding (McLeod et al., 2021). This Special Issue therefore represents an opportunity to reflect on the experience of reading qualitative studies with the aim of informing one's practice.

Bognarne et al. (2024) looks at the emotional and relational responses of men around the pre-term birth of a child. Sani et al. (2024) documents what it is like for an individual when end-of-life care for their spouse involves the use of sedation. Finegan (2024) explores the experiences of guidance counsellors in schools, following the suicide of a student. Csekő et al. (2024) provides a case analysis of the meaning of body tattoos for one person, in relation to themes of loss in their life. Bahrs (2024) analyses the interaction between a medical doctor and a patient, around developing awareness of the emotional significance of bodily symptoms. Viou & Georgaca (2024) investigates how shifts in the direction of greater self-awareness and self-compassion within members of a therapy group are expressed in the way that they talk with each other. Other papers in the Special Issue focus on making sense of the pros and cons of different ways of conceptualising and conducting research. Talens (2024) critically addresses the underlying concept of the person that underpins much mainstream psychotherapy outcome research. Smith (2024) considers the potential value for counselling and psychotherapy research of developments in longitudinal qualitative approaches that focus on how people change over time. Ullmann (2024) argues that ideas from existential philosophy introduced into psychotherapy by Irvin Yalom are highly relevant for qualitative inquiry, but suggests that it is necessary to appreciate that these themes have come to be expressed in different ways over the course of recent history. Bryniarska (2024) demonstrates how the use of medical records as qualitative data can be used to generate new ways of understanding the process of therapy for individuals receiving psychotherapy for eating disorders. Winship et al. (2024) discusses recent developments around the kind of ethical consent that is needed to publish a psychotherapy case study, and the implications of consent procedures for the ongoing viability of such studies within the psychotherapy literature.

These studies showcase the potential of qualitative research to contribute reliable knowledge that can be used to enhance practice and service provision in the fields of counselling, psychotherapy and mental health (Levitt et al., 2024). In the remaining sections of the present commentary piece, I share some of the ways that I – or you – can read with a purpose, to use such written texts as resources for practice.

Reading research articles to inform practice

It is possible to identify a set of core skills that underpin the capacity to read research to inform practice. It is necessary to know how to search for, and access, relevant research articles, using search tools within on-line University and college libraries, Google Scholar, ResearchGate, and journal websites. It is also helpful to know one's way around the counselling and psychotherapy research literature for example, to have an idea of which keywords to use in searches, or why certain topics may be under-represented. A key skill is understanding how and why research articles are structured in a particular style – typically along the lines of the format developed by the American Psychological Association. Such understanding allows readers to have confidence that particular types of information (e.g. the aims of a study, the methods used to collect and analyse data, etc.) can generally be found in the same place within an article. When using research to inform practice, it is essential to appreciate that one of the central principles of science is that a study should be written-up in a manner that would allow another researcher to replicate it (i.e. test the validity or generalisability of its findings). As a consequence, in many research articles, the task of informing practice by providing rich clinical detail is only a secondary consideration. This means that reading a research article can be a frustrating experience for practitioners because the information that is most meaningful for them is either highly condensed or only available by following up references that lead to other sources where practice-relevant material is available (e.g. in a treatment manual).

Knowing your practice

It is not possible, or useful, to try to read all the research that is produced because there is too much of it. Instead, it is necessary to be selective, and be guided by a sense of what you are interested in or want to know more about, or where you have identified gaps in your knowledge and competence. To read with the purpose of informing your practice, it is therefore necessary to know your own practice. Within the field of counselling and psychotherapy, it is possible to identify many different patterns of practice. Some colleagues devote their careers to becoming specialists in a particular area, such as neurodiversity, eating disorders, working with college students, or providing personal therapy for other therapists. By contrast, others operate in general practice therapy, such as in front-line community counselling agencies used by clients with a wide range of issues. Many therapy practitioners combine seeing clients with a variety of other therapy-related roles, such as supervision, training, management, research, writing, and involvement in professional organisations or as public intellectuals. Others work at the interface between counselling/psychotherapy and other disciplines. Beyond these broad categories of practice, there may be specific elements of the process of therapeutic work that are significant, either at a particular stage in one's career or over an extended period. For example, some practitioners develop a particular interest in therapy endings, using expressive arts techniques, or how to facilitate effective between-session client homework and behavioural experiments. A strong interest in an aspect of therapy practice may be motivated by a realisation that it is something that one is struggling with, or because it represents an area where one's life experience makes it possible to make a distinct contribution to the profession as a whole. In some instances, both of these factors may be relevant.

As I read the articles in this Special Issue, I was very aware of how my response and curiosity were shaped by my pre-existing practice interests. I have had very little experience of working with eating disorders, so the specifically eating disorder-related findings reported in Bryniarska (2024) did not connect in a strong way with my practice. On the other hand, I have a strong interest in the implications of different ways of delivering therapy, so the findings of Bryniarska (2024) that described the effects of a residential mode of treatment helped me to gain a better understanding of how that form of provision can have an effect on the relationships between the patient and members of their family. As a therapist and supervisor, an important guiding principle of my practice is that different people are helped by different things at different times (McLeod, 2018). Reading Bryniarska (2024) had the effect of enhancing my capacity to engage in conversations with clients and supervisees about the potential value of finding residential opportunities that might offer opportunities for intensive therapeutic or sanctuary.

Sometimes, also, reading a research study can reveal a gap in one's competence. I am part of a generation in which tattoos were rare, have never really understood what they might mean to a person, and as a result, have never broached discussion of this topic with clients who exhibit tattoos. Reading Csekő et al. (2024) helped me to develop a capacity to engage with clients around the personal and relational meaning of their tattoos, where such a theme might be relevant to their goals for therapy.

As a counselling educator, I have had a longstanding interest in supporting practitioners in fields such as education and health and social care, to develop ways of embedding counselling skills and psychotherapeutic perspectives into their work with clients and service users (McLeod & McLeod, 2022). Several of the papers in this Special Issue expanded my awareness of specific areas of frontline embedded counselling practice: Bognarne et al. (2024), Sani et al. (2024), Finegan (2024) and Bahrs (2024).

When reading such studies, I do not necessarily expect that any of them will have an immediate impact on my practice. My aim at first reading a paper is to decide on whether it is in principle relevant to an area of my practice. If it seems potentially relevant, I then save it in a folder. For instance, within a general embedded counselling folder, I have created sub-folders around topics such as childbirth, bereavement and GP-patient consultations. When I am faced with a situation – in teaching, supervision or my own practice – in which such an aspect of my work emerges as problematic in some way, I am then able to immerse myself in the resources within that sub-folder. An important aspect of this strategy of collecting or curating sets of studies that are potentially relevant, is that no single study on its own is likely to provide a sufficient guide to practice. Instead, significant practical insights depend on being able to compare, contrast and triangulate across and between several articles.

Reading with love

Because we read all the time, there is a tendency to take the act and process of reading for granted – it is just something that one does. However, reading research articles to inform practice calls for a particular *way* of reading. Anyone who doubts this is recommended to consult a truly wonderful and inspirational paper by Elliott Kuecker (2024), who makes a distinction between the kind of distanced, cognitively focused reading (i.e. collecting information) that most of us learn at school and an alternative type of reading in which we enter – and are touched by – the world and reality being depicted by the author. A detailed example of what this second type of reading looks like is illustrated by Mercieca and Mercieca (2014) in a reflection on how one of them (a teacher of children with disabilities) was moved by reading a book written by the mother of a child with severe cerebral palsy. In this instance, being moved entailed revisiting and reframing their own experience as a practitioner, at both cognitive and emotional levels. Borrowing from the French philosopher Gilles Deleuze, this process is described by Mercieca and Mercieca (2014) as *reading with love* – an intensive experience with similarities to 'plugging into an electric circuit'. In other words, the text being read is not being appraised in relation to other texts, but instead has the effect of energising the reader by evoking personally significant meanings and memories. The effect of reading with love is not that the reader stays essentially the same, but better-informed. Rather, the reader is changed by the act of reading.

What does this have to do with becoming a better therapist? How can reading with love equip one to be more responsive with clients? Two concepts that might help us to make sense of these questions are *therapeutic imagination* and *mindlines*. The idea of therapeutic imagination was introduced in a book by the psychoanalytic psychotherapist Jeremy Holmes (2014) as representing an essential core process within the therapist. First, the therapist attends closely to the client through intensive listening. There then follows a phase of what Holmes describes as *reverie*, in which the therapist allows the client's experience, story and way of being to 'flow through' them (Holmes, 2014, p. 7). At some point, the therapist then needs to formulate this imaginative state into some kind of verbal response. Finally, out of this process there emerge possibilities for action. The capacity and willingness of the therapist to engage in reverie or imagination, based on the interplay between what the client brings and the inner world and life experience of the client, is a crucial element in this sequence. This way of relating is similar to reading with love, and in fact Holmes (2014) book is organised around examples of how reading literary fiction can be viewed as practice and rehearsal of the ability to use therapeutic imagination. What Kuecker (2024) and Mercieca and Mercieca (2014) show us is that reading with love need not only occur in response to literary fiction – it can also take place in response to other forms of writing. Even – one might suggest – research articles. Also, while Jeremy Holmes is grounded in a theoretical tradition in which free-floating attention and reverie are highly valued, the importance of therapeutic imagination has been recognised within other therapy approaches (see, for example, Rubinstein & Lahad, 2023).

The notion of clinical mindlines was developed over 20 years ago, as a way of understanding how doctors and other health and social care practitioners made use of a range of sources of evidence to inform their work with clients (Gabbay & Le May, 2022; Greenhalgh, 2023). Interviews with medical practitioners and ethnographic studies of interactions between patients and doctors in general practice settings showed that practitioners did not apply clinical guidelines and research evidence in a straightforward, linear manner. Instead, they appeared to create complex, holistic forward-branching internal mental networks of possible lines or directions that treatment might take. While the ideas and information included in mindlines might well refer to recommendations from clinical guidelines, they would also incorporate conversations with colleagues, learning from earlier cases, personal experience, inputs from the patient's support network and community, and many other sources. Just as an expert chess-player can imaginatively think several moves ahead, these physicians were able to create uniquely individualised maps of how a patient's condition might unfold over time in response to a range of contingencies Although there do not appear to have been any studies or analyses of the use of clinical mindlines by counsellors and psychotherapists, it seems highly likely that such capabilities comprise an essential element of what it means to be able to 'think like a therapist'.

Returning to the experience of reading research studies to inform practice, it becomes possible to see that the two styles of reading described by Kuecker (2024) and Mercieca and Mercieca (2014) serve different functions. The more emotionally-distanced, information-oriented reading operates as a type of horizon-scanning around new ideas and evidence generated by the research community, and as a strategy for identifying and collecting articles that might possess practical value at some point in the future. By contrast, being faced with some kind of practice dilemma, and intensively reading a group of relevant studies from a position of love, has the effect of enriching one's therapeutic imagination or mindlines, in respect of that aspect of one's work. This deeper type of reading calls for an ability to imaginatively recreate the experiences of both participants in a study and those who are conducting the investigation, and to allow one's own experience of similar situations to be viewed from a new perspective.

A valuable means of facilitating reading research articles with love is to meet with colleagues or learning partners to read and discuss a published paper together. This kind of activity can take place in workshops and seminars within training programmes, as well as through journal clubs that operate within organisational settings and communities of practice (New et al., 2024; Western Cape HPSR Journal Club Team, 2022). What tends to happen in such situations is that different members of the group are drawn to different segments of the text or exhibit quite different emotional responses to what is being read. This has the effect of expanding the horizon of understanding each member of the group, in a way that requires them to move beyond their initial interpretation of the source article.

The discussion of reading research articles within the present paper has largely focused on reading qualitative studies and case studies. However, reading with love, as a means of developing therapeutic imagination, is also possible in relation to quantitative studies such as reports of randomised clinical trials. For example, McPherson et al. (2020) conducted workshops in which key stakeholders – clients, family members, GPs – were able to read about and hear presentations on a controlled statistical study of psychotherapy for depression. In the ensuing group discussion, it was clear that engaging with that research study had acted as a catalyst for participants to become more aware of, and articulate, what therapy meant for them. This project demonstrates that even if quantitative research is primarily oriented toward the production of objective cumulative knowledge, readers are still able, in appropriate circumstances, to imaginatively grasp the human experience behind the numbers.

Conclusions

The qualitative and methodological articles brought together in this issue of the *European Journal of Psychotherapy and Counselling* represent a welcome addition to the psychotherapy and mental health literature. My aim, in the present paper has been to offer an invitation to reflect on how these articles might be read, and the practical psychotherapeutic purposes to which such readings might be applied. At the outset, such an endeavour may seem awkward and difficult. My own experience has been that reading research in ways that meaningfully informed my practice only really started to make a difference when it became a skill and a habit.

Looking forward, it is possible to identify strategies that might support a broader appreciation within the counselling and psychotherapy professional community of the potential value of routinely reading research articles. At the present time, there is a curious absence of a genre of critical/appreciative commentary on research articles. Our critical understanding of novels, poems, plays, and other cultural products is supported by an ability to access critical reflection offered in newspaper and magazine articles, as well as in academic texts. There is an absence of similar sources with respect to therapy research articles. In addition to helping readers to engage with research articles, in the sense of being better able to see what they offer, such writing might also have the effect of enabling authors to learn about how to write more effectively for different audiences – to write with love. Some academic journals already enable critical reflection on published articles by commissioning commentary pieces or through discussion threads in which readers can engage in dialogue around their reactions to articles. It would also be useful to know more about the reading patterns of therapy trainees and practitioners. In the present article, I have described some of my own ways of reading research – it is highly likely that there are many other strategies that are equally effective.

It is also essential to be sceptical about reading – to be alert for what is not being said in an article or cannot be said and the intrinsic limitations of the written word. Reading research can be enlightening and helpful when it affords a way of knowing that provides balance and creative tension when set against other ways of knowing. However, placing too much weight on text has the effect of buying into colonialist strategies for 'wording the world', that elevate the worldview and epistemology of the privileged while suppressing everyday wisdom (Mika et al., 2020). Ultimately, therapy is a form of practical action – a performance that is embodied, creative, intuitive, improvised and relational. The process of 'wording' therapy – describing it through any kind of written text – inevitably struggles to do justice to these elements of its lived experience. Decolonised therapy training and practice involves the ability to understand how academic and scientific writing abstracts the interconnected and emergent reality of the world into linear causal sequences. In the context of therapy training and ongoing therapist development, reading research runs the risk of reinforcing a top-down expert-driven position if it is treated as a uniquely privileged form of knowing. By contrast, reading research reinforces solidarity and collaboration when it constitutes one element in a broader communitarian way of being (Mendoza-Newman & Erickson Cornish, 2023).

Disclosure statement

No potential conflict of interest was reported by the author(s).

ORCID

John McLeod http://orcid.org/0000-0002-8545-2844

References

Bahrs, O. (2024). The body as mediator: Case understanding in salutogenic-oriented General Practitioner consultation. *European Journal of Psychotherapy & Counselling*, this issue.

Bergner, R. M. (2006). The many secure knowledge bases of psychotherapy. *American Journal of Psychotherapy*, *60*(3), 215–231. https://doi.org/10.1176/appi.psychotherapy.2006.60.3.215

Betan, E. J., & Binder, J. L. (2010). Clinical expertise in psychotherapy: How expert therapists use theory in generating case conceptualizations and interventions. *Journal of Contemporary Psychotherapy*, *40*(3), 141–152. https://doi.org/10.1007/s10879-010-9138-0

Bognarne, E., Márta, G., Monostori, D., & Lampek, K. (2024). "Lost in space and time": Fathers' experiences of preterm birth. *European Journal of Psychotherapy & Counselling*, this issue.

Bryniarska, A. (2024). Using medical records in qualitative research. Advantages and limitations. *European Journal of Psychotherapy & Counselling*, this issue.

Csekő, C., Szél Csekő, A., & Bodor, P. (2024). Living with and living by tattoos – discursive analysis of a bodily practice. *European Journal of Psychotherapy & Counselling*, this issue.

Finegan, C. (2024). School organisational trauma during student suicide crisis. *European Journal of Psychotherapy & Counselling*, this issue.

Gabbay, J., & Le May, A. (Eds.). (2022). *Knowledge transformation in health and social care: Putting mindlines to work*. Taylor & Francis.

Goates, J. D., Szymanski, D. M., Pulice-Farrow, L., & Gonzalez, K. A. (2023). "Me being myself isn't a barrier": Identity and praxis of nonbinary psychotherapists. *Journal of Counseling Psychology*, *71*(1), 48–62. https://doi.org/10.1037/cou0000718

Greenhalgh, T. (2023). Books: Knowledge transformation in health and social care. Putting mindlines to work in knowledge construction. *British Journal of General Practice, 73*(731), 274–275. https://doi.org/10.3399/bjgp23X733101

Holmes, J. (2014). *The therapeutic imagination: Using literature to deepen psychodynamic understanding and enhance empathy.* Routledge.

Kuecker, E. (2024). A closer kind of reading. *International Journal of Qualitative Studies in Education, 37*(6), 1577–1584. https://doi.org/10.1080/09518398.2024.2342694

Levitt, H. M., Hamburger, A., Hill, C. E., McLeod, J., Pascual-Leone, A., Timulak, L., Buchholz, M., Frommer, J., Fuertes, J., Iwakabe, S., Martinez, C., Morrill, Z., Knox, S., Langer, P., Muran, J. C., Oddli, H., Řiháček, T., Tomicic, A., & Tuval-Mashiach, R. (2024). Broadening the evidentiary basis for clinical practice guidelines: Recommendations from international qualitative psychotherapy researchers. *The American Psychologist.* Advance online publication.

McLeod, J. (2015a). Reading case studies to inform therapeutic practice. *Psychotherapie Forum, 20*(1–2), 3–9. https://doi.org/10.1007/s00729-015-0036-5

McLeod, J. (2015b). Reading qualitative research. *European Journal of Psychotherapy & Counselling, 17*(2), 194–205. https://doi.org/10.1080/13642537.2015.1038729

McLeod, J. (2016). *Using research in counselling and psychotherapy.* Sage.

McLeod, J. (2018). *Pluralistic therapy: Distinctive features.* Routledge.

McLeod, J. (2022). *Doing research in counselling and psychotherapy* (4th ed.). Sage.

McLeod, J., & McLeod, J. (2022). *Embedded counselling; A practical guide for helping professionals.* Open University Press.

McLeod, J., Stiles, W. B., & Levitt, H. (2021). Qualitative research: Contributions to psychotherapy practice, theory and policy. In M. Barkham, W. Lutz, & L. G. Castonguay (Eds.), *Bergin & Garfield's handbook of psychotherapy and behavior change* (pp. 51–86). Wiley.

McPherson, S., Rost, F., Sidhu, S., & Dennis, M. (2020). Non-strategic ignorance: Considering the potential for a paradigm shift in evidence-based mental health. *Health: An Interdisciplinary Journal for the Social Study of Health, Illness and Medicine, 24*(1), 3–20. https://doi.org/10.1177/1363459318785720

Mendoza-Newman, M., & Erickson Cornish, J. A. (2023). Creating a communitarian, multiculturally sensitive, and socially just training culture. In R. A. Schwartz-Mette, E. A. Hunter, & N. J. Kaslow (Eds.), *Supporting trainees with competence problems: A practical Guide for psychology trainers* (pp. 9–24). American Psychological Association.

Mercieca, D., & Mercieca, D. (2014). Reading with love: Reading of life narrative of a mother of a child with cerebral palsy. *Ethics & Education, 9*(3), 264–275. https://doi.org/10.1080/17449642.2014.974855

Mika, C., Andreotti, V., Cooper, G., Cash, A., & Silva, D. (2020). The ontological differences between wording and worlding the world. *Language, Discourse & Society, 8*(1), 17–32.

New, K., Fox, K., Church, H., & Moorman, F. (2024). The development and evaluation of an online journal club: Perspectives from student participants and practitioners. *Open Learning: The Journal of Open, Distance and E-Learning*, 1–19. https://doi.org/10.1080/02680513.2024.2349234

Rubinstein, D., & Lahad, M. (2023). Fantastic reality: The role of imagination, playfulness, and creativity in healing trauma. *Traumatology*, *29*(2), 102–111. https://doi.org/10.1037/trm0000376

Sani, L., Chemrouk, Y., Le Berre, R.,Ducos, M., Peyrat-Apicella, D., & Bacqué, M-F. (2024). Exploring the grief journey of bereaved spouses: Insights into the impact of sedation within palliative care. *European Journal of Psychotherapy & Counselling*, this issue.

Smith, J.A. (2024). Travelling in time: Using interpretative phenomenological analysis (IPA) to examine temporal aspects of the personal experience of issues in mental health and well-being. *European Journal of Psychotherapy & Counselling*, this issue.

Talens, P. (2024). Psychotherapeutic research and practice: Do we need to talk about 'efficacy'? *European Journal of Psychotherapy & Counselling*, this issue.

Ullmann, T. (2024). Uncertainty and existential thinking. *European Journal of Psychotherapy & Counselling*, this issue.

Viou, M. and Georgaca, E. (2024). Developing reflexivity and self-compassion in group psychotherapy: A dialogical and narrative approach. *European Journal of Psychotherapy & Counselling*, this issue.

Winship, G., Scott, A., & Edgar, J. (2024). Towards a psychotherapy publishing ethics concordat. *European Journal of Psychotherapy & Counselling*, this issue.

Western Cape HPSR Journal Club Team. (2022). "Not just a journal club–It's where the magic happens": Knowledge mobilization through co-production for health system development in the Western Cape Province, South Africa. *International Journal of Health Policy and Management*, *11*(3), 323.

Endnote: The possibility of phenomenology and psychotherapeutic knowledge?

Julia Cayne

Introduction

It seems rather different to be writing for this article when it is based on a talk, which is more in the moment as is the nature of such things. However, I would like to maintain some of the sense of that. When I was considering whether to speak to the title of this article it was tempting to say no, it being difficult to explain what is essentially tacit and acquired over years of experience, including 30 years as a psychotherapist overlapping with 25 years as a nurse. Learning in such practice disciplines tends more to the tacit although all disciplines have a praxis, that is, a set of theories and how they are embodied in cultural practices. These ideas about praxis run through philosophy (e.g. through Plato, Aristotle, Kierkegaard, Marx, Arendt, Freire) and also within psychoanalysis (e.g. Lacan). One thread that seems to run throughout is that praxis is action orientated and there is the idea that we have to be involved in what we practice through reflection and critical awareness.

When thinking about psychotherapeutic practice and research, it seems that much of what is known is tacit and could be considered as concerned with what has become part of my being and is unknown to me except in allusive, elegiac, contemporaneous, non-intentional ways emerging as new ways of knowing through being in relationships. Therefore, if I were to consider this title tomorrow or next week it would be different; this is important.

In consideration of this title, the approach is phenomenological and being concerned with how phenomenology and psychotherapeutic theories, here the particular example of psychoanalysis, approach questions of knowing rather differently. In a phenomenological approach meaning is multiple, contextual, temporal and therefore always on the way, whereas theorising has to some extent fixed meaning in time and certain ways – ways of certainty. However the certainty is, to some extent, also to do with how we read and utilise theory. The fluidity of meaning can of itself induce uncertainty, although it doesn't mean that the next meaning invalidates the previous although it might. Furthermore, in this paper no distinction is being made between practice and research. The differing methodologies to be considered (phenomenology and psychoanalysis) with their different ontological and epistemological underpinnings hold influences over both practice and research and some would consider practice to be an ongoing inquiry in any case.

The thinking about this article involved a to-and-fro between conversations with others, odd opportunities, and more deliberate reading. I would also like to convey something of the journey I have been on along the way with thanks to all those others. As so often happens the beginning of this paper was arbitrary, a reaction to being asked to speak about phenomenology and psychotherapeutic theory and for me that juxtapositioning is problematic, raising a question of whether can such differing epistemological foundations work together, can they, should they? This was mixed up with a dose of possibility!

Experiences

At this arbitrary start of a process, there were two conversations that proved fertile! In one, the film *Oppenheimer* was referred to and how what they didn't initially understand was that the process they were starting (splitting the atom) led to a chain reaction that can go on forever. This might be to do with how abstract theorising can be taken as real, whereas the world of practice throws up unexpected things and therefore we might be well advised to be more concerned with our experience. Although experience is tricky Boud (1993) reveals:

> Much experience, however, is multifaceted, multi layered and so inextricably connected with other experiences, that it is impossible to locate temporally or spatially. It almost defies analysis as the act of analysis inevitably alters the experience and the learning which flows from it (7).

Further:

> experience always says less than it wishes to say, there are many readings of it, it is never exhausted and total clarity may never be reached (Boud 1993:16).

In the same week someone else told me of their visit to a graveyard in Copenhagen to see the grave of the physicist Niels Bohr who was involved with atomic structure and quantum theory. In fact Bohr is considered to have been a philosopher too, having read particularly Kierkegaard. As it turned out Kierkegaard was also buried in the same cemetery as was Hans Christian Anderson. A couple of things about this conversation; the first is that the person knew I would enjoy this which I think speaks to the importance of relationship and the capability for aliveness, through which something can emerge.

These two conversations got me moving, so to speak, on how to approach a question of phenomenology and theory such as in a psychoanalytic approach.

I was thrown back to my love of science especially physiology where I first learned a bit about Bohr and my love of stories and reading, and later philosophy where I found myself at home. These have always been mixed up for me within my own praxis as a nurse, nurse teacher, and then psychotherapist. I think its fortunate for me that I had this mix, holding these differing ways of approaching the world never seemed problematic; it seemed pretty obvious that these differing views could operate together in a praxis.

However, imagine my surprise when I realised that science and philosophy became split off, some locate this split between 16C and 19C but Descartes (1596–1650) and Kant (1724–1804) are particularly implicated. Descartes, through the notion of a mind/body, subjective/objective split, and Kant seen as separating natural philosophy (science) from philosophy when it had been under the same umbrella, with a porosity between different viewpoints. To some extent the phenomenology of Husserl (1859–1938) is informed by these thinkers. Thus, we have ended up with philosophy/phenomenology, not seen as scientific when considered from the perspective of what is now the dominant discourse for scientific method. The phenomenological approach, with its concern with inquiry about our lived experience, does not mistake such experience as reality. For example, from the perspective of Merleau-Ponty (1963), perception is a lens through which we view the world and is seen as a creative act, not simply viewing what already exists. In Kierkegaard's thinking such a creative act might be considered to have possibility. Such an approach is in comparison to logical positivism where theory so easily can be taken as reality whereas for Kierkegaard such theoretical or empirical knowledge is only ever an approximation.

Approximation in Kierkegaard

I have been engaged with an idea in Kierkegaard for years and here it is again! In Kierkegaard (1992) there is an idea that knowing is in relation to the knower so the best that knowledge can be is an approximation. There are several reasons for this:

1. Human knowers are in the process of becoming, the knower and the known are changing, so conformity of thought is unattainable.
2. The beginning of empirical knowing cannot be located and so the start of an inquiry is arbitrary. The knower decides the focus and limits of the study; thus, there are also problems with generalisation.

The issue of generalisation belongs to a scientific research paradigm whereas if we are more concerned with what it means to be human and how our responses to that might come from more tacit knowing then a different paradigm is needed. Rather than generalisability we could be more concerned with what has possibility which is taken up later through Kierkegaard. Further, I have written elsewhere about the need to be located through beginnings or origins which could be seen as seeking causal explanation (Cayne 2014). For Merleau-Ponty (1968), the search for such beginnings is seeking reassurance, which is already a closure, our investigations are emanating from what we already know. The origin is a place to hide from the existential struggle that "we are not at home" (Merleau-Ponty 1968:104) and as such leads us in circular, self-repeating, self-reinforcing paths.

3. Empirical knowledge lacks necessity because the being it seeks to know lacks necessity, in other words human beings are more than what can be determined. It is easily forgotten that what is taken as empirical 'reality' is in constant change, dependent on the perspective of the knower, thus beginning with arbitrary choices however human beings are contingent, that is, there are many possibilities. For Kierkegaard (1992), truth about human existence is not located in objectivity rather only as approximations. We see this problem in theories such as psychoanalysis, for example, when we speak of the unconscious or anywhere we make an object of human experience.

This doesn't, however, mean that there aren't truths. My own therapist once made a rather playful interpretation about sibling murder and hatred (without even saying the words) drawing on the cuckoo in the nest. He didn't draw explicitly on theory around sibling rivalry but was able to say something pertinent for me, funny too! No further explanation was needed. So it's not that we know nothing but what is crucial is how the knowing comes into being through relationship, and it is this 'coming into being' that is so different from the already known of theory and that Kierkegaard calls possibility!

Possibility in Kierkegaard

What emerges from the above is this notion of possibility a word Kierkegaard used again and again. But what does Kierkegaard mean? Possibility is concerned with how things come to be, the change from not being to being. A consideration of this is so important for our practice as psychotherapists, that is in terms of how knowing something comes into our being, for example, does it emerge through experience in a relationship or is it applied from a theory? I would link these two very different ways of approaching the world with our relationship with despair. For Kierkegaard, both ways have the possibility to slide into despair depending on the balance between possibility (how things come into being) and necessity (what is). He says that possibility's despair is to lack necessity and necessity's despair is to lack possibility.

Therefore, we can become caught up in endless possibilities in imagination/fantasies, lose touch with ourselves, and hold things open almost infinitely. Alternatively, we can be caught up in losing ourselves in what others tell us. Both are in despair.

In the first above, there is inability to submit to the necessity of one's life, such as our limitations, or perhaps we might say this is when we cannot be subject to the other. This might include holding things open too much, not listening to what others have to say. It is also possible that a phenomenological approach, through remaining open to the way meaning is always shifting, could also lead to this position.

In the second, one forgets oneself becoming lost in necessity, a copy. This is the determinist. Hence, too much adherence to theory could here be taken as a form of despair too.

There is a tension between these positions although importantly not a synthesis of one into the other as in a more Hegelian position, which seems to involve an incorporation of the thesis/antithesis. The tension between is very important, permitting more of a continual to-and-fro and allowing contradiction and paradox, and as Winnicott (1990) once said, these are to be born not solved! There is thus a chance for possibility in tension where something new might break though is allowed to come into being. This all speaks to the importance of the relationship with self, the world, and others.

Here is an example of an experience of realising something I did not know I knew until it came into being. A child was afraid to go upstairs where I suggested to the parent that they simply go with the child whenever asked, always with good humour and without any push to make things get better. There was a certainty in the suggestion, but at the same time, the unknown and having some clarity about the difference. Here, not thinking we knew the child, which could be seen as an act of incorporation, can still permit a response, where an action is required. Importantly no explanation, either required of the child or told to them, was necessary, anyway doesn't explanation kill the possibility of understanding?

The idea of the unknown also emerges in the work of Schon (1983, 1992, who developed his ideas about reflective learning in response to what he saw as the messy world of experience in practice where difficulties could not always be reduced to clearly solvable problems that fell within easily identified categories of what is already known. He saw such categorisation of the world as based within a technical rational epistemology which was unable to deal with divergent situations. He predicted that in any discipline involving practice there would arise unique cases that did not fit with such certainty and indeed practitioners would be faced with the uncertainty of not knowing (Schon 1983). I would add that every case should be considered as unique though!

Donald Schon's work (1983) on practice disciplines and how knowledge is built up over time through many examples is rather helpful. However, it's not that such experiences are directly applicable or appliable; but, rather one becomes more able to think in the unique situations that practice throws at us. Is this being open to possibility?

In another conversation, about possibility, someone spoke of how impossibility is to be stuck on the same note! Perhaps we can easily become like a record on a turntable repeating the same notes, hearing the same notes or is it hearing the notes the same. Phenomenology is about returning to familiar notes anew, getting out of the groove. One could say that theory, which from a phenomenological viewpoint would be considered as an abstraction because of the way it is removed from the contextuality of being, can become more about the impossible of enclosure than about the opening of the possible.

Different epistemological assumptions

Medard Boss (1963) in "Psychoanalysis and Daseinanalysis" writes about much of what Kierkegaard is saying. This is useful here because of the direct comparison he makes, between psychoanalysis and his existential position that he called daseinanalysis, without throwing out the baby with the bathwater. In particular, the problematic dichotomy between theory and practice where theory could be viewed as psychological and derived from practice as opposed to a praxis that is intuitive and tacit in its understanding (Boss 1963:58).

According to Boss (1963:75), psychoanalytic theory is based in an epistemology in the natural sciences where he outlines basic assumptions as follows:

- There is an external real world.
- Real can only be what can be measured, calculated, and established with certainty.
- Connections between objects are predictable and the relations in the chain of cause and effect are always unbroken.
- All that is real fits into three dimensions, space, temporal order, and the movements of the sun and the other stars.

As so often happens I came across something contemporaneously to do with causality that had not occurred to me and that Bohr is credited with pointing out, which is that we cannot measure cause because it's not there; it is not an object.

Boss (1963:76–77) further summarises a logical rational/scientific approach which leads to a theoretical framework in psychoanalysis as follows:

- Mental phenomena are products of an object (psyche) that pictures extraneous objects within itself and functions like a reflex.
- The systems run on energy (libido) from body organ excitations, manifestations having the character of wishes, and also stimuli from the external world. These stimuli are transmitted to the psychic apparatus as energy.
- External and internal stimuli are transformed while being cathected with libido, producing perceptions, by the psych, of the external world as ideas, memory, traces, unconscious, preconscious, and conscious strivings. This process is causal.
- The aim of the above process is motor discharge in order for maintenance without excitation (accumulation of which is unpleasure).
- There are then two kinds of thinking: correct – external, objective reality, or secondary-process thinking. Incorrect, irrational thinking – unconscious processes or primary process thinking.

For Boss (1963:77) this leads to the primacy of right or rational thinking and as such the avoidance of contradictions or one could say of experiences that do not seem to fit with what is already known.

He further argues that the basis of psychoanalysis fails to begin from a position of understanding the nature and essence of the person and in relationship with others as follows:

> *As long as we do not understand man's essential nature as being of a meaning-disclosing, elucidating character, we remain unable even to understand how someone is able to perceive a fellow man as a fellow man, let alone how he could enter into so-called interpersonal relationships (Boss 1963:80).*

Once one is too caught up with all kinds of theories, we miss the obvious. For me this can mean that theory can become an approximation of our relationship with the other. Or rather our relationship with knowing replaces our relationship with the other a problem of knowing that I will return to. You could further add that theories start from the arbitrary place that Kierkegaard speaks of, mentioned earlier.

Boss (1963), from the point of view of daseinanalysis, gives the example of a different view of dreams pointing out that they are not the royal road to the unconscious but to the 'core' of our existence. This puts us in such a different place in terms of how we approach working or researching with others. However on a cautionary note, whilst I was initially taken with this idea I then found myself questioning the notion of a 'core'. Some would take issue at the idea of a core. Boss perhaps misses what he himself has already said about the movement of the sun and stars; we are not the centre of the universe. Here he seemed to be critiquing notions of a centre but then proposes it? One could say that such a notion is more about the necessary than possibility where the idea of the 'core of existence' could lead to locating human existence as an object that can be discovered rather than the possibility of our existence coming into being. This is a problem that Merleau-Ponty (1968) highlights where we become caught in trying to locate an origin in order to find a solution to a problem. Further he states:

> *The world and reason are not problematical. We may say, if we wish, that they are mysterious, but their mystery defines them : there can be no question of dispelling it by some 'solution', it is on the hither side of all solutions (Merleau-Ponty 1962:xx).*

Two issues emerge here: Firstly, the importance of understanding the epistemological assumptions underpinning theories; it is not enough to just learn theories. Secondly, consideration needs to be given to how these assumptions can unknowingly influence even as we question them, for example, while Boss is critiquing a positivist foundation, one can see that he is also informed by it.

The problem of mastery

One difficulty, as above, is that in proposing a theoretical idea the practitioner, researcher, or theorist can fail to realise how embedded in certain cultural ways we are. Furthermore, there is a question of how our own position in the world can unknowingly lead us to use or develop knowledge through mastery. Consideration of psychoanalytic theories about mastery reveals something of this problem which can then be further understood through Derrida's (1998) critique.

Some of Freud's (see, e.g., Gay 1995) papers, such as the papers on technique, remembering repeating and working through, screen memories, the case studies, and of course dreams, seem to have more room for possibility. These, for example, seem to emerge from practice compared to more psychological, scientific papers that tell us what is. There is also the issue that the problem can be noticed in the telling, that is in the difference between the saying or how things are written and the said or what is written. I have always found the former more useful as I just cannot take the latter as real and, when writing this, came to realise my own block with some aspects of theory, or some might say it is resistance! However, I have found that there are some ways of presenting ideas that resist me in that it is difficult to play with them. For me playing with ideas is where possibility emerges through a kind of creative process. In fact as will be discussed the resistance is not totally in the patient or therapist but can also be located in the very nature of theory.

According to Sarup (1993), Lacan might seem to offer a different approach to Freud; he does seem to claim his approach is not scientific/biological. He was influenced by phenomenology and ideas about meaning and therefore the linguistic chain being concerned with associations rather than causal links. There is also a more post-modern view where the subject is decentred; that is, there is no core or centre as considered in humanistic, existential thought.

This notion of decentring is best seen for me in terms of Lacan's ideas about language, where words speak us, where we are always somewhere else, and the chain of signifiers keeps meaning always on the move (see, e.g., Sarup 1993).

The main ideas about the move into language are Lacan's (1977) reference to Freud's thinking about the 'fort da' (gone/there) game and his own theory of the mirror stage. These are also useful for thinking about the decentring of the subject caught in an illusory (the imaginary) register. It is also these crucial tenets of psychoanalysis along with Freud's work on dreams that are the basis for Derrida's critique and deconstruction of psychoanalysis which will be linked to Kierkegaard's notion of possibility.

For Freud the fort da game was seen as a way for the child to manage the anxiety of the unpleasure of absence linked with the comings and goings of the mother. These ideas came to him through the experience of noticing how a child threw a reel away and said 'gone', and on its return the child said 'there'. It occurs to me that perhaps also the child is no longer being at the centre of the mother's concerns. It is also the beginning of symbolisation in that the return of the reel stands in for the mother's presence. Lacan took these ideas up as the child's entry into language (the symbolic) where there is a move from the mother to the reel and from the reel to language; the words fort da symbolise what is happening. Both Freud and Lacan saw this as gaining mastery over anxiety. I would add that absence hints at death. However, there is a play on the word reel in that the entry into language creates a distance from what Sarup (1993) calls the "lived experience of the real".

This entry into language is necessary for becoming aware of oneself as separate and the journey into the social, cultural world continues through the Mirror stage (6–18 months). However, there is also an issue here that this mastery comes at a price, which is alienation, in that we are caught up by the imaginary.

Derrida (1998) in *Resistances of Psychoanalysis* draws particularly on Freud's work on dreams and Lacan's on the Mirror stage to deconstruct psychoanalysis and what runs throughout that is the misrecognition that the masters too are masters of the image not themselves. In other words they are caught in the very game they theorise on.

To go back to the dream work, he undertakes a close reading of Freud's text of the dream of Irma's injection. There is a lot of word play around threads, knots, solutions, and dissolving. He says that Freud had a premonition that something exceeds the analysis of the dream, which means the analysis cannot be carried far enough – as if there was a solution out of reach. Indeed, Irma did not accept his solution; you could say she resists him and he introduces the idea of the navel of the dream beyond which psychoanalysis cannot go. The dream knot (oomphalos) represents what is unknown. What I understand of this is that Derrida is saying that what Freud cannot see is that it is not the dream that resists interpretation and it is not because of a lack of meaning that makes the dream resist understanding. Rather the resistance is set up by psychoanalysis itself, by the nature of theory or as I would add, it is the theoretical threads that tie one up in knots.

It seems that for Derrida it's all about mastery that comes with the misrecognition and misunderstanding leading us to an endless fort da game. Further, the fort da game begins to be linked with death or perhaps the avoidance of thinking about it, hence the endlessness of the game. As Derrida (1998:118) says: "*.....mastery and death, that is, the same-death and the master, death as the master*".

Conclusions

So, what of my title: what of the question of "The possibility of phenomenology and psychotherapeutic knowledge"?

Firstly with regard to possibility it seems that Kierkegaard is saying something about how possibility can be too much for us. Allowing things to come into being rather than forcing them onto the other puts us in touch with unknowns, what we don't know, what we don't know about the other, what we don't know about ourselves. To be open to possibility is quite a fearful place; we don't know what might emerge. Having clarity about the very nature of theory and its use is therefore important so that we can recognise its limitations in understanding the contextual, temporal, and uniqueness of human being. Derrida usefully shows how theory can lead to resistance and I would add that the resistance can be to the permitting of such uniqueness. And then there is the ultimate unknowable death from which mastery helps us to escape, also avoiding the gaps, the breaks, or unknowns.

In terms of research, there is a question of what approach to research is most helpful for psychotherapeutic practice. This does depend on what kind of praxis we are engaged in and whether one sees psychotherapeutic practice as being concerned with the tacit, uncertainty, and unknowns. Furthermore, what has possibility as opposed to the endless repeating of what is already known. One argument here is that phenomenological approaches can be more open to possibility. However, there is also a question of what happens to phenomenology when it is reduced to a meta method. For Merleau-Ponty, such methods can be seen to be still within a positivist domain. This can lead to locating ourselves in an origin which is generally the place of the already known with a tendency for repetition and reassurance rather than opening to possibility.

The question was also about whether differing epistemological foundations work together, can they, should they? One thought is that I have found much thinking about integration, in the sense of integrative models, problematic in that this can tend to mean an incorporation where one is reduced to the other in a synthesis, rather than permitting difference. Whereas Kierkegaard's meaning of synthesis has more to do with tolerating the tensions between, such as conflicting epistemologies. It's the very differences, epistemological or relational, that create the tensions and the fertile ground for possibility.

References

Boss M. (1963) *Psychoanalysis and Daseinanalysis.* Basic Books Inc., New York.

Cayne J. (2014) Review Essay: The Visible and the Invisible by Maurice Merleau Ponty. *Self and Society, 41* (3) pp46–48.

Derrida J (1998). *Resistances of Psychoanalysis.* Stanford University Press, Stanford.

Freud S. (1920) *Beyond the Pleasure Principle* in Gay P. (1995) *The Freud Reader.* Vintage, London.

Kierkegaard S. (1992) *Concluding Unscientific Postscript to Philosophical Fragments.* Princeton University Press, New Jersey.

Lacan J. (1973) *Four Fundamental Concepts of Psycho-Analysis.* Penguin, London.

Lacan J. (1977) *Ecrits.* Routledge, London.

(ppMerleau-Ponty M. (1963) *The Phenomenology of Perception.* Routledge, London.

Merleau-Ponty M. (1968) *The Visible and the Invisible.* Northwestern Press, Evanston.

Sarup M. (1993) *An Introductory Guide to Post Structuralism and Postmodernism.* Harvester Wheatsheaf, New York.

Schon D. (1983) *The Reflective Practitioner: How professionals think in action.* Temple, London.

Schon D. (1992) The Crisis of Professional Knowledge and the Pursuit of an Epistemology of Practice. *Journal of Interprofessional Care, 6* (1) pp49–63.

Winnicott D. W. (1990) *The Maturational Process and the Facilitating Environment.* Karnac, London.

Index

Note: Figures are indicated by *italics*. Tables are indicated by **bold**.

FSC
www.fsc.org
MIX
Papier | Fördert gute Waldnutzung
FSC® C083411

Kolibri 360 GmbH
Ferdinand-Jühlke-Straße 7
99095 Erfurt, Deutschland
produktsicherheit@kolibri360.de